Newgate

*'Prototype of hell' is a quotation
from Henry Fielding, novelist,
playwright and magistrate*

Newgate

LONDON'S
Prototype of Hell

STEPHEN HALLIDAY

SUTTON PUBLISHING

First published in 2006 by
Sutton Publishing Limited · Phoenix Mill
Thrupp · Stroud · Gloucestershire · GL5 2BU

British Library Cataloguing in Publication Data
A catalogue for this book is available from the British Library.

ISBN 0-7509-3895-1

Endpapers, front: The execution of Lord Ferrers, Tyburn, 1760.
(Guildhall Library, London); *back*: George Dance's design, built
after the Gordon Riots of 1780. *(Guildhall Library, London)*

Typeset in 11/14.5pt Sabon.
Typesetting and origination by
Sutton Publishing Limited.
Printed and bound in England by
J.H. Haynes & Co. Ltd, Sparkford.

'A hell such as Dante might have conceived.'

Giacomo Casanova

'An emblem of hell itself.'

Daniel Defoe, *Moll Flanders*

Contents

List of Illustrations

PREFACE

Newgate in the English Penal System

'That horrid place . . . an emblem of hell itself'

Newgate occupies a unique place in the history of the English penal system, though the gaol itself has not existed for over a century, having been demolished in 1902. Its reputation was such that in the eighteenth century Daniel Defoe, who had himself been a prisoner in Newgate, described it in his novel *Moll Flanders* as 'that horrid place . . . an emblem of hell itself'. His fellow writer, Henry Fielding, whose work as a magistrate required him to visit Newgate, described it as 'one of the dearest places on earth' on account of the cruel exactions the gaolers imposed upon the inmates. It has given its name to a phrase which has entered the language as a simile for blackness and filth, 'as black as Newgate's knocker'. Such is its reputation abroad that New York adopted the name Newgate for one of its early gaols, Sing Sing later replacing it.

The name itself is a misnomer, arising from a mistaken belief that the Medieval gatehouse which served as the first gaol in the reign of Henry II was a later addition to the four Roman gates to the City of London. In the early years of the twentieth century excavation of the site revealed that Newgate was itself of Roman origin. There have been five gaols at Newgate. The original gatehouse was substantially reconstructed in the early fifteenth century through a bequest in the will of Richard Whittington, four times Mayor of London, who had been appalled by the filth and disease that beset Newgate during his last period as mayor. This building survived until the Great Fire of 1666, which destroyed most of Whittington's gaol, including the statue of Whittington himself accompanied by a cat. Its successor, the third Newgate, fell into disrepair and was in the process of re-construction when the Gordon Riots of 1780 destroyed it and much else besides. The fifth and final Newgate was completed to the designs of George Dance the Younger and opened in 1785.

Newgate owes much of its notoriety to its association with execu-tions. In the sixteenth century its proximity to Smithfield made it a convenient place in which to hold Dissenters who were to be burned at the stake to satisfy the religious whims of Tudor monarchs. In the seventeenth and eighteenth centuries Newgate served as the embark-ation point for those who were to be hanged (or worse) at Tyburn, near the present site of Marble Arch. The execution developed into a macabre ritual, preceded by the 'condemned sermon' preached in the prison chapel itself by the prison chaplain or 'Ordinary' who would then write up an account, preferably containing a last-minute confession on the scaffold. These accounts became a recognised literary genre, the *Newgate Calendar*, to be sold to the crowds who habitually gathered along the route to Tyburn or, if they were able to afford a seat, at Tyburn itself. Executions became a gruesome form of public entertainment, accompanied by drunkenness, violence, attempted rescues and the occasional riot. James Boswell, a man not usually noted for his sensitivity, found himself unable to sleep after attending a Tyburn execution. The Tyburn rituals and other events associated with Newgate were celebrated by artists such as William Hogarth and James Gillray. In 1783 executions were transferred to Newgate itself, a scaffold being erected outside the gaol's 'debtor's door', so the building itself became the focus of the mayhem associated with public executions until they were moved inside the gaol in 1868.

Charles Dickens and William Thackeray were among those who attended the 'Newgate drop' on execution days and wrote about it. To theirs may be added many other names which became associated with Newgate and its victims. Bulwer Lytton, author of *The Last Days of Pompeii*, helped to found that distinctive literary form, the Newgate Novel. The name of the incompetent, bungling axeman Jack Ketch became synonymous with that of a brutal executioner and he also gave his name to Jack Ketch's Kitchen, within the gaol itself, where cadavers were boiled and dismembered. The notorious perjurer Titus Oates sent many to their deaths at Newgate before himself being incarcerated there. The Italian libertine Casanova passed through the gaol while the Cato Street conspirators were beheaded there (after first being hanged) in 1820. Jack Sheppard was hanged at Tyburn, having in the meantime become a popular hero for his many audacious escapes from Newgate. He was quickly followed on the scaffold by his accuser, Jonathan Wild, the eighteenth-century criminal and 'supergrass' whose exploits were soon celebrated in John Gay's *The Beggar's Opera* and, in the twentieth century, by Bertold Brecht's *The Threepenny Opera*. The Newgate Monster, who quite possibly did not exist except in the imaginations of his victims, spent six years in Newgate in the 1790s for sticking sharp implements into ladies' bottoms. A gentler association is with the memory of Elizabeth Fry, who began the process of making Newgate a more wholesome place in the nineteenth century.

Newgate prison's reputation is thus perpetuated not only in the phrase that it has given to the English language, but in the events and the people associated with it. It was eventually demolished to make way for another building on the corner of Newgate Street, which has similar associations with foul deeds and their conse-quences: the Central Criminal Court, better known as the Old Bailey. This volume records the history of one of London's most notorious buildings, which served the capital for more than 700 years, from the reign of Henry II to that of Edward VII.

Stephen Halliday
November 2005

ONE

The Heinous Gaol of Newgate

By reason of the foetid and corrupt atmosphere that is in the heinous gaol of Newgate many persons are now dead who would be alive.

> (Proclamation of Richard Whittington,
> Mayor of London, 1419)

A merciless race of men and, by being conversant with scenes of misery, steeled against any tender sensation.

> (William Blackstone's description
> of the qualities of a gaoler, *c.* 1770)

Alexander, the severe keeper of Newgate, died miserably, swelling to a prodigious size, and became so inwardly putrid that none could come near him

> (Foxe's *Book of Martyrs*, *c.* 1554, noting
> the fate of a cruel gaoler of Newgate)

NEW CATHEDRAL, OLD GATE

In the first years of the twentieth century, as the old gaol of Newgate was being demolished to make way for the Old Bailey, excavation of the site revealed unmistakable traces of Roman construction, suggesting strongly that the original gate was built by the

1

Romans in the wall which they had built to protect the community of Londinium on the banks of the Thames.[1] Six Roman gates are still remembered by names associated with surviving street names or areas of the City. To the east, Aldgate gave access to the roads that led towards Colchester and from 1374 the gatehouse itself accommodated Geoffrey Chaucer and his family when the poet was Controller of Customs for Richard II. To the north, Bishopsgate opened on to Ermine Street, while Aldersgate opened on to Watling Street, with Cripplegate not far away. To the east, Ludgate (allegedly founded by the mythical Kind Lud in 66 BC) and Newgate gave access to the west and to important towns such as Silchester, Cirencester and Bath. Excavations for the construction of Holborn Viaduct in the nineteenth century revealed that Newgate was itself aligned with Watling Street. There was probably also a gate, later known as the Postern gate, north of the present site of the Tower of London. To the south, the City was bordered by the River Thames and there was probably a gate which opened on to London Bridge, later referred to as Bridgegate. By Anglo-Saxon times other gates had been created at Dowgate, Billingsgate and Moorgate.

In 1087, the final year of the reign of William the Conqueror, the Saxon cathedral of St Paul in the City of London was destroyed in a fire. The first, built in 604, had lasted only 71 years before being burned down. It was rebuilt before being destroyed by Vikings in the tenth century and reopened in 962. This Saxon cathedral, therefore, survived for a little more than a century before suffering a fate common to many buildings at a time when wood was the principal component in construction work and precautions against fire were rudimentary. The Norman Bishop of London, Maurice, decided to build a magnificent stone cathedral on a much greater scale than its Saxon predecessors. It was completed in 1310 and would survive until it was itself destroyed in the Great Fire of London in 1666 and was replaced by Sir Christopher Wren's masterpiece.

Maurice's ambitious cathedral required a much greater expanse of land than did its modest Saxon predecessors. In particular, the site of the new cathedral lay across the thoroughfare which gave access to the Ludgate at the foot of what is now Ludgate Hill. In the twelfth century, as Maurice's successors oversaw the construction of the new cathedral, the ever-expanding building site, occupying something like the area of Wren's later cathedral, began to cause problems to those wishing to travel from the busy trading area of Cheapside, to the east of the cathedral, through the Ludgate on their way to the growing community of Westminster. This was by now becoming the royal residence and seat of government.

As Ludgate became less accessible, Newgate became more important for travellers entering and leaving the City to the west. John Stow, in his *Survey of London*, first published in 1598, explains that:

> The next gate, on the west and by north, is termed Newgate, as latelier built than the rest, and is the fifth principal gate. This gate was first erected about the reign of Henry I . . . This gate hath long been a jail or prison for felons and trespassers.[2]

Stow was wrong about the date of construction, as we have seen, since Newgate had existed in one form or another since Roman times. The most likely explanation for Stow's error is that, as a result of the construction of St Paul's, Newgate replaced Ludgate as the principal access point to the west of the City.

NEWGATE THE PRISON

The legal reforms instituted by Henry II (1154–89) gave the king a far more important role in the administration of justice than had applied in the chaotic reign of his predecessor, Stephen, whose nineteen-year rule had amounted to little more than a prolonged civil war over who should be king. Henry's Assize of Clarendon (1166), reinforced in 1176 by the Assize of Northampton, required that gaols be constructed in every locality in which the king's judges would administer the process known as 'gaol delivery'. Those confined within the gaols would have their cases considered by the king's justices at regular intervals, normally twice a year, according to a common set of principles ('Common Law'), which would grad-

John Stow (*c.* 1525–1605): John Stow was born in the vicinity of Cornhill, the son of a tallow chandler (a candle maker). John himself became a tailor and was admitted to membership of the Merchant Taylors' company. In 1561 he took to literature, his first work being an edition of the works of Chaucer and it was at this time that he began to assemble his substantial collection of books, spending as much as £200 a year on this hobby. He contributed to *Holinshed's Chronicles*, a somewhat fanciful account of British history which was first published in 1577 and on which Shakespeare drew for his history plays. Thereafter, Stow was exclusively concerned with historical works including *Chronicles of England from Brute unto the Present Year of Christ* (1580) and the work for which he is best remembered, his *Survey of London* (1598), which is based partly upon his own observations of Tudor London and partly upon his extensive collection of original sources. He died in 1605 and was buried in the church of St Andrew Undershaft.

ually come to apply throughout the kingdom. These courts came to be known as assizes and they continued until they were replaced by the Crown Courts in 1971. Hence Henry II may claim to be the father of the Common Law. Some communities resented the intrusion of royal judges, despatched from Westminster, into local justice and it was probably for this reason that Edward III agreed that one of the justices responsible for gaol delivery at Newgate would be the mayor of the City of London.[3] The gaol in the gatehouse of Newgate may have been one of the first to be established to meet the needs of gaol delivery since the first reference to it serving this purpose occurs in 1188, the penultimate year of Henry's reign. It was not London's first gaol. Apart from the Tower of London itself, whose many roles included that of prison, there is a record of repairs being made to the Fleet prison, to the north of the present site of Ludgate Hill, as early as 1155. Newgate appears to have acquired early its bad reputation as a place of incarceration since an early letter book held at the Guildhall refers to the 'heinous gaol of Newgate'.[4] It was sufficiently unpopular to be attacked by Wat Tyler's followers in the Peasants' Revolt of 1381.

Over the centuries that followed, Newgate was a frequent object of official and, particularly, royal attention. In 1218 the young Henry III (1216–1270) ordered the Sheriffs of the City of London 'to repair the gaol of Newgate for the safe keeping of his prisoners'[5] and in 1253 a much angrier Henry sent the City Sheriffs to the Tower of London for a month because they had allowed the escape from Newgate of a prisoner who had had the temerity to kill the Queen's cousin.[6] The prison, or threat of it, was also employed when His Majesty needed to raise some money by exploiting some sinister prejudices. In 1241 some Jews had been hanged in Norwich for allegedly circumcising a Christian child. Henry took the opportunity to inform their London brethren that they would have to pay him 20,000 marks 'or else to be kept perpetual prisoners in Newgate'.[7] The unfortunate Jews appear to have paid up. Newgate was also used as a warning to potential malefactors. In 1345 four servants were executed at Tyburn for murdering their master, a member of the King's household. The murder of a master by a servant was classified as 'petty treason', as against high treason, which was committed against the King. Their heads were exhibited on poles at Newgate.[8]

An examination of Medieval records reveals the wide variety of offences for which incarceration in Newgate (usually for an unspecified and thus indefinite period) was the remedy. Thus in 1378 a parish clerk was sent to Newgate because he spoke ill of John of Gaunt, Duke of Lancaster, a younger son of Edward III, who was thought by orthodox clergy to be unduly sympathetic to the heretical John Wycliffe and the Lollards. This clerk did not claim 'benefit of clergy', an arrangement by which clergymen were exempt from the harsher provisions of the criminal law. This clerical privilege had lain at the heart of the dispute between Henry II and Thomas à Becket. Nuns also qualified. Since clergymen were among the few citizens who were literate, the benefit was effectively extended to anyone who could read or write. The arrangement eventually deteriorated to the point where anyone who could read the first verse of Psalm 51, 'Have mercy upon me, O God, according to thy loving kindness', was deemed to qualify for benefit of clergy. Experienced but illiterate criminals therefore took the precaution of learning these few words (known as 'the neck verse') by heart. Many judges went along with this deceit in order to mitigate the savagery of the law since the ecclesiastical courts imposed far milder sentences than did the king's.

The crimes for which people were sent to Newgate reflected, then as now, public anxieties. Thus towards the end of the reign of Edward I there was public concern about street robberies, which we would call muggings. Accordingly, the act of drawing a dagger was punished with fifteen days in Newgate while drawing blood was punished with forty days. One Roger le Skirmisour was sent to Newgate for keeping a fencing school, an activity that was forbidden by a statute of 1287 since it was thought to encourage sword fights. Riotous assemblies were rewarded with a year and a day in the gaol.[9]

Others were not so coy as John of Gaunt's critic about taking advantage of this legal anomaly. In 1406 William Hegge, a burglar, was sentenced to death by hanging, but when he claimed benefit of clergy he was sent to Newgate to await the arrival of an 'Ordinary' (a representative of the bishop), who could impose a sentence in an ecclesiastical court. In 1487 those claiming benefit were branded on the thumb and thereafter forfeited benefit of clergy for future offences unless they could prove that they genuinely were clergy. The ecclesiastical courts kept much of their jurisdiction until 1576 and benefit of clergy was not finally abolished until 1827.[10]

BARBAROUS PRACTICES

Some penalties were savage and reflected both the barbarous practices of the time and also a desire to avoid the expense of providing prisons for long sentences. In the reign of William the Conqueror mutilation replaced the hangings that had been favoured by the Anglo-Saxons for many offences, so castration, amputation of hands or ears, slitting of noses, excision of eyes and branding with a hot iron became common punishments for many offences of dishonesty.[11] Vagabonds were branded with a V, thieves with a T and brawlers with the letter F to signify 'fraymaker'. The letter S signified a serf without a master. The Conqueror's son, William Rufus, reintroduced hanging for those who poached royal deer and his successor, his brother Henry I, adopted it for a wider variety of crimes. The first hanging at Tyburn was recorded in 1196, though other sites were also used for prisoners from Newgate, notably at St Giles' Fields near the present site of Tottenham Court Road Underground station. From the thirteenth century capital punishment became more common, particularly for crimes against property or its owners. By Tudor times the death sentence could be imposed for theft of property worth 1s (five new pence) or more. Smithfield, close by Newgate, was a common execution place in Medieval times where crowds could assemble to watch the spectacle.

Those hanged or beheaded could count themselves fortunate. The gruesome penalty of hanging, drawing and quartering for treason was introduced by Edward I in his campaigns against the Welsh and Scots, being inflicted on William Wallace at Smithfield in 1305. In November 1330 Edward's grandson, Edward III, seized power from his mother and her lover Roger Mortimer, who had deposed and murdered the King's father, Edward II, three years earlier. The Queen Mother was sent into exile while Mortimer was found guilty of the murder and executed at Tyburn. He was spared the ritual disembowelling and suffered the less gruesome penalty of a public hanging. In 1531 the cook to the Bishop of Rochester, a man called Rouse, was boiled alive at Smithfield for attempting to poison his master and inadvertently poisoning several colleagues. Near Newgate there was one possible refuge from these grisly penalties. From 1439 the College of St Martin-le-Grand, founded in 1056 in the reign of Edward the Confessor by two of that king's cousins, offered sanctuary to those fleeing justice administered both by the royal and ecclesiastical courts. Thieves and debtors were granted sanctuary, but Jews and traitors were turned away. One of those who sought refuge there and 'rotted away piecemeal', according to the account of Sir Thomas More, was Miles Forest, one of the alleged murderers of the Princes in the Tower. Enterprising criminals continued to take advantage of this opportunity to escape the noose, the axe, or worse, until the arrangement ended in 1697.

Lesser crimes, such as vagrancy, were punished with a public whipping, the stocks or the pillory. From 1405 every parish was required to maintain stocks and most had a pillory and whipping post as well.[12] Whippings were regarded as a form of public entertainment, drawing large crowds. Elizabeth Fry successfully campaigned to end the public whipping of women in 1817.[13] The Museum of London's exhibits include such a whipping post. The object of the stocks and the pillory was to humiliate the culprit by exposing him to the ridicule, as well as the missiles, of the crowd, but the outcome was sometimes fatal. In 1384 two defendants failed to appear at their trials because they had been left in the stocks and forgotten. Their feet had rotted in the cold winter weather and they died.[14] The pillory was more hazardous since this device constrained the victim's hands and neck so that he had no means of defending himself from the assaults of the crowd and it was not unknown for an angry or drunken mob to launch such an onslaught that the victim died. As late as 1570 an unfortunate prisoner called Penedo, who had counterfeited the seal of the court of Queen's Bench, was nailed to the pillory by his ears and was only able to escape at the expense of losing them.

In 1380 some malefactors were lodged in Newgate for three nights and brought out to be pilloried for three days for 'pretending to be dumb'. They had exhibited what they claimed were their tongues, mounted in silver frames, which had supposedly been extracted by a hook, also on show. The whole enterprise had been designed to improve their earnings from begging. Sometimes the pillorying was attended by some ceremony as with John de Hakeford in 1364. He was sent to Newgate for perjury for one year and 'within the year to be pilloried four times, once in every quarter of the City'. He would be preceded on the journey to his place of punishment by two trumpeters with a stone hung round his neck covered by a placard reading 'false liar'.[15] Jurors could themselves be pilloried if they did not carry out their task conscientiously. In 1468 jurors who had returned a false verdict in return for a bribe were obliged to ride from Newgate to the pillory at Cornhill with 'miters' (dunces' caps) on their heads.[16] The pillory survived into the nineteenth century. In 1790 two valets convicted of homosexuality were pelted by a huge mob with potatoes, stones and, more expensively, eggs (one of the culprits was called Bacon), and barely escaped with their lives.[17] Twenty years later, 1810, two men were pilloried in Leadenhall in London and fifty women assailed them with stones, dung, dead cats (a favourite missile) and offal thoughtfully provided by butchers from the nearby market. They were taken away blinded and unconscious. The pillory was finally abolished in 1837.

PEINE FORTE ET DURE

One of the most gruesome practices was associated with Newgate's 'pressing room'. Felons (an archaic term used to describe those who had committed serious crimes, including theft) who were found guilty forfeited all their property, leaving families destitute. Such forfeiture was not abolished until 1870.[18] The only way to avoid this penalty was to refuse to enter a plea. Prior to 1426, those who took this course were starved to death, one victim being Hugh de Beone who died in Newgate in the late fourteenth century[19], but so many prisoners made this grim choice that the authorities decided to subject such recalcitrants to 'peine forte et dure'. In the words of Sir Thomas Smith, written in 1583, 'he is judged mute, that is dumb by contumacy, and to his condemnation is to be pressed to death, which is one of the cruellest deaths that may be'.[20] The prisoner was made to lie prostrate and almost naked on the ground beneath a board on which metal or iron weights were placed. More weights were added each day, a process which continued until he was pressed to death. An eighteenth-century occupant of the prison, the robber John Hall, described these wretched prisoners 'having no Food or Drink but Black Bread or the Channel Water which runs under the gaol, if his fainting pains should make him crave to eat or drink'. Few could endure the suffering, but some hardy souls died in this way in order to secure the welfare of their families. The penalty was last used at Cambridge Assizes as late as 1741, after which it was abolished. For obstinate female prisoners pressing could be replaced by the practice of tying cords tightly round the thumbs – a penalty inflicted on Mary Andrews in 1721 until her thumbs snapped.[21]

Not all offences attracted such savage punishments. In the reign of Edward III one Nicolas Mollere was sent to Newgate 'until such time' as the Sheriffs saw fit to release him for the offence of 'circulating lies' – in particular for spreading a rumour that Newgate was to be closed and its occupants all sent to the Tower of London. Others were sent to Newgate for cheating at dice, highway robbery, 'nightwalking' (being out and about after 9 p.m.) and, a more modern offence, for using fishing nets with too fine a mesh so that the smaller fish (referred to as 'fry') could not escape: hence the expression 'small fry'. In the fourteenth century, traders who sold bread or cheese which was of poor quality or less than the appropriate weight were liable to be sent to Newgate with their defective merchandise, which was used to feed their fellow prisoners.

RICHARD WHITTINGTON

By the early fifteenth century the conditions in Newgate were causing concern to the mayor, Aldermen and Sheriffs who were responsible for administering the gaol. Thomas Knowles, a grocer, paid for a supply of fresh water to be piped to the gaol from St Bartholomew's Hospital,[22] though this did not stop one of the later keepers from charging the inmates for its use. In 1406 three worthy citizens expressed their concern that male and female prisoners were being housed together. A tower was built adjacent to the Medieval gaol to accommodate the women.[23] In 1382 a prison had been opened in what remained of the old Ludgate to accommodate citizens (male and female) who had been imprisoned for debts, trespasses, contempt and what would now be called false accounting. These culprits had offended their fellow citizens rather than infringed the king's peace – broadly speaking they had committed civil rather than criminal offences. These were the 'respectable' criminals, many of them tradesmen and freemen of the city who had fallen on hard times. They had once associated with the mayor, Sheriffs and members of the governing body, known as the Court of Common Council, which ran the Square Mile, as it still does. Unfortunately, some of them were too comfortable in their surroundings, as explained in an ordinance passed in June 1419 by the mayor, William Sevenoke. Referring to the complacent residents of Ludgate he declared:[24]

> Many false persons of bad disposition and purpose have been more willing to take up their abode there, so as to waste and spend their goods upon the ease and licence that there is within, than to pay their debts.

Sevenoke duly closed the comfortable quarters at Ludgate and transferred its occupants to the harsher conditions at Newgate where, later the same year, more than sixty of them succumbed to 'gaol fever' (probably typhus). The new mayor, who had been elected to the office for the third time, was Richard Whittington, a man of more humane disposition, who was to play a significant role in the history of Newgate as well as that of pantomime.

Many of the facts that are known about Richard Whittington (he was never Sir Richard) fit the later legend. He was born in Pauntley, Gloucestershire, in about 1359. He was the son of a local landowner and Member of Parliament Sir William Whittington and he married Alice Fitzwaryn, the daughter of another Gloucestershire landowner. Richard's father died at about the time of his celebrated son's birth, thus possibly creating the 'orphan' legend, and Sir William's estate (in which certain creditors appear to have had an interest) all passed to Richard's elder brother, this combination of misfortunes perhaps explaining the impoverishment of the legend. In fact, Richard went to London in the 1370s, as many younger sons of gentry did, and quickly became wealthy and well connected. He became a member of the Mercers' Company (literally dealers in small quantities, or retailers) and himself traded in cloth, which at the time was England's

> **The officers of the City of London:** the oldest office in the City of London (the 'Square Mile') is that of Sheriff, which dates from Saxon times. Two Sheriffs were appointed by the king to administer the City and collect taxes. Aldermen also date from this period though their role in the governance of the City in the Court of Aldermen dates from the thirteenth century. The Sheriffs were the executive officers of the court whose responsibilities included running Newgate and other gaols. The first mayor, Henry Fitzalwyn, was appointed in 1189. Since 1395 the City has been administered by the Court of Common Council on which now sit twenty-five Aldermen, one elected for each City ward, and a much larger number of elected Council members. The two Sheriffs, whose office is now largely ceremonial, are elected on Midsummer Day each year in the Guildhall by the City livery companies. Their responsibilities include attendance at the Old Bailey sessions, as in the time of Newgate. Election to the post of Sheriff is normally followed by eventual election to the post of Lord Mayor who remains Chief Magistrate of the City of London.

principal export. By 1385 he was a wealthy member of the Court of Common Council and in 1397 he was appointed mayor by King Richard II upon the death in office of the previous mayor.[25]

A number of contemporary legends quickly grew up about his fabulous wealth, notably the claim that, at a banquet which he gave in honour of Henry V, Whittington consigned to the fire £60,000 worth of the King's bonds, representing money borrowed to pursue his expensive foreign adventures in France. The mayor thus, according to this account, wrote off this early portion of the national debt. What is certain is that Richard Whittington was held in such high esteem by his monarch, for whatever reason, that in 1415 he was nominated as one of only four grandees whose permission had to be sought before any buildings in London could be demolished and he was also put in charge of the construction works for the rebuilding of Westminster Abbey. He is also credited with commissioning the *Liber Albus* (White Book), which was compiled by John Carpenter at about this time and remains one of the principal sources of information about the customs of the Medieval City of London.

Shortly after he was elected mayor for the third time (thus making four mayoralties, because the first time he had been appointed by the King), Richard reversed the decision of his predecessor to close the Ludgate prison. In November 1419 he issued a new ordinance which proclaimed that:

> 'By reason of the foetid and corrupt atmosphere that is in the heinous gaol of Newgate many persons are now dead who would be alive.' He therefore decided to reopen Ludgate 'to keep therein all citizens and other reputable persons whom the Mayor, Aldermen, Sheriffs or Chamberlain of the City shall think proper to commit and send to the same'.

The lesson was not learned since a few years later, in 1431, after Whittington's death in 1423, Ludgate prisoners were again sent to Newgate for a time. Whittington, however, did not forget the unfortunate prisoners at his death. Most of his estate, valued at the huge sum for the time of £5,000[26], was left to the Mercers' Company and was the foundation of the enormous wealth of this, the first in precedence of all London's livery companies. However, a substantial sum of Whittington's money was used by his executors to 're-edify [rebuild] the gaol of Newgate which they did with his goods'.[27] We have no record of this later Medieval gaol, but when Newgate was rebuilt after the Great Fire of 1666 one of its features was a figure with a cat, supposedly placed there in honour of Richard Whittington, the earlier benefactor.

THE GAOLERS

The Newgate prisoners did not have to wait for the sentence of the court to begin their punishment. For some of them the pillory would have been a blessed relief compared with the torments inflicted upon them by their gaolers. The head gaoler (known as the 'keeper') was chosen by the Sheriffs and formally appointed by the City's Court of Aldermen. However, at a time when taxes were low and sources of revenue for the Corporation very few, it was common practice for a candidate to purchase the office and then set about recouping his outlay by exploiting the prisoners in his care. In some cases this amounted simply to charging prisoners for privileges, such as being freed from iron shackles. To avoid the worst abuses of this practice, the Court of Aldermen in 1393 set the fee for removing irons at a maximum of £5 – a substantial sum for the time.[28] Another source of profit arose from the supply of food to prisoners who were otherwise dependent upon charitable gifts, which were themselves likely to be pilfered by the keepers and their turnkeys. In an attempt to prevent the worst profiteering an edict of 1370 forbade brewing, baking and victualling within the prison, but the experiment cannot have been successful since it was amended in 1393 with the proviso that exorbitant prices should not be charged for these services.[29] The Sheriffs themselves, who were technically responsible for the prisoners, sometimes took advantage of their positions by offering accommodation in what came to be known as 'sponging houses' to more acceptable prisoners, notably debtors, in return for sometimes exorbitant payments.[30]

Some keepers resorted to desperate measures to profit from their investment. In about 1330 Edmund Lorimer, Keeper of Newgate, was himself sent to the Fleet prison for torturing and blackmailing prisoners.[31] One of his predecessors had actually been hanged in 1290 for murdering one of his charges.[32] His successors did not learn from this example, because in 1449 the keeper was imprisoned for raping some of the female prisoners confined in their tower, following which the Court of Aldermen appointed a board of visitors to carry out inspections of the gaol. William Blackstone described such gaolers as 'a merciless race of men and, by being conversant with scenes of misery, steeled against any tender sensation'. Nor were they noted for their deference to authority. In 1447 the keeper, James Manning, left the corpse of one of his prisoners in the road outside the gaol 'causing a nuisance and great danger to the King who was passing there'. When he refused to remove it and after 'shameful words' had been exchanged with the King's messenger, Manning and his wife were themselves gaoled.[33]

William Blackstone (1723–80): born in 1723, four months after the death of his father, Blackstone was sent to Oxford by his uncle and in 1741 entered the Middle Temple, being called to the bar in 1746. He was a notably unsuccessful barrister when, in 1758, he began to give a series of lectures at Oxford, which later became Blackstone's 'Commentaries on the Laws of England'. It was published in America as well as England and soon translated into French, German and Russian, earning Blackstone the huge sum of £14,000. In 1761 he was elected to Parliament and, on the strength of his *Commentaries*, became a King's Counsel and later a judge. His great work set out the principles of the Common Law and, among other things, argued for religious toleration and against slavery at a time when these were not popular causes. It influenced the American Declaration of Independence and Constitution, led the new nation to adopt a justice system based on the English Common Law and prompted the American jurist and Librarian of Congress, Daniel Boorstin, to comment that no other book but the Bible had so influenced the United States of America. In 1834 Abraham Lincoln, when asked how to set about becoming a lawyer, replied, 'Begin with Blacksone's *Commentaries*.' Blackstone died in 1780 of dropsy, an abnormal swelling of the body caused by the accumulation of water. His early influence in America and the continued appearance of his name on legal texts published in the twenty-first century suggests that his *Commentaries* is possibly the most influential law book ever written in the English, or perhaps any language.

John Stow, the chronicler of Tudor London, was himself involved with the case of the keeper of another gaol in Bread Street. This wretched man, Richard Husband, was brought before a jury of which Stow was a member and found guilty of maltreating prisoners whereupon he was himself set in irons in Newgate. This prompted Stow to note that 'gaolers buying their offices will deal hardly with pitiful prisoners'.[34]

THE TUDOR PRISON

The advent of the Tudor dynasty in 1485 led to some changes at Newgate, notably the construction of the first Old Bailey court-house which would eventually replace the gaol. This arose from a petition by the City Aldermen for a suitable building from which the task of gaol delivery could be carried out. The result was the construction, in 1539, of a 'sessions house'. Sessions houses, where magistrates and judges presided over Quarter Sessions, were once a feature of many substantial towns. The former Middlesex Sessions House, dating from the eighteenth century, is an attractive feature of Clerkenwell Green in London, where it remains in use as a Masonic building. The Newgate Sessions House was built 'over against Fleet lane in the Old Bailey' on part of the present site of the Old Bailey itself. The name is a reference to a fortification in the Roman Wall derived from the Latin word *ballium* meaning a wall for defence. This building, conveniently situated for the adjacent gaol, remained in use until it was destroyed in the Great Fire of London in 1666.

The changing religious convictions of Tudor monarchs ensured that a growing number of their subjects would pass through the new sessions house and be consigned to Newgate before their gruesome deaths at nearby Smithfield. Some of the most vivid, if not the most reliable, accounts of this time are to be found in John Foxe's *Book of Martyrs*, which describes not only the sufferings of the Protestant martyrs of Mary's reign but also the fates which befell some of their tormentors.

16

John Fox (or **Foxe**) (*c*. 1517–1587): born in Boston, Lincolnshire, John Fox studied at Oxford and became a Fellow of Magdalen College, but the college expelled him when his heretical (anti-Catholic) opinions became known before such views were acceptable. He became tutor to the children of Sir Thomas Lucy at Charlecote, near Stratford-upon-Avon, a gentleman who was quite possibly lampooned in the character of Justice Shallow in *The Merry Wives of Windsor* after a dispute with the young William Shakespeare. Fox later became tutor to the children of the future Duke of Norfolk. During the reign of Mary, Fox fled to the Continent, settling in Basle, Switzerland, with a group of his Protestant countrymen. He returned to England and to the patronage of the Duke of Norfolk upon the accession to the throne of the Protestant Elizabeth. His *Book of Martyrs*, which he began to compile during his Swiss exile and first published in 1554, is best remembered for its lurid tales of the Inquisition and the English martyrs of Mary's reign, though it begins with the early Christians and subsequent writers have added to it so that later editions of the work include accounts of John Bunyan, the oppression of the Quakers and the work of John Wesley. Fox died in 1587 and was buried in St Giles', Cripplegate, where he had once been vicar.

PROTESTANT MARTYRS

The first monarch to persecute Protestants was Henry VIII who, even after his break with Rome, adhered to many Catholic doctrines, such as belief in the Real Presence of Christ's body and blood in the mass, and was averse to the practice of reading the scriptures in English. Like all good authoritarians, Protestant or Catholic, Henry believed that if the common people could understand the scriptures in their own language they might start to ask questions about them. Andrew Alexander was appointed Keeper of Newgate in Henry's reign and was in the worst traditions of his oppressive Medieval predecessors. Alexander was a man with two passions: music and the maltreatment of prisoners, especially if they were heretics. One prisoner was favoured with the prison's best quarters in return for entertaining Alexander and his wife by playing the lute, but this fortunate gentleman was nevertheless overcome by a 'burning ague' brought on by the prison's evil smells. At this time, also, there was a report of eleven monks being chained in a standing position in the gaol and left to starve to death.[35] Prisoners who were unable to pay Alexander to have their fetters removed were consigned to Newgate's deepest dungeon to await death. Foxe, in *Book of Martyrs*, described Alexander's excesses, but added with some satisfaction that 'Alexander, the severe keeper of Newgate, died miserably, swelling to a prodigious size, and became so inwardly putrid that none could come near him. This cruel minister of the law would go to [bishops] Bonner, Story and others, requesting them to rid his prison, he was so much pestered with hereticks.'[36]

The favoured way of ridding Alexander of his troublesome hereticks was to burn them at nearby Smithfield, though sometimes they were sent back to the place where their offence had been committed. Sometimes, mercifully, the victim would be suffocated by smoke before the flames reached him, but Richard Bayfield, who had been identified as a trader in banned books, was denied this comparatively humane fate. Bayfield had repented of his heresy, but then resumed it, 'like a dog returning to his vomit', in Sir Thomas More's unflattering phrase.[37] Bayfield was burned at Smithfield in December 1531 and 'there, for lack of a speedy fire, was two quarters of an hour alive'.[38] There arose the legend of a black dog, which supposedly walked the surrounding streets before an execution, though in later centuries the expression 'making the black dog walk' signified the brutal treatment inflicted by existing inmates on new prisoners. Eighty years later a highwayman called Luke Hutton turned to writing while awaiting execution and attributed this mythical beast 'ringed about the nose with a golden hoop' to 'a black conscience, haunting none but black conditioned people, such as Newgate may challenge to be guests' and composed some sinister and unmemorable verses in its memory.[39]

An early victim of Queen Mary's concern with heresy was John Rogers, Vicar of St Sepulchre's, which still stands opposite the site of Newgate and whose bell was, in later centuries, rung to signal forthcoming executions. Rogers had befriended William Tyndale and Miles Coverdale, translators of the Bible into English and, while chaplain to the Merchant Adventurers in Antwerp, had translated part of it himself. He held unorthodox views on the nature of the Eucharist. The Bishop of London, Edmund Bonner (*c.* 1500–69), known at the time as 'Bloody Bonner' had him committed to Newgate, 'there to be lodged among thieves and murderers' in Foxe's words, before being burned at Smithfield in February 1555. John Rogers's wife and eleven children met him on the way to his death and when the driver of the cart which was bearing him from Newgate to Smithfield stopped to enable Rogers to take leave of his family, a City Sheriff, named Woodroffe, struck the driver on the head. Foxe records that shortly afterwards Woodroffe was 'struck with a paralytic affection, and languished a few days in the most pitiable and helpless condition' before expiring. Royal connections were no guarantee of safety from suspicion of heresy. In July 1546, during the penultimate year of Henry VIII's reign, a huge crowd gathered at Smithfield to see Anne Askew led to the stake. The fact that she had worked in the household of Henry's last Queen, Catherine Parr, did not save her when the authorities discovered that she denied the Real Presence at mass.

One of her questioners was 'Bloody Bonner', to whom Foxe referred as 'this Catholic hyena'. Bonner had denounced papal supremacy in the reign of Henry VIII, but upheld it under Mary when he was among the most zealous in the persecution of Protestants. During the intervening reign of Edward VI (1547–53) he had been confined to the Marshalsea prison to which he was again sent by Elizabeth for the last ten years of his life. Bonner had been instrumental in securing the committal to Newgate of a fellow bishop, Hooper of Gloucester, before sending him back to be burned in his diocese, but he also found time to deal with less exalted prisoners. John Rough, a clergyman from the north of England, was brought before Bonner and Watson, Bishop of Lincoln, whom Rough had sheltered during the Protestant persecutions of Edward VI's reign. When the grim pair condemned him, Rough cried to Watson, "Is this, Sir, the reward I have for saving your life?" before being taken to the stake at Smithfield. A teenage youth named William Hunter was sent by Bonner from Newgate to Brentwood in Essex to face the stake.

One of Foxe's particular *bêtes noires* was 'that arch-persecutor' Stephen Gardiner (1497–1555), Bishop of Winchester, who had at one time been a threat to Foxe himself while he was tutor to the children of the Duke of Norfolk and who vied with Bonner in his zeal to burn Protestants. Foxe reported that, on the day that Latimer and Ridley were burned in Oxford, Gardiner declined to begin his dinner until he heard that the fires were lit, following which Gardiner was seized with mortal illness. Gardiner survived the two martyrs by barely a month. Other persecutors and perjurers, according to Foxe's account, suffered such fates as 'a fit of the palsy', and a broken neck, while in another case 'his bowels suddenly gushed out'.

In the reign of Elizabeth, Catholic martyrs were executed at Tyburn. On 1 December, 1581, the Jesuit martyr Edmund Campion was dragged on a hurdle to Tyburn, there to be hung, drawn and quartered. As he passed the arch of Newgate, he raised his racked body to salute the image of the Virgin. The charges against Campion were trumped up and his heroic death led others to adopt the Catholic faith. He was canonised in 1970. Five years later there was not much doubt about the guilt of those involved in the plot of 1586, led by the Catholic Anthony Babington. The crowd, and the Queen, were so appalled by their suffering at their execution on 20 September, 1586, that the remaining conspirators were executed by the comparatively civilised method of hanging the following day.

It was not only those who offended against the current sovereign's religious views that were sent to Newgate. In the reign of Henry VIII, 278 apprentices were arrested for inciting riots against immigrant workers who were supposedly undercutting their wages. Such was their number that Thomas Wolsey sent some to the Tower and others to Newgate before parading them through the streets accompanied by a mobile gallows, as a reminder of their possible fate. Most were reprieved and the gallows packed away, and the disorder appears to

Sir Anthony Babington (1561–1586): born into a Catholic family in Derbyshire, Anthony Babington became a page to Mary, Queen of Scots, in 1577 and seems to have become infatuated with the exiled Queen and her cause. From about 1580 he was a fashionable courtier who was accepted at Elizabeth I's court despite his Catholic sympathies, though he aroused the suspicion of Sir Francis Walsingham, Elizabeth's spymaster. In the 1580s Babington travelled frequently on the Continent where he seems to have made contact with Spanish and other Catholic elements who were planning to assassinate Elizabeth and replace her with Mary, who had a claim to the throne. He carried letters to Mary on behalf of others and exchanged letters with her. This was his downfall, since Walsingham was aware of the plot from a very early stage and intercepted and deciphered the correspondence which damned Babington, his fellow plotters and Mary herself. In September 1586 he and his fellow plotters were arrested and Babington pleaded for his life, begging Elizabeth to spare him and placing the blame for the conspiracy on others. On 20 September he was hanged, drawn and quartered and the following February Mary was herself beheaded after Elizabeth had, with great reluctance, signed the warrant for her execution.

have ceased.[40] At about the same time, in 1526, some bakers were sent to Newgate because they had boycotted the Bridge House, the official supplier of wheat, in favour of cheaper and better supplies from elsewhere. The authorities were anxious to support the Bridge House since profits from this source were used to maintain the nearby London Bridge. At the end of the century, Thomas Green, a goldsmith, was drawn from Newgate to Tyburn on a hurdle and there hanged, drawn and quartered for the 'petty treason' of 'coining' – clipping coins in order to create more, thereby undermining the currency and the economy.

ATTEMPTS AT REFORM

In the reign of James I, disorder within the decaying gaol led the Lord Mayor to issue a proclamation 'for Reforming Abuses within the Gaol of Newgate', a state of affairs that was attributed to the practice of the keepers 'permitting them [the prisoners] strong wine, tobacco, excessive strong drink and resort to women of lewd behaviour'. At a time when disagreements about religion underpinned many controversies more commonly associated with politics, the authorities were concerned to learn that, in 1611, the keeper was allowing Catholic mass to be celebrated in Newgate and there was even a suggestion that a Catholic priest had conducted a marriage ceremony in Newgate in the last decade of Elizabeth's reign.[41] This was, at the time, scandalous, but others were sent to Newgate for crimes that were more innocuous but resonate with the concerns of later centuries as well as Stuart politics.

Thus, in the reign of Charles I, some coachmen were briefly imprisoned for taking the wrong route to Richard Burbage's theatre at Blackfriars. This sounds like an early attempt at traffic management, but may have more to do with the controversial character of the theatre itself. It had been founded in the reign of Elizabeth by Richard Farrant (1535–80), a court musician and Master of the Choristers at Windsor. Theatres were unwelcome within the precincts of the City and were normally banished, with other undesirable activities such as bear-baiting and brothel-keeping, to the south bank of the river at Southwark. This was the site of the Globe and the Rose theatres, but Farrant successfully campaigned to convert the old Blackfriars monastery into a theatre featuring children 'for the better training them to do her Majesty service' at the chapel royal. The boy actors were popular with the public and royal patronage protected it from the disapproving City authorities, but they seized the opportunity to close it in 1608 when the French ambassador complained about an offensive production. By this time Farrant was long dead, but it was reopened by the actor Richard Burbage in company with a number of partners, including William Shakespeare who had lived nearby. Skirmishes between the authorities and the company over controversial productions continued and the erring coachmen may have been among the casualties of these encounters. The theatre was closed in 1642, demolished in 1655. Its former site is marked by Playhouse Yard.

At about the same time one William Cooke, a stationer, was arraigned for what sounds like an infringement of twentieth-century planning regulations. Cooke had erected a wooden shed in which to store his stationery near Furnival's Inn, an Inn of Court associated with Lincoln's Inn and situated on the present site of Holborn Bars (formerly the Prudential Building) in Holborn. Cooke was sent to Newgate pending the demolition of the offending structure, but his incarceration appears to have been a failure since, in the complaining words of Inigo Jones, 'He lies in prison and the shed continues'.[42]

In 1628 a Committee of Aldermen was created 'to view the ruins of Newgate' and, as a result, the City fathers began to execute some repairs. These were piecemeal and could only be carried out by releasing some prisoners from the notoriously overcrowded gaol. Its residents often numbered twice its approximate capacity of 150, particularly before the sessions at the Old Bailey which would despatch many of them to Tyburn. Many were freed by royal pardon provided that they joined the army or navy. William Dominic, a young boy sentenced to death for stealing a purse containing four pounds, was released, 'this being his first offence and he an excellent drummer, fit to do the King service,' in the words of the time.[43] The need for recruits grew as a result of the foreign adventures of Charles I and his favourite Buckingham, whose misguided attempts to use the Royal Navy to relieve the beleaguered Protestants of La Rochelle from Cardinal Richelieu's siege failed despite the infusion of ex-convicts into the ranks of the sailors.

NEWGATE AND STUART POLITICS

Others had to depend upon the politics of the gaoler to secure their release. Just as, in the Tudor era, the occupants of Newgate had reflected the religious whims of sovereigns so in the reign of Charles I they were victims of Charles's disputes with Parliament over taxation.

Thus, in the 1630s the Keeper of Newgate was reprimanded for releasing one Richard Chambers who had been gaoled for refusing to pay ship money. This was a tax that had traditionally been levied on coastal communities under the royal prerogative (that is without the need for Parliamentary consent) to equip a navy. Charles levied the tax on all counties as a form of general taxation in order to avoid the need to bargain with Parliament. It became a major source of controversy in the process that eventually led to the Civil War and Richard Chambers, along with more celebrated opponents such as John Hampden, was one of the casualties. His release from Newgate presumably reflected the Parliamentary sympathies of the keeper.

A less obvious victim of Charles's financial difficulties was Edward Powell, who was sent to Newgate because he had been agitating in Ely against plans 'for the losing of the fens'. This referred to a proposal by the Dutchman Cornelius Vermuyden to drain the Great Fen of East Anglia in Norfolk and Cambridgeshire. Much of the land in these counties lay below sea level and was flooded for most of the year. The Isle of Ely was, literally, an island surrounded by lakes, rivers and marshes. In 1629 Vermuyden, who had already undertaken drainage work on similar land in Lincolnshire and South Yorkshire, informed Charles that, with the King's support, he could create almost 300,000 acres of rich agricultural land from the flooded areas, which would yield substantial revenue to the Crown after the existing landowners, such as the Earl of Bedford, had themselves been paid off. This would have gone a long way towards solving Charles's financial problems. The scheme was opposed by Parliamentarians, led by Oliver Cromwell who was Member of Parliament for the area and a resident of Ely and who did not want to support any plan that would make the King less dependent on Parliament. The King could not imprison Oliver Cromwell at this delicate stage in his quarrel with Parliament, so Edward Powell was sent to Newgate as a more vulnerable opponent of his plan. The argument continued and on 25 January 1641, the year before the dispute with the King became a war, the Long Parliament decided, 'Sir Cornelius Vermuyden shall be forthwith summoned to attend this House, to give an Account by what Authority he goeth on with his Works in the Fens'.[44]

Paradoxically, once he had defeated the King, Cromwell supported the drainage plans and even supplied Vermuyden with some labourers in the form of Scottish prisoners captured at the battle of Dunbar in 1650. Edward Powell's brief confinement in Newgate thus represented a small incident in the sequence of events that led to war.

Further problems followed in 1642 when the reprieve of six Jesuit priests caused other prisoners to riot in the increasingly decrepit gaol. This was another indicator of the politics of the time since Charles's wife, Queen Henrietta Maria, was a French Catholic who was known to be sympathetic to the Jesuit cause. In the same year some sailors were apprehended travelling from France to Ireland by boat and were sent to Newgate by order of Parliament upon suspicion of intending to join a rebellion against its authority. One of the more frequent occupants of Newgate at this time was 'Freeborn John' Lilburne, who managed to spend time in Newgate by offending both Parliamentarians and Royalists. In 1637, together with William Prynne (who had his ears cut off), Lilburne was charged with distributing Puritan pamphlets which opposed the policies of archbishop William Laud. He was sentenced to be pilloried, but his punishment turned into a demonstration against the policies of Laud and the King so he was sent to Newgate. When the Long Parliament was summoned in 1640, Cromwell denounced Lilburne's oppressors and he was released from the prison by order of Parliament. During the Civil War which followed, Lilburne was an effective officer in the Parliamentary army and fought at Edgehill and Marston Moor, in which latter engagement he fought with Cromwell. In 1645, as the Parliamentary cause gained the advantage after the battle of Naseby, he fell out with Parliament and refused to give an account of his actions before the House of Lords, explaining, 'I cannot, without turning traitor to my liberty, dance attendance to their lordships' bar'. For this offence he was now sent by Parliament to Newgate, which was also, at that time, filling up with captured Royalist officers. Lilburne was eventually banished and upon his return in 1653 he was sent to Newgate yet again, this time by Cromwell, despite his acquittal at a trial in the London Guildhall amid popular rejoicing. Never has anyone been sent to Newgate so many times for so many different reasons by so many different people, his fate reflecting the politics of the time, as did that of the Fifth Monarchy men.

This strange sect was a quasi-political movement which flourished during the period of the Protectorate, 1649–61, and whose beliefs were based on a passage in the Old Testament Book of Daniel which predicted five kingdoms, the last of which, the Fifth Monarchy, would make way for a new kingdom on earth. However one of their concerns was the more earthly desire that Cromwell's New Model Army should receive its arrears of pay. The movement's early support for Cromwell collapsed after he put down mutinies in the army and suppressed the Leveller movement. After Cromwell's death a group of Fifth Monarchy men, led by a cooper named Thomas Venner, tried to seize power in January 1661 to prevent the restoration of Charles II. Following the suppression of the rebellion, many of the Fifth Monarchists spent time in Newgate before their execution at Tyburn and one of them, John James, was asked for twenty pounds by the hangman. Upon James (who was probably innocent) protesting that he did not have this sum, the hangman suggested a minimum payment of five pounds unless he wanted him to 'torture him exceedingly'.[45]

Amid all this confusion and in circumstances in which tax revenues were being devoted to more pressing and warlike activities, repairs to the decaying gaol proceeded slowly, a contemporary chronicler recording only that Newgate was 'now well-faced and headed' as the Civil War approached.[46] Work was further interrupted by the exigencies of the war itself, the Protectorate and the restoration of Charles II. A few years after Charles resumed his throne *force majeure* ensured that the rebuilding of Newgate could no longer be postponed.

TWO

An Abode of Misery and Despair

Worse than the worst of the Men, not only in respect to Nastiness and Indecency of Living, but more especially as to their Conversation, which to their great Shame is as profane and wicked as Hell itself can possibly be.

(A description of female prisoners in Newgate
in the early eighteenth century)

I saw the heads when they were brought up to be boiled; the hangman fetched them in a dirty dust basket; setting them down among the felons he and they made sport of them. They took them by the hair, gloating, jeering and laughing at them. The hangman put them into his kettle and par-boiled them with camphor to keep them from putrefaction.

(An inmate's description of a Newgate ritual
of the early eighteenth century)

An abode of misery and despair, a hell such as Dante might have conceived

(Casanova's description of Newgate
in the late eighteenth century)

27

THE GREAT FIRE ·

On the evening of Saturday 1 September 1666, Thomas Farynor, baker to King Charles II, retired to bed after his day's work at his premises in Pudding Lane in the heart of the Medieval buildings of the City of London. He failed to douse the fire in his oven, the embers of which set light to some firewood stacked nearby. By one o'clock the following morning the bakery was ablaze and Farynor, with his wife and daughter, escaped the conflagration by climbing through an upstairs window and making their way along the roofs of adjacent buildings. A maid, who was too frightened to climb on to the roof, remained in the bakery and was one of only six recorded victims of the fire. There were probably many more of whose deaths no record was kept. There were casualties among the animal population, too, as Samuel Pepys recorded in his diary for 2 September, as the fire gathered strength: 'The poor pigeons, I perceive, were loth to leave their houses but hovered about the windows and balconies till they were, some of them, burned [on] their wings and fell down.' Fires were a common hazard in the City, where buildings were mostly constructed of wood, thatch and pitch. Indeed, it was an earlier fire, of 1633, which now saved Southwark since it had destroyed some buildings on the old London Bridge and thereby created a firebreak. However, the strong winds which prevailed on that fateful Sunday ensured that the crude apparatus of buckets and ladders which parishes were obliged to provide against such eventualities were inadequate to the task they confronted.

Samuel Pepys carried a report of the fire to the King at Whitehall, which prompted Charles to send Pepys with a message to the Lord Mayor, Bludworth, ordering that firebreaks be created by demolishing houses in the paths of the flames. Bludworth was very reluctant to do this, fearing the compensation claims that might fall upon the City Corporation. He was also no doubt troubled by the fact that, in the early stages of the fire, he had underestimated the threat it posed, declaring that 'a woman might piss it out'. By the time Pepys delivered the King's instruction Bludworth was in despair. Pepys described the scene in his diary of 2 September:

To St Paul's; and there walked along Watling Street, as well as I could, every creature coming away laden with goods to save and, here and there, sick people carried away in beds. Extraordinary goods carried in carts and on backs. At last my Lord Mayor in Cannon Street, like a man spent, with a handkerchief about his neck. To the king's message he cried, like a fainting woman, 'Lord, what can I do? I am spent: people will not obey me.'

By the Monday the fire had engulfed Lombard Street and Cornhill and was approaching St Paul's, which was duly destroyed in the two days that followed, some of its stones exploding in the heat while molten lead ran from the roof into the streets. By the time the fire burned itself out it had reached Fetter lane, off Fleet Street in the west, approached Smithfield in the north and stopped just short of the Tower of London in the east. Around 13,000 buildings were destroyed, some 80 per cent of the City, including the Medieval St Paul's. Thomas Farynor insisted that the fire had been started deliberately so a scapegoat for the conflagration had to be found and several were available: French, Spanish, Irish and, in particular, Catholic residents. Suspicion fell on 'one Grant, a papist' a shareholder in the New River Company who had supposedly turned off the water supply needed to extinguish the fire.[1] Fortunately for Grant he did not buy his shares until after the fire had done its work. Instead, the blame fell upon a young Frenchman, Robert Hubert, who confessed to starting the fire despite evidence that he had arrived in England two days after it started. He was hanged at Tyburn and when Sir Christopher Wren's Monument was erected in 1667 on the site of Farynor's bakery it included an inscription which attributed the disaster to a Catholic conspiracy. The inscription was removed in the nineteenth century at the behest of the solicitor to the City Corporation, Charles Pearson (1794–1862), and in 1986 the Bakers' Company issued a belated apology for the fire.

Whittington's Newgate prison, at the north-western extremity of the fire, was almost entirely destroyed and had virtually to be rebuilt. The rebuilt prison, completed in 1672, 'maintained the connection with Whittington and was referred to as 'The Whit'. It occupied a relatively small site, measuring about 26 metres by 16 metres, though it was five storeys in height. Henry Chamberlain, in his *History and Survey of the Cities of London and Westminster*, written in 1770, described the main gate of this gaol shortly before its replacement by a new prison. The old gaol had four niches, each containing a lifesize figure. Three of the niches were occupied by figures representing Peace, Security and Plenty. The fourth he described in some detail. In it:[2]

> is a figure, representing Liberty, having the word *Libertas*, inscribed on her cap; and at her feet lies a cat, in allusion to the story of Sir Richard Whittington, a former founder, who is said to have made the first step to his good fortune by a cat.

The eighteenth-century antiquarian Thomas Pennant (1726–98) claimed that the new cat was a replacement for one that had been there in the Medieval gaol before the fire. Pennant had written of the rebuilding of Newgate by 'the executors of the famous Sir Richard Whittington' and added that 'his statue, with the cat, remained in a niche to its final demolition, on the rebuilding of the present prison'.[3] There is no reason to disbelieve Pennant, who was chronicling the buildings of the City rather than compiling a legend. Perhaps there is some truth in the story of the cat after all.

PRISON CONDITIONS

The condition and management of the prisoners in the old prison had been a source of concern for some time before it was destroyed in the fire. In the 1620s prisoners had occasionally been released to relieve overcrowding, either as an act of royal mercy or on condition that the freed prisoners join the army. In 1626 Sir Nicholas Poyntz, who had been gaoled for killing a man in a brawl, complained that a shortage of beds meant that he had been obliged to sleep in a coffin. In 1649 a group of seventeen prisoners, attending their own funeral in the prison chapel the day before their planned execution, started a mêlée with knives, which had been smuggled to them by their wives who had joined them in the congregation. Fifteen of them escaped. In 1662, shortly before the destruction of the prison, Colonel James Turner wrote that the prisoners in the condemned cell 'lie like swine upon the ground, one upon another, howling and roaring – it was more terrible to me than death'.[4]

A number of accounts of the rebuilt prison testify to the fact that conditions were no better and, for 'common' prisoners, could hardly have been worse. Immediately beneath the entrance gate was a dungeon known to the inmates as 'Limbo', which served as the condemned cell. An open sewer ran through the middle of this chamber, emptying its contents into the River Fleet, which ran beneath the Farringdon Road a short distance to the west. The condemned cell also served as a reception area for new arrivals who were fettered in heavy irons and thereby prepared for the exactions which were to be inflicted upon them by their gaolers and fellow inmates. Batty Langley (1696–1751) left an account of the process, which was based on his experience of Newgate in 1724.[5] Langley was an architect and garden designer on which subjects he was the author of more than fifty works. He was confined in Newgate for debt at this time, but was sufficiently in funds to be able to pay for admission to the some of Newgate's more salubrious accommodation. Manacles could be attached to the wrists, shackles to the ankles and iron collars to the neck and these could in turn to be attached to rings and staples in the walls and floors. In Langley's words, 'It is customary when any felons are brought to Newgate to put them first in this condemned hold where they remain till they have paid two shillings and sixpence, after which they are admitted to the masters' or common felons' side'. The irons could remain in place until the victims paid 'easement' of 2s 6d[6] to have them removed. One prisoner died when a neck iron was fastened so tightly that it broke his spine. These were the first of many such charges, which were exacted by the gaolers or 'keepers' in order to repay the investment they made in purchasing the office. The gaolers thus had every reason to keep the gaol full of prisoners. One Newgate keeper paid £40 per annum to Sir Francis Mitchell, a Justice of the Peace for Middlesex, in return for which Mitchell sent all his prisoners to Newgate.

MASTERS AND COMMONS

Once the prisoners were discharged from the reception area they proceeded, with or without their fetters, into one of the eight sections into which the prison accommodation was divided. First, as in the late Medieval prison, there was separate accommodation for men and women, though in 1700 a keeper, William Robison, was found to be charging the male prisoners sixpence for the privilege of admission to the women's quarters. This was not always unwelcome to the women since a woman condemned to hang could, by becoming pregnant, 'plead her belly' and escape the noose for the sake of her unborn child. There was then a further division between felons, who had committed serious criminal offences (against people or property) and debtors who had been gaoled at the behest of their disappointed creditors. The segregation between these groups was not complete and one commentator complained that, 'The debtor, rendered unfortunate by the vicissitudes of trade, undergoes the ignominy of being confined in the same prison with the most abandoned villains'.[7] Finally, within each of these categories there was the more sinister and alarming division between the Masters' side and the Commons'.

The masters were those who could afford to pay for better accommodation and the charges were recorded by Batty Langley.[8] Upon entry, debtors paid 6s 6d and an additional 10s 6d for 'garnish' – a supply of coal and candles. The expression 'garnish' was in common use at the time in connection with apprenticeships, new apprentices being called upon to pay for drinks for their older workmates when they began their indentures. This payment was made to the 'steward' of the ward to which the prisoner was admitted, this post normally being filled by the longest-serving inmate. The most recent arrival, the 'constable', was responsible for keeping the ward clean and making up the fires. Langley makes the

Masters' side sound rather like an English public school of later centuries, with a prefect in charge (the steward) and a fag (the constable) to keep the place clean and tidy.

This theme continues in Langley's very complimentary verdict on the prison regime of Pitt, the governor at this time. In the preface to his work he gives a dedication 'in Justice to Mr Pitt, by the care he reposes in Mr Rowse and Mr Perry (his principal Turnkeys) the *Decorum* [his italics] maintained in Newgate is not inferior to that of a well-regulated family'.[9] The reason for his favourable view of Newgate becomes clear in the sentences which follow, in which he declares that, 'The Master debtors' side is an absolute Paradise compared to the best of Sponging-Houses'. These establishments, which were later caricatured in the novels of William Makepeace Thackeray and Charles Dickens, were relatively comfortable semi-official places of confinement run by bailiffs or Sheriffs. Debtors were taken to them and were detained there under threat of being taken to Newgate or other prisons until such time as they reached an accommodation with their creditors. While they were held in these establishments the unfortunate debtors were grossly over-charged for food, wine, tobacco and other essentials, most of which would be consumed by their gloating 'hosts'. In Langley's words, 'The chief Swine of the Herd comes to you and, after some few Judas compliments he calls for Pipes, Tobacco and a Bottle of Wine . . . you must understand that Good Manners amongst Bailiffs are as scarce to be found as Honesty.'[10] Langley estimated that twenty-four hours in Newgate under Pitt's regime cost him 1*s* 7½*d* compared to 17*s* 6*d* in the bailiff's sponging house.

Things did not go so well with those who were unable to pay the customary exactions. In the words of a contemporary report, those 'not having the wherewithal to pay were stripped, beaten and abused in a most violent manner'.[11] Garnish was also paid by felons, but they paid a higher entry charge – 14*s* 10*d*. Beds cost 3*s* 6*d* a week while a daily charge of 1*s* 6*d* was made for visitors who were received in a room known as the 'gigger'. Prisoners also had to pay a fee to be discharged, even if they had been found not guilty of the offences of which they were accused. Many remained in custody because they lacked the discharge fee or owed money for food, and attempts by well-wishers to pay these debts could themselves be frustrated by avaricious gaolers. A Frenchman visiting England in the 1720s offered 1s to a young woman in this situation only to find the gaoler demanding half of it as his fee.[12] In the mid-eighteenth century there were thirteen Common wards (cells occupied by several people) and four Masters' wards. The prison was designed to hold 150 prisoners, but normally contained at least 250 – a number substantially exceeded immediately prior to the sessions in the Old Bailey next door.

The situation that prevailed on the 'Common's' side beggars description. Batty Langley wrote that 'such Wickedness abounds therein that the Place seems to have the exact aspect of Hell itself' and added, as if to remove any doubts in the mind of the reader, that 'the Augean Stable could bear no Comparison to it'.[13] There were no beds and food was of the poorest quality served in the smallest portions: a daily portion of bread, with beef served once a week. They were supervised by 'cellarmen' or 'partners'. These were themselves prisoners who had bid for the office and, in return, sold candles to the inmates to provide some relief to the Stygian gloom in which they lived. The partners were also responsible for removing fetters, upon payment to the keepers, and for distributing food to the inmates. The conditions were described by Daniel Defoe during his brief incarceration in words he put into the mouth of his heroine Moll Flanders who, in his novel *The Fortunes and Misfortunes of Moll Flanders who was Born in Newgate* described it as 'an emblem of hell itself and a kind of entrance to it'.[14]

In putting these words into Moll's mouth Defoe may have reflected the experience of Batty Langley who had described the female inmates as being 'exceedingly worse than the worst of the Men, not only in respect to Nastiness and Indecency of Living, but more especially as to their Conversation, which to their great Shame is as profane and wicked as Hell itself can possibly be'.[15] The Italian libertine Giacomo Casanova, who spent some time in Newgate following a 'misunderstanding' over a marriage proposal, described it as an 'abode of misery and despair, a hell such as Dante might

have conceived'.[16] As we will see, these were not the only commentators to compare Newgate with the infernal regions. Lice and fleas
helped to spread the typhus ('gaol fever') which killed far more
inmates than the gallows. In 1726, for example, twenty-one
prisoners from Newgate were hanged at Tyburn while eighty-three
died from gaol fever.[17]

The keepers and their 'partners' or cellarmen found other ways of
supplementing their pay. In 1724 the Corporation investigated
complaints from prisoners that the partners had stolen charitable
donations intended to relieve the suffering of the Common prisoners
and, further, that they had sold to shopkeepers much of the bread
intended to feed the prisoners. The charges were well founded and
the Corporation insisted that, henceforward, the partners should be
elected by the prisoners rather than appointed by the keepers as
their accomplices in exploiting their fellow inmates.[18] Further
payments could be exacted from the families of prisoners who died
in Newgate before the corpse was released for burial, the clothes
having been removed and sold in the meantime.

THE PRESS YARD

The most salubrious accommodation was to be found in the Press
Yard, that grim place of torture which had fallen out of use at
Newgate by the time that Langley was writing. It was described as
being for 'prisoners of note', but these were in practice inmates who
could pay fees ranging from £20 to £500 upon admission, 'in
proportion to the Quality of the Prisoner' according to Batty Langley
– in other words according to the amount the keeper could extort at
any one time. These privileged prisoners could live in the Press Yard,
with their families, in conditions which were little different from
their homes. A cleaner could be provided for 1s a week while the fee
for a visiting prostitute was 1s a night. A Major John Bernardi
married and raised three children in the Press Yard in the 1720s.

The atmosphere in the Press Yard was described by a contemporary chronicler, the anonymous author of *History of the Press*

Yard, published in 1717. He was welcomed to Newgate by an inmate called George who had been gaoled for wearing his best suit of clothes on the birthday of the Old Pretender, 'King James III', who had instigated an uprising against the Hanoverian monarchy in 1715 – a victim of the politics of the time. The author described himself as one of the 'Brethren of the Quill',[19] who had been gaoled for writing in disparaging terms about the Hanoverian succession. He explained that he had been sent to Newgate 'there to reflect with myself on my past indiscretion and to cool my Heels, till the Act for suspending the Habeas Corpus Act should be out of force'.[20] He described the reception which he experienced on arriving at the gaol – a process which has all the characteristics of a ritual designed to demoralise its object and prepare him for the exactions of his gaolers.

He entered first the Keeper's Lodge, which was on the opposite side of Newgate Street from the prison itself, joined to it by a bridge which formed an arch across the road. The writer recorded that 'this tomb of the living was once the Phoenix Inn by Newgate Street and being contiguous to the Gaol[21] of that name was added to it in the Times of Usurpation' – presumably a reference to Cromwell's Protectorate by this supporter of the Stuart monarchy. He was first greeted by a turnkey who, having looked him over, declared loudly, 'We shall have a hot supper tonight, the Cull [fellow] looks as if he had the Blunt [money] and I must come in for a share of it after my few Masters have done with him.' The new arrival then received a measure of brandy from 'a short thick protuberance of female flesh not less than five yards in the Waist'.[22] This lady appears to have been a prisoner. There followed a loud discussion between the turnkey and the protuberance as to whether 40lb weight of irons would suffice for the newcomer or whether a greater burden would be required to subdue him.

Shortly after this alarming conversation ended the author heard a disembodied voice coming from above his head. The voice cried, 'Sir, I understand that you are a Gentleman too well Educated to take up your abode in a vault set aside only for Thieves, Parricides and Murderers . . . you may be removed to a Chamber equal to one in any private House where you may be furnished with the best Conversation.' Having been softened up by his reception it is not surprising that the writer took up the gaoler's offer, at his own expense: an entrance fee of twenty guineas and a weekly charge of 11*s*: far more than the exactions demanded for admission to the Masters' side. The author speculated on the origins of the term 'Press Yard' and dismissed the suggestion that it referred to its use for applying *Peine Forte et Dure* ('strong and harsh punishment', see Chapter One) to those who refused to plead,[23] preferring to believe that it referred to the oppressive charges levied on those who resided there. The turnkey explained that the charges were necessary because the keeper had paid £5,000 for his post and needed to recoup his investment.[24]

His description of the Press Yard, to which he was now admitted, makes it sound like a gentlemen's club. His companions included a number of army officers who had backed the wrong dynasty when George I ascended the throne in 1714 as the first Hanoverian monarch. One of them was a contemporary of the Duke of Marlborough and this officer, together with another who was a septuagenarian, had both married while in Newgate. A third resident was described as an orange merchant who had been forging bills of the relatively new Bank of England by means of the application of lemon juice to their surface in some unspecified way and had been betrayed by a fellow conspirator. Others included a mathematician and a classical scholar. Evenings were spent smoking, drinking, playing skittles and conversing about former inmates of the Press Yard, with particular emphasis on the finer points of their last journeys to Tyburn. On these occasions friends, relatives, admirers and curious visitors were admitted to their circle to add to the blend of gossip, cultivated conversation and light entertainment, though they also served a less refined purpose 'to comfort the distressed Inhabitants of this Place by the only method that is capable viz. by inordinate drinking'.[25] In defence of the residents it should be added that those who, on one of these occasions, 'had gone beyond the Rules of Decency in their Cups' paid a fine (in drink of course) to the turnkey the following morning.

THE 1715 REBELLION

A popular subject of conversation at these gatherings concerned the prospects of the 1715 uprising, which aimed to restore the Stuart dynasty to the throne in the form of James III, the Old Pretender, son of James II who had been deposed in the Glorious Revolution of 1688. The uprising was beginning as Batty Langley entered the gaol and was the subject of much confident and optimistic speculation as the inmates contemplated the restoration of their freedom and fortunes by a newly restored Stuart dynasty. As news of the collapse of the insurrection reached the gaol it was greeted initially with disbelief and then with a learned discussion among the inmates of the faulty tactics adopted by the rebel commanders. Several of these were shortly to join the residents of the Press Yard and the chronicler was allowed to watch their arrival from a vantage point in the Keeper's Lodge opposite the entrance to Newgate – no doubt in return for a suitable fee.

These new inmates included the notably incompetent rebel general Thomas Forster (1675–1738), who had been given the command of the largely Scottish force because of his status as a Member of Parliament rather than because of any military experience. Faced with a Royalist force at Preston, Forster lost heart and the result was the collapse of the Jacobite cause. Forster complained about his incarceration in Newgate, arguing that his status as MP entitled him to be sent to the Tower of London, the traditional lodging for high-level traitors. He was probably glad that his protest was ignored since he managed to escape from Newgate with the assistance of a key made by his servant. Pitt, the Keeper of Newgate, was taking wine with Forster, as was his custom, when he was induced to go from the room to the cellar. There Pitt was locked in while Forster made good his escape. Forster fled to France, despite a reward of £1,000 for his recapture, and died of asthma in Boulogne in 1738.

Pitt was arrested for this lapse while his Jacobite prisoners enjoyed a luxurious lifestyle thanks to the venison, ham, chicken and other comestibles supplied to these glamorous residents by female admirers.[26] The mood changed, however, when the trials and executions began of those involved in the rebellion. Some of them petitioned to be treated as prisoners of war rather than traitors, hoping to persuade the retired Duke of Marlborough himself to intercede on their behalf. This stratagem having failed, some of the rebels who were executed took advantage of their dying speeches on the scaffold to trumpet their defiance. Thus, William Paul, who was executed in July 1716, advised the onlookers to 'remember that King James III is your Rightful Sovereign . . . do all you can to restore him to his crown'.[27]

One of the evening discussions was joined by the executioner who rejoiced that one of the prospective outcomes of the 1715 uprising and the fiasco at Preston would be a significant boost to his income. He anticipated payment of £3 for beheading a peer and the same for hanging, drawing and quartering a gentleman. Additional perquisites were expected to include the clothes worn by the victims, any money in the pockets and additional fees he described as 'respective gratifications they shall make me for a quick and easy despatch, provided the king does not spoil my market by reprieves and pardons'. Provided there was no such misguided mercy on the part of the monarch the executioner foresaw a bumper harvest of as many as seventy victims. He outlined with satisfaction his plans to invest the proceeds: 'I shall not only purchase the title of an Esquire but the Estate too'.[28]

This first Jacobite uprising was even more profitable for Pitt, the Keeper of Newgate who needed to recoup the outlay of several thousand pounds that he had paid for the post. His brief incarceration for allowing Forster to escape did not prevent him from reaping a handsome profit from the remaining prisoners. They were put in Newgate's dungeons until, in the words of an observer 'for better lodgement they had advanced more money than would have rented one of the best houses in Piccadilly'.[29] Nearly ten years later Batty Langley recorded that the weekly rents in the Press Yard had increased greatly 'when the Preston Gentlemen were imprisoned therein'.[30] Having settled into their more salubrious accommodation these unwilling guests then made further payments for fine wines, games and the admission of visitors. Pitt made about £4,000 from his exactions in four months.

JACK KETCH'S KITCHEN

There was also a punishment room known as the 'Bilbows' and a sinister room occupied by those about to be taken to execution known as 'Jack Ketch's Kitchen' after the prison's most notorious executioner. According to Batty Langley this room was 'that place in which that honest fellow [the executioner] boils the quarters of such men as have been executed for treason', this being a necessary preparation for their gibbeting, a process described in a later chapter.[31] The grim ritual was described in 1661 by a visitor named Ellwood at a time when there was a steady flow of regicides' violated corpses following the restoration of Charles II and the vengeance which he inflicted upon those who had executed his father. The procedure was carried out by the hangman assisted by some felons:

I saw the heads when they were brought up to be boiled; the hangman fetched them in a dirty dust basket; setting them down among the felons he and they made sport of them. They took them by the hair, gloating, jeering and laughing at them. The hangman put them into his kettle and par-boiled them with camphor to keep them from putrefaction.

The heads would then have been taken away to be impaled on spikes at such vantage points as Westminster, London Bridge and Newgate itself as a warning to others. The remaining bits of the victims' quartered corpses could then be reclaimed, upon payment, for burial by their families.[32]

Prisoners who could no longer afford to pay for the better accommodation could be subjected to persecution in the hope that their families would come to their rescue and thereby line the gaoler's pockets. The most notorious case occurred at the nearby Fleet prison in 1728 and was revealed by the Member of Parliament James Oglethorpe, who later founded the colony of Georgia for discharged debtors. The Keeper, Thomas Bambridge, had paid £5,000 for the office and was alarmed when a prosperous inmate, named Robert Castell, declined to make further payments for the accommodation he was renting. Bambridge therefore moved Castell to a part of the prison where there was a smallpox epidemic. Castell duly died of the horrible disease. Bambridge also had a dungeon called the Strong Room, which he kept as a place of punishment and which he sometimes used for storing corpses to keep the inmates company.

EXACTIONS BY INMATES

The financial penalties were imposed not only by the keeper and his accomplices, the cellarmen and stewards. Long-term inmates had their own methods of exacting payment from newcomers who, upon arriving at the gaol, were told to 'pay or strip'. Either they paid out 'rhino' or 'chummage',[33] a sum of money to buy drink for their fellow prisoners or their clothes were removed and sold for the same purpose.[34] In the words of a contemporary:

If any prisoner comes in and has not the wherewithal to pay the garnish money he or she is presently conveyed to a place they called *Tangier* and there stripped, beaten and abused in a very violent manner.[35]

Batty Langley described the atmosphere in 'Tangier' in forthright terms:

The Air in this Ward is very bad, occasioned by the Multitude of Prisoners in it and the Filthiness of their Lodgings.[36]

An inmate called John Hall described it, at about the same time, as 'the nastiest place in the gaol' and stated that most of its occupants were debtors, which presumably meant that they owed money to the prison authorities rather than to creditors outside the gaol. If so, Tangier was no doubt designed to encourage them to settle their debts.[37]

The plight of one unconvicted prisoner, by profession a lawyer, was described by his distressed wife who told of:[38]

The wretches making game of him and enjoying my distress . . . though they could not force him to gamble he was compelled to drink and I was obliged to let him have five shillings to pay his share, otherwise he would have been stripped of his clothes.

PRISON ROUTINE

The prison routine was described in the *Memoirs of the Right Villainous John Hall*, published in 1708 by a robber of that name who spent his time before his execution at Tyburn in 1707 compiling an account of his experiences in the infamous gaol. Hall had previously been whipped at the cart's tail and narrowly escaped death and transportation for housebreaking so, on his final committal to Newgate, he was not without experience of the criminal justice system. Even he was awed by Newgate. Hall's experience of the Common side of the gaol may be contrasted with the author of *The History of the Press Yard*, referred to above. Upon arrival, Hall was pinioned by two 'truncheon officers' (turnkeys), while two others picked his pockets. He was then handed over to two convicts 'who hovered about him like so many Crows about a Piece of Carrion' and demanded *6s 8d* garnish money 'otherwise they strip the poor wretch if he has not the wherewithal to pay it'. Having thus 'matriculated' he was taken to a ward 'which, to give the Devils their due, is kept very neat and clean' whereas another ward, for those unable to pay, 'one would take to be Old Nick's backside . . . the Lice crawling under their feet make such a Noise as walking on Shells which are strewed over Garden Walks' in Hall's evocative words.[39] Adjacent to this was a small room known as the 'Buggering Hold', possibly because it contained those convicted of sodomy. The women's quarters contained residents whose behaviour caused even this hardened robber to blush since 'the Licentiousness of the Women on this side is so detestable that it is an unpardonable Crime to describe their Lewdness'.[40] The staff were little better. The gaoler was described as one who 'distils money out of poor Prisoners' Tears and grows fat by their curses' while the condemned sermon,[41] preached to those about to be taken to execution, is described as being on the subject of 'Holy Dying; for to preach up Amendment of Life, would here be Eloquence thrown away'.[42]

Hall also provides an interesting insight into the hierarchy which prevailed among the prisoners and the strange prison vernacular, many of whose expressions have entered the language. Thus 'hoisters' helped to lift fellow criminals over walls while 'Sneaking Badgers' stole from market stalls – early shoplifters. A 'Buttock and Twang' was a woman who picked up men on the street and then confronted them with a 'pretended husband' who would demand money. Some idea of the low esteem in which pickpockets were held may be inferred from Hall's comment that 'a Pickpocket is no more a Companion for a Reputable Housebreaker than an Informer is for a Justice of the Peace'.[43] He compares Newgate with a university where a first-time offender has a Bachelor's Degree, a more experienced inmate a Master's Degree or a Fellowship, while one who hears the condemned sermon is 'Head of his Order'. 'Blunt' is money, 'booze' is already in use meaning strong drink, a 'cove' is a man, a 'tye' is a neckcloth, a 'nutcracker' is the pillory, while the word 'fence' already signifies one who deals in stolen goods. A 'café' is a bawdy-house, while Newgate is referred to as 'The Whit', in reference to Richard Whittington's rebuilding.

At 7 a.m. the prisoners were awoken by a bell which summoned them from their wards to empty their chamber pots and to be counted before having their breakfasts. From breakfast until mid-afternoon the prisoners were left to their own devices, much of the time being devoted to drinking, which was a critical element of the Newgate regime and fulfilled the needs of both prisoners and gaolers. Liquor was plentiful and many prisoners lived in a state of almost permanent inebriation in order to mitigate the effects of incarceration until death mercifully released them from their sufferings. Wine was relatively costly at 2s a bottle, but a condition of senselessness could be achieved fairly cheaply with brandy at 4d for a quarter bottle.[44]

For the keepers, who ran the taphouse, liquor was a source of profit estimated as about £400 per annum in the eighteenth century and it was also a means of maintaining order in the overcrowded gaol. In the words of one keeper in 1787, 'When the prisoners are drunk they tend to be docile and quite free from rioting.'[45]

In 1699 the Society for Promoting Christian Knowledge (SPCK) appointed Dr Thomas Bray, one of its founders, to investigate conditions in Newgate and he reported on 'the personal lewdness of the keepers' and the practice of 'old criminals corrupting newcomers', the latter being a feature of prison life that would be recognised by twenty-first-century criminologists. One observer commented that, 'instead of employing their time in the amendment of life and a religious preparation for their trial, prisoners are forced to drink, riot and game to curry favour with the gaoler and support his luxury'.[46]

Dr Thomas Bray (*c.* 1658–1730): born near Oswestry, on the Welsh borders, Bray was the son of a farmer, and was educated at the local grammar school and at All Souls, Oxford, as a poor scholar. In the seventeenth century the American colonies were technically the responsibility of the Bishop of London who in 1696 sent Bray to the colony of Maryland to find ways of increasing the numbers of Anglican clergymen available to minister to its growing population. He was remarkably successful both in recruiting clergy and in raising funds to equip them with clerical regalia and a selection of over fifty texts with which to spread the Gospel. He also founded lending libraries for poor clergy at home and overseas. In 1717 he founded 'Dr Bray Associates' which was devoted to the education of plantation slaves. In 1701 he persuaded William III to grant a Royal Charter for the foundation of what became the Society for Promoting Christian Knowledge. He devoted much energy to the reform of prison conditions, one of the first to do so. He ended his days as incumbent of St Botolph's, Aldgate, back in the heart of the diocese of London.

At this time there were no ordinances in place to govern the routine of the prison so in 1730 a particularly enterprising prisoner called Joseph Woolan and his wife opened a rival taphouse which, at the request of the indignant keepers, was closed by order of the City Sheriffs. Seven years later the same fate befell a still which had been designed by another inmate, but a few years after that, in 1756, the Sheriffs compelled the keeper to reimburse prisoners who had complained that the official taphouse was supplying them with 'hogwash' – watered-down beer. Later in the century a group of prisoners organised the 'Free and Easy Club', a drinking club whose avowed aim was 'to promote tumult and disorder' and which survived until it was banned in 1808.[47]

Other occupations included badger-baiting and gambling, a pastime which was especially popular among those awaiting execution and who presumably felt that they had nothing to lose by it. William Robison, the Keeper of Newgate from 1700 to 1707 referred to earlier, provided more diverse forms of entertainment by admitting whores to the prison and encouraging them to bring with them stolen goods, thus providing a ready market for this merchandise. He was only maintaining a well-established tradition since forty years earlier a Recorder had observed that 'the Keeper of Newgate hath at this day made his house the only nursery of rogues, prostitutes, pickpockets and thieves in the world'.[48] Those who had not the means to gamble could amuse themselves by tormenting the neighbours and passers-by who were liable to be bombarded with insults, the contents of chamber pots and the output of urinating and excreting prisoners, some of whom climbed on to the roof the better to spread their output.[49]

In the afternoon the main meal of the day was served. This included roast meat for the Masters' side and bread and water for the Common side, where meat was served perhaps once a week unless it was purloined by the keepers and sold to local merchants. At ten o'clock the prisoners were herded to their wards by the keepers and cellarmen, 'like drivers with so many Turkish slaves' according to Hall.

CRIMINAL CONTACTS

Some of the minor officials at the gaol established beneficial liaisons with local criminals. Ralph Briscoe, a seventeenth-century clerk of Newgate, formed a liaison with a former inmate, the notorious Mary Frith, better known as Moll Cutpurse. Briscoe would organise the packing of a jury or a reprieve for one of Moll's associates and in return she would lay on a particularly savage example of Briscoe's favourite sport of bull-baiting.

The City authorities remained indifferent to these appalling conditions until, in 1750 forty-three officials, including two judges at the nearby Old Bailey, along with the Lord Mayor and many jurymen, succumbed to gaol fever (typhus). This encouraged them to install a

Moll Cutpurse (*c.* 1584–1659): born Mary Frith, in the Barbican, Moll quickly established a reputation as a hoyden, or tomboy, more interested in bull-and bear-baiting than in traditional feminine activities. An attempt by her uncle to send her to America was frustrated when she escaped from the ship before it set sail and, dressed as a man, she became a prominent member of a gang of thieves operating in the City. They specialised in the art of the cutpurse, or pickpocket, for which she was branded and spent time in Newgate, but her career as a robber ended when she carried out a highway robbery on the Parliamentary General Thomas Fairfax. After this she was caught and condemned, but secured a pardon by a payment of £2,000. She then became a 'fence', disposing of property stolen by others, and an organiser of crimes carried out by others. She devised a new crime, which involved stealing the unguarded ledgers of traders, containing records essential to the businesses, and charging for their return. She died shortly after the death of Oliver Cromwell and, a keen Royalist, she left £20 in her will to celebrate the forthcoming restoration of Charles II.

Dr Stephen Hales (1677–1761): born in Kent, Hales was a clergyman, botanist and biologist. He served as curate at Teddington, Middlesex. Like many clergymen of the age, including Gilbert White and George Crabbe, he devoted his considerable leisure time to the study of science. He was a pioneer in botany, particularly in the study of the mechanisms by which plants used water and in demonstrating that plant sap flows upwards. He studied the effect of electrical impulses on the physiology of animals and devised a method for measuring blood pressure. He became a Fellow of the Royal Society in 1718 and in 1754 was a founder of the Society for the Encouragement of Arts, Manufactures and Commerce, later the Royal Society of Arts. He campaigned against the practice of drinking spirits and advocated the distillation of fresh water from seawater. In his honour an annual Stephen Hales prize is awarded by the American Society of Plant Biologists to a scientist who has made a noteworthy contribution to that science.

windmill on the roof of the gaol, designed by a Dr Hales, to improve ventilation, but seven of the eleven labourers employed in installing the device themselves succumbed to the fever which is carried by fleas. The authorities now began to make plans to replace the foetid and decaying gaol with a new one designed by George Dance.

THE OLD BAILEY

Newgate's neighbour and provider of many of its inmates, the Old Bailey courthouse, had also been destroyed in the Great Fire and had been reconstructed in a more enlightened manner. In 1673 it was rebuilt as a three-storey brick building in an Italianate style, described by the contemporary chronicler John Strype as 'a fair and stately building'. The ground floor, where the courtroom was situated, was

open to the elements – a device designed to ensure the free circula-
tion of air and hence reduce the incidence of typhus passed on by the
residents of the gaol when they were brought before the court. The
courtyard outside accommodated spectators, some of whom were
drawn by the curiosity which accompanied the trials of celebrated or
notorious defendants. Others, it was suggested, were professional
criminals who wished to familiarise themselves with court layout
and procedure in order to plan their escapes or to devise suitable
strategies for their defence should the need arise. A third category
consisted of friends of infamous criminals on trial, their presence
designed to 'influence' the deliberations of the juries.

In 1737 the building was remodelled and the open courtroom on
the ground floor was enclosed, supposedly to keep out the weather,
though it may have been prompted by a desire to reduce the influence of the crowds assembled in the courtyard. Thirteen years later,
as we have seen, an outbreak of typhus killed forty-three people at
the courthouse. This did not deter the spectators. Their visits to the
courtroom itself were profitable to the court officials who levied an
entry charge. In 1771 John Wilkes, then Sheriff of London, tried to
stop this practice as being undemocratic, but he was persuaded to
rescind his prohibition when the press of people trying to enter the
court led to a near riot.

TWO CELEBRITY PRISONERS

Just as Newgate and nearby Smithfield had become notorious for the
sufferings of those whose religious beliefs did not accord with the
whims of Tudor monarchs, so the Stuart and early Hanoverian
period became associated with prisoners who owed their celebrity
either to their notoriety or to their beneficial influence on their
fellow citizens. Daniel Defoe, the author of *Moll Flanders*, was one
of these whose brief stay in Newgate provided him with material for
his novel without inflicting undue hardship on the author. Defoe was
born Daniel Foe in 1659 or 1660 and added the 'De' to his name in
1703 for reasons unknown. He was the son of a butcher of

Presbyterian belief and Flemish descent in the parish of St Giles, Cripplegate. Daniel was intended for the ministry, but instead followed a chequered career as merchant, brickmaker, insurance agent and pamphleteer. He was bankrupted on more than one occasion and rescued from his creditors by patrons who valued his talents as a propagandist on behalf of the Whig party. He escaped the potentially fatal consequences of joining the Duke of Monmouth's ill-judged rebellion in 1685 and became a supporter of William of Orange. This did not save him from Newgate and the pillory for publishing, in 1702, *The Shortest Way with Dissenters*, which lampooned the established Church's intolerant view of those who deviated from its doctrines.

However, such was the sympathy of the London mob that Defoe did not suffer the painful consequences that could result from exposure in the pillory. In his honour the pillory was draped in flowers and he survived the process unscathed.[50] Defoe is remembered as one of the fathers of the English novel with *Robinson Crusoe*, published in 1719, and *Moll Flanders* (1722) in which he made full use of his brief experience of Newgate. Despite these successes he was, as usual, in straitened financial circumstances at the time of his death in 1731.

An earlier, and more heroic inmate was William Penn. He was born in London in 1644 to an English father, an admiral in the navy who served both the Stuart monarchs and Oliver Cromwell with distinction. His mother Margaret was described by Samuel Pepys as a 'well-looked, fat, short old Dutch woman, but one who hath been heretofore pretty handsome'. He entered Oxford University, but was expelled in 1661, aged 17, for views which were eventually to send him to Newgate. He showed what the authorities regarded as an unhealthy interest in dissenting religions and protested against the requirement to attend college chapel. He then attended a French Protestant university in Saumur during a brief period of comparative religious toleration in France before entering Lincoln's Inn and acquiring the knowledge of the Common Law and judicial procedure which he would shortly need.

In 1667 he was arrested while attending a meeting of the Quakers, or Society of Friends, a sect founded by George Fox in 1647 whose emphasis on the direct relationship between believers and God, without the need for intermediaries such as clergymen to expound Christian doctrine, was regarded by the secular and ecclesiastical authorities as particularly seditious and threatening. During a short spell as a prisoner in the Tower of London Penn wrote much of the early Quaker literature which presented a historical case for religious toleration and declared, 'I owe my conscience to no mortal man.'

He was by now identified as a serious dissident voice. The authorities duly closed the Quaker meeting house in Gracechurch Street which Penn attended, whereupon he and a fellow preacher, William Meade, held their meeting in the street. He was taken to Newgate and tried in the Old Bailey before a bench, which included the Lord Mayor,[51] under a rather strangely framed charge of sedition which claimed that he and Meade, by preaching, had 'met together with force of arms to the terror and disturbance of His Majesty's liege subjects'. Penn, with his sharp mind and legal training, was able to challenge this absurd charge so effectively that the enraged Lord Mayor interrupted his courtroom speech, crying, 'Stop his mouth! Bring fetters and stake him to the ground.'

The jury were not impressed and the foreman, Edmund Bushell, returned a verdict of 'not guilty' at which point The Lord Mayor informed them, 'You shall not be dismissed till we have a verdict that the court will accept. You will be locked up without meat, drink, fire or tobacco. We will have a verdict by the Grace of God or you shall starve for it.'[52] This rather unusual judicial pronouncement led to the incarceration of the jury in Newgate, which failed to move them, as did the fines that the Mayor imposed on the recalcitrant jurors. They were rescued from the infamous prison by a writ of habeas corpus and a decision of the Lord Chief Justice that jurors could not be coerced or punished for their verdicts: a critical decision for the rights of juries. Penn was sent to Newgate the following year by a more compliant jury. Upon entering the Common side he commented, 'When we came to Newgate we found that side of the prison full of Friends [i.e. Quakers].' Penn is usually remembered as the founder of the state of Pennsylvania, under a charter granted by Charles II in 1681, perhaps because the King was anxious to despatch his well-intentioned but troublesome subject across the ocean. The colony flourished, but Penn was no administrator and his own fortunes declined. He returned to England and died in 1718. He is buried in the Quaker village of Jordans, Buckinghamshire, not far from his ancestral village of Penn in the same county.

POLITICS

Penn, like many other inmates of Newgate, had been consigned to the prison by the justices of the Old Bailey for reasons that reflected the politics and fears of the age. Whereas in the reigns of the Tudors and the earlier Stuarts many of the victims had been incarcerated and executed, because their religious opinions differed from those of the sovereign, in the 1690s anxieties shifted to the coin of the realm. The foundation of the Bank of England in 1694 and the cost of William III's wars with Louis XIV placed a new emphasis on the need to preserve the integrity of the currency. In 1696 Sir Isaac Newton, already renowned throughout Europe for his mathematical work, was appointed Warden of the Royal Mint, one of his tasks being that of preventing the debasement of the coinage. He pursued 'coiners' relentlessly and at this time Newgate acquired hundreds of prisoners convicted of this crime. The offence was regarded as 'petty treason', which meant that men were liable to be hanged, drawn and quartered while female coiners were burned. This was the fate of Elizabeth Hare who was burned in Bunhill Fields, the reprieve that was customary in such cases being opposed by the Treasury unless her accomplices were identified.

Highwaymen were also becoming a problem and some of the most notorious prisoners of the seventeenth century fell into this category, though it was not until the Hanoverian period that they acquired the status of major celebrities. Rewards as high as £40 were offered for their arrest and those suspected of the crime were paraded before the door of Newgate on horseback in the hope that their victims would recognise them – an early if crude form of identity parade. One of the most notorious was Jack Cottington, known as 'Mulled Sack' because of his legendary capacity for that drink (warm sherry). Having failed to pick Oliver Cromwell's pocket at Westminster, he robbed a wagon on the Oxford Road of a sum alleged to be £4,000 intended as wages for the army. He escaped justice by bribing the Abingdon jury, which had been empanelled to try him. The abduction of heiresses was another popular crime at this time, as in the case of a Captain Clifford who spent a year in Newgate in 1683 for abducting a wealthy widow, taking her to Calais and forcing her to marry him.

As in previous centuries the pillory remained in use as an alternative or additional punishment to gaol, though the effects of this device were unpredictable and could be either fatal or benign. Thus, in 1732 John Waller, who had given false information against those accused of highway robbery, was pelted to death in the pillory by an enraged rob who looked with some favour on highwaymen, partly because of their audacity and partly because those who travelled on the highway, especially in coaches, were thought of as wealthy and well able to afford their fate. In 1765 James Williams, publisher of John Wilkes's *North Briton*, was treated as a hero. The offending issue of the paper, number 45, had accused the King's government, led by Lord Bute, of falsehood. Wilkes had escaped a charge of seditious libel when the Lord Chief Justice ruled that his status as a Member of Parliament exempted him from prosecution, so the government proceeded against Williams instead. Far from pelting Williams, the crowd protected him, collected 200 guineas for him and executed Lord Bute in effigy. A Dr Shebbeare, who was pilloried for a similar offence a few years earlier, was driven to the pillory by an under-sheriff whose footman then stood by with an umbrella to protect Shebbeare from the elements.

By this time Newgate was once again in a poor state of repair. In 1770 a programme of reconstruction began and in 1774 this was extended to its neighbour, the Old Bailey. The work was barely completed when the events of 1780 determined that the new gaol would have a very short life and would swiftly be replaced with a new design by a famous architect.

THREE

The Bloody Code: Punishment in Hanoverian England

The Bloody Code was monstrous and ineffectual. Its vice lay in the enormous disproportion it maintained between offences and penalties. It gave the impression of a world in which 'great thieves hang little ones'. It was not justice that was administered; it was a war that was waged between two classes of the community.

(*The Times*, editorial, 25 July 1872)

Instead of making the gallows an object of terror, our executions contribute to make it an object of contempt in the eye of the malefactor; and we sacrifice the lives of men, not for the reformation but the diversion of the populace.

(Henry Fielding, magistrate at Bow Street)

THE PENAL CODE

In 1582 William Lambard of Lincoln's Inn applauded the fact that the English penal code no longer included 'pulling out the tongue for false rumours, cutting off the nose for adultery, taking away the privy parts for counterfeiting of money' or certain other punishments associated with the Medieval period. That is not to say that the

53

remaining penalties were altogether humane. Lambard divided them into three categories – infamous, pecuniary and corporal.[1] Infamous punishments were reserved for crimes such as treason and involved such hideous processes as hanging, drawing and quartering. Pecuniary penalties involved fines for such offences as swearing, playing a musical instrument on the Sabbath or failing to attend church. They were mostly imposed by Justices of the Peace and constituted an important source of revenue for the clerks who advised the Justices. The third category, corporal punishments, Lambard divided into 'either Capital or not Capital. Capital (or deadly) punishment is done sundry ways, as by hanging, burning, boiling or pressing. Not Capital is of diverse forms as of cutting off the hand or ear, burning, whipping, imprisoning, stocking, setting in the pillory or ducking stool'.

From this description it is evident that imprisonment was only one of many punishments available and was, in fact, comparatively unusual, partly on account of the expense involved in constructing and maintaining prisons. Newgate itself, London's largest prison, had a capacity of only 150 prisoners until the late eighteenth century, though this was often exceeded. Fines, on the other hand, were a useful source of revenue for the courts, while mutilations and public whippings were a popular if gruesome public spectacle. Thus, in 1572, an 'Act for the Punishment of Vagabonds' prescribed that such reprobates as 'fortune tellers, pedlars, players and jugglers' should be whipped and 'burnt though the right ear' as evidence to their fellow citizens of 'his or her roguish kind of life'. Players of course, were actors, but fortunately for the cause of English literature this statute, passed when Shakespeare was 8 years old, did not apply to companies that enjoyed the patronage of prominent courtiers, as Shakespeare's companies did. The act further prescribed that ears could be cut off for vagrancy while hands were removed from those who were responsible for publishing seditious books – a common punishment at a time when the publication of unorthodox religious opinions was regarded as little short of treason.

The financial motives for punishing vagrants with a public whipping were illustrated by an example cited by Lambard. Destitute beggars were liable to become a charge upon the parish, so Lombard proclaimed that 'Any Justice of the Peace may appoint any person to be publicly whipped naked until his or her body be bloody that shall be taken begging or wandering', this punishment being visited upon a 'sturdy vagrant' named John Stile, who was then returned to his place of birth to avoid further expense for the parish where he was apprehended.[2] These attitudes prevailed well into the eighteenth century. An Act of 1744 divided such citizens into three categories. 'Idle and disorderly persons' and 'rogues and vagabonds' were to be publicly whipped; the third category, 'incorrigible rogues' (repeat offenders), were to be offered to the army or navy. Other criminals, rather than being imprisoned, were subject to transportation, which was first permitted by an Act of 1598, but did not become a regular feature of the penal system until 1719 when convicts were sent to North America. The American War of Independence ended this convenient outlet for Britain's penal system, but criminals continued to be sent to Cape Town until 1849 and to Australia until 1864.

A further device for keeping the prisons empty was the enactment, from the late seventeenth century, of what became known as the Bloody Code, whereby those found guilty of an increasing number of offences, principally involving property, were made subject to the death penalty. In 1688 there were about fifty capital crimes, most of which had been added by Acts of Parliament to the Common Law offences of treason, murder, arson, robbery and grand larceny, but from that date there followed a series of statutes creating new capital offences. During the reigns of the first four Georges, 1714–1830, such statutes created a steady flow of such penalties, so by the latter date the number was approaching 300. Under this code an offender could be hanged for stealing goods worth 5s (25p), impersonating a Chelsea Pensioner, cutting down a tree or damaging Westminster Bridge. A statute of 1721 designed to discourage resentful weavers from damaging clothes made from imported cloth was to have strange consequences in the trial of the Newgate Monster later in the century.[3] The most notorious of the statutes that created the Bloody Code was the Waltham Black Act of 1723, which was brought in to deal with roving bands who, with blackened faces, were stealing deer in royal forests. This act alone created fifty capital offences, including the poaching of deer. Some commentators have attributed this savage code to the fact that the interests of property were very well represented in both the Houses of Parliament which passed the statutes, an interest underpinned by the influential philosophy of John Locke (1632–1704) whose writings emphasised the role of just government in preserving property rights. In his *Second Treatise of Government*, published in 1690 as the Bloody Code began its monstrous progress, Locke defined political power as the right to make 'Laws with Penalties of Death, and consequently all less Penalties, for the Regulating and Preserving of Property'. The 1830s were the high-water mark of the Bloody Code. In 1831 George Widgett was the last person to be hanged at Newgate for sheep stealing and the following year John Barrett was the last to be hanged for stealing from the Royal Mail.[4] In 1842 the efforts of penal reformers saw the gradual removal of capital offences from the statute book until in 1861 there remained only the old Common Law offences of murder, treason, robbery and arson in the royal dockyards. After the demise of the Bloody Code, *The Times*, in an indignant leader, drew attention to the injustices that it had inflicted in defence of property:

> The Bloody Code was monstrous and ineffectual. Its vice lay in the enormous disproportion it maintained between offences and penalties. It gave the impression of a world in which 'great thieves hang little ones'. It was not justice that was administered; it was a war that was waged between two classes of the community.[5]

In practice many juries refused to convict defendants for petty offences which carried the death penalty, while in other cases the judges simply declared stolen items to be worth less than 5s and sentenced offenders to a flogging rather than the scaffold. This did not, however, eliminate appalling miscarriages of justice. William Cobbett left an account of a 19-year-old mother of two children whose husband had been pressed into the navy and who had stolen a small quantity of cloth in London. She was hanged, as was another young woman under a law which, in the words of the judge who sentenced her, was 'aimed not at her death but at the death of her crime' – in other words to set an example to others.[6] This sentiment reflected the philosophy of the eminent Anglican divine William Paley, who held that a wide variety of crimes should carry the death penalty to act as a deterrent. He wrote that, 'The proper end of human punishment is not the satisfaction of justice but the prevention of crimes', and advocated the hanging of thieves because 'property being more exposed requires the terror of capital punishment to protect it'. Paley, however, mitigated the severity of this judgment by the further argument that the death penalty should rarely be inflicted, believing that the resulting uncertainty would deter criminals: 'The humanity of this design furnishes a just excuse for the multiplicity of capital offences which the laws of England are creating beyond those of other countries'.[7] The weakness of his reasoning is illustrated by the fact that a large proportion of the crowds that attended public executions were habitual criminals. A nineteenth-century governor of Newgate reported that in his fifteen years as a governor he had never known a murderer who had not previously attended an execution.

William Paley (1743–1805): born in Peterborough, William Paley trained as an Anglican priest at Christ's College, Cambridge. Paley's book, *Natural Theology or Evidences of the Existence and Attributes of the Deity, Collected from the Appearances of Nature*, presented God as a watchmaker and the creation as a carefully designed organism, each part, down to the wings of an insect, having its part in the order of things. *Paley's Evidences*, as the volume was known, was required reading at Cambridge into the twentieth century, and it made a favourable impression on the young Charles Darwin when he was himself studying at Christ's College in the nineteenth century. Darwin's own work on evolution later overturned that of Paley. Paley became Archdeacon of Carlisle, a prebendary of St Paul's Cathedral and Subdean of Lincoln where he was living when he died in 1805. He was an early campaigner against the slave trade.

THE PROCESS

The process by which defendants from Newgate were tried, sentenced and conveyed to their execution, originally at Tyburn, was a macabre ritual, though the trial that preceded it was often marked by unseemly haste. In the 1780s only one defendant in eight tried for a property offence at the Old Bailey was represented by a lawyer[8] while an account of proceedings there, which was published in 1833, estimated that trials took, on average, less than nine minutes.[9] The proceedings were no doubt on occasion expedited by the use of 'men of straw' who stood outside the courts with pieces of straw protruding from their footwear to indicate that they were prepared to give evidence for whichever side was willing to pay them. After sentence of death was pronounced by the judge wearing, of course, the black cap, the convict was taken to Newgate's condemned cell to await his transfer to Tyburn and execution.

Under an Act of 1752 those found guilty of murder were taken to execution within forty-eight hours of the sentence (there being no Appeal Court at that time) while those convicted of lesser crimes were give about a week to await their execution. During this time the occupants of the condemned cell were objects of interest to well-meaning clergymen who wanted to prepare them for death. In the words of a contemporary, 'The prison is beset with applications for admittance by persons who wish to be allowed to administer consolation to the unhappy malefactors.' These were often Wesleyan clergymen whose attentions were resented by the Newgate chaplains, known as 'Ordinaries' who had their own reasons for ministering to the condemned. Curious visitors were also admitted to the condemned cell upon payment to the keepers so that 'the parties may go home and say they have seen the prisoners under sentence of death in the condemned cell at Newgate'.[10] Some of the more recalcitrant prisoners welcomed the celebrity conferred upon them by their condition, but were less impressed by the ministrations of the clergy. Jack Sheppard, Newgate's most notorious escaper, told one clergyman that 'one file's worth all the Bibles in the world'.[11]

Some of those condemned to death escaped the sentence through the intervention of the Privy Council, which could give reprieves in the name of the king. Many of these were sentenced instead to transportation which, in Batty Langley's time, took them to work on the American plantations in Maryland and elsewhere.[12] A typical sentence of seven years would involve their being sold to a plantation owner by the captain of their ship. They would then work, virtually as slaves, for four years after which they could settle in America with a grant of land. If they returned to Britain before their sentence had expired they would, if caught, be sentenced to death.[13]

THE ORDINARIES AND THE CONDEMNED SERMON

In 1544, at the request of the Aldermen of the City of London, a chaplain from nearby St Bartholomew's Hospital was appointed to minister to the needs of the Newgate prisoners. From 1694 these Ordinaries, as they became known, of Newgate were appointed by the Bishop of London. In the eighteenth century ten people altogether filled the post, each receiving a salary of £35 a year together with a house on Newgate Street, near the gaol. The Ordinary's task was to minister to the needs of the prisoners, take the regular chapel services, preach the condemned sermon and attempt to bring to repentance those who faced execution. The last of these tasks enabled many of the Ordinaries to earn four or five times their salary by publishing 'Accounts' of the confessions of the prisoners. These were often published in the form of chapbooks, cheap and often poorly printed publications that were frequently rushed into print at short notice. The robber John Hall remarked upon the Ordinary's persistence, on the morning of execution, when he 'is as diligent in inquiring out the Particulars of their Lives, as though he were to send a Catalogue of their sins along with them', thereby furnishing material for the Accounts.[14]

Over 200 such Accounts survive from the eighteenth century.[15] They were long considered to be little more than fiction of the most sensational kind whose purpose was to make money for the publishers, but Peter Linebaugh, an authoritative source, has observed that many of the facts they contain can be verified from other accounts such as parish records.[16] The Accounts normally included a report of the trial, a description of the crimes attributed to the condemned, an account of his or her confessions and, finally, a description, often lurid, of the hanging at Tyburn. Individual Accounts, as pamphlets, sold for between 2*d* and 6*d*, depending upon the notoriety of the prisoner, and bore such revelatory titles as *The Ordinary of Newgate, His Account of the Behaviour, Confession and Dying Words of the Malefactors who were Executed at Tyburn.* They were advertised in the *Old Bailey Proceedings*, which were published during the time that the court was sitting. It was in the interests of the more predatory Ordinaries to extract sensational confessions from the condemned in order to raise the price of the Accounts and some of them went to great lengths to achieve this. In the following century, the reformer Francis Place protested that 'the Ordinary used to torture the person under sentence of death for confessions'. John Allen, who served as Ordinary in the early eighteenth century, offered to recommend reprieves for prisoners who were prepared to give especially colourful accounts of their crimes. Allen also ran a funeral business, which provided an additional source of revenue from the families of his unfortunate clientele.

Samuel Pepys's former secretary, Paul Lorraine,[17] served as Ordinary at the execution of the notorious pirate Captain Kidd. Kidd was hanged at Execution Dock, Wapping, the traditional site for those convicted of piracy. Kidd was drunk by the time he reached Wapping and rejected Lorraine's ministrations. The rope that was used to hang him broke, at which point Kidd's nerve also broke and he repented before being successfully hanged at the second attempt. Following these executions the pirate's body would be left for three tides to wash over it, during which time it was guarded by a Sheriff's officer who prevented souvenir hunters from removing pieces of body or clothing as souvenirs or lucky charms. Lorraine was less successful with a young pickpocket who steadfastly refused to confess, prompting the frustrated Ordinary to exclaim, 'Such case hardened rogues as you would ruin the sale of my paper.' Another prisoner declined to confess on the grounds that he did not want the Ordinary to profit.[18]

The Ordinaries were not without competitors in compiling and marketing Accounts, which were openly sold at the execution scene. Tobias Smollett's (1721–51) novel *Roderick Random*, includes an account of a penniless poet, imprisoned in the Marshalsea, describing his own attempts to earn a living from such literary productions. He explained, 'I have made many a good meal on a monster; a rape has often afforded me great satisfaction; but a murder, well-timed, was my never failing resource.' Such hack writers were bitterly resented by the Ordinaries as intruders upon their livelihoods and were themselves the objects of satire by authors like Defoe, Pope, Swift, Gay and Goldsmith. This did not prevent these writers from themselves penning highly colourful accounts of these events. Daniel Defoe, whose frequent state of financial embarrassment has already been noted,[19] was the author of a colourful account of the career of the serial escaper Jack Sheppard, though it was presented as an account written by Sheppard himself. Written in the first person and illustrated with a sketch of one of Sheppard's escapes, it is a skilful blend of lurid accounts of daring exploits and pious homilies on the consequences of crime. Thus Elizabeth Lyon, one of Sheppard's accomplices who had escaped with him from Newgate and later denounced him, is described as a 'wicked, deceitful and lascivious wretch' followed by the request that 'God forgive her'.[20] Later accounts of Sheppard's exploits are based largely on this account which spares no details of his daring and ingenuity.

Some Ordinaries exhibited impatience with anything that threatened to compromise the profitability of their publications. John Villette was the Newgate Ordinary in the 1770s and was required to accompany a young boy to Tyburn. Before the execution was carried out another person confessed to the crime, but when Villette learned that this had prompted a request for a reprieve for the unfortunate young man he told the executioner to proceed, exclaiming that it was no time to worry about 'details of this kind'.[21] Despite Villette's haste, the boy was spared. A reprieve was not invariably fatal to the success of a publication, however. One minister, not an Ordinary, sent an account of the crimes, confession and death of a prisoner to a news-paper which duly published it. In the meantime, the man had been reprieved and was thus able to read an account of his own death.[22]

The chapel services could be noisy affairs. In 1716 one Ordinary complained that prisoners were 'eating and drinking on the Communion table that is now broken' and urinating in the corner of the building.[23] On other occasions prisoners would shout or spit at the Ordinary or even threaten to shoot him.[24] In 1719 the service was disrupted when a prisoner circulated a bawdy pamphlet that he smuggled into the service by concealing it in his hat. An attempt by the City authorities to raise the tone of the prison by providing two Bibles was frustrated when they were stolen and had to be replaced by new ones which were chained in accordance with Medieval usage.

On the Sunday before the execution those to be executed the follow-ing day were obliged to attend chapel, where the Newgate Ordinary preached the condemned sermon, calling the guilty to repentance. To emphasise the solemnity of the occasion a coffin, to be called into use very soon, was laid out in the chapel in full view as those due to die the following day sat in the condemned pew. In the nineteenth century a humane Ordinary, Horace Cotton, tried to dispense with the coffin, but the City Aldermen sternly insisted on its reinstatement. The condemned services were very popular with local residents, so the keepers were able to charge handsomely for admission to these grim occasions. The proceedings were likely to be interrupted by insistent whispering among the onlookers and noisier quibbling with the turnkeys about the entrance fee for admission to the spectacle. In 1729 it was estimated that the turnkeys could make over £20 on a good day.[25] The congregation included a number of what *Punch* called 'Old Bailey Ladies' who attended these macabre events in order to have 'their Christianity and their morals mightily refreshed by the discipline' on what the magazine termed an Old Bailey Holiday:[26]

Who would seek the vulgar playhouse when, with Newgate interest, ladies may be on the free list for all condemned sermons, when they may witness real agony, may behold a real murderer writhing in all the hell of horror and despair.

The condemned themselves were not always in repentant mood and it was not unusual for the Ordinary to have to shout his sermon in the small chapel in order to be heard above the hubbub of chattering spectators and loud threats from prisoners. In May 1762 the chronicler James Boswell, better known for his *Life of Dr Samuel Johnson*, visited Newgate and was moved by the plight of a former seaman, Paul Lewis, who had been condemned to hang at Tyburn. Boswell described him as a 'genteel, spirited young fellow. He was dressed in a white coat and blue silk vest with his hair neatly queued and a silver-laced hat . . . Poor fellow! I really took a great concern for him and wished to relieve him. He walked firmly and with a good air, with his chains rattling upon him to the chapel.'[27]

The ritual did not end with the chapel service. In 1605 a wealthy citizen had bequeathed to the City a legacy which would pay for a bell to be rung outside the cell of the condemned at midnight, thus waking them from any slumber they had managed to achieve.[28] The bell was rung by the sexton of St Sepulchre's Church, which lay opposite the gaol, and it was accompanied by a recital of a verse that was calculated to instil repentance rather than cheerfulness:

> All you that in the condemned hold do lie,
> Prepare you, for tomorrow you shall die;
> Watch all and pray: the hour is drawing near
> That you before the Almighty must appear;
> Examine well yourselves; in time repent,
> That you may not to eternal flames be sent.
> And when St Sepulchre's bell in the morning tolls,
> The Lord above have mercy on your souls.

THE PROCESSION TO TYBURN

The following morning, as the bells of St Sepulchre's tolled twelve times, the condemned would be led into the prison Press Yard where their chains would be struck off. In Batty Langley's words, 'then they are bound with the same fatal Hempen String [hemp rope] which shortly after finally determined their wicked days'.[29] By this time the prisoners were often drunk, having been plied with fortifying liquors the previous night by sympathetic inmates. Occasionally, the hangman was also in this condition. These proceedings could be viewed by those who had been guests of the governor at the earlier 'Governor's Execution Breakfast' where devilled kidneys were the customary fare. The prisoners were handed over to the under-sheriff who, with a troop of soldiers, was responsible for escorting them to the scaffold, a necessary precaution since it was not unknown for rescue attempts to be made. The procession to Tyburn consisted of a line of carts containing the prisoners, their coffins, the hangman and the Ordinary, a strict order of precedence being observed. Carts containing highway-men who had robbed the Royal Mail went first, followed by lesser criminals. Traitors brought up the rear. They were denied the dignity of a cart, being dragged instead on hurdles. By the time the procession left Newgate a huge crowd would have gathered, since execution days were often regarded as public holidays. They lined the route from the prison along Holborn, Oxford Street (then called Tyburn Road) to the scaffold itself in the south-east corner of Connaught Square, close to the present site of Marble Arch, the site now being marked by a brass triangle set into the highway.[30] The reconstruction of the site in the 1820s revealed a number of bodies, which suggests that some victims were buried at their place of execution.

Immediately after leaving the prison the convoy would stop at St Sepulchre's where, to the accompaniment of the tolling bell, the sexton would make a further plea for those about to die:

> All good people, pray heartily under God for these poor sinners who are now going to their death, for whom this great bell tolls . . . You that are condemned to die repent with lamentable tears . . . Lord have mercy upon you . . . Christ have mercy upon you.[31]

Fortified by these wishes, and by the nosegay and cup of wine each prisoner was handed at this point, the carts continued on their journey, cheered and occasionally booed by the excited crowds, among the more drunken of whom there developed a tradition of throwing dead cats and dogs into the air. Unpopular prisoners would be pelted with missiles. The procession would pass through a notorious slum district, The Holy Land, which was demolished when New Oxford Street was created in 1847. It would stop at Resurrection Gate, in the grounds of the church of St Giles in the Fields, a former place of execution close to the present site of Centrepoint. Further stops were made at inns on the route for more strong liquor, gin being particularly favoured for the Dutch courage that it conferred. The last such stop was at the Masons Arms in Seymour Place. More affluent prisoners dressed for the occasion, usually in wedding or funeral attire. John Hall wrote that, 'One would take them for Bridegrooms going to espouse their old Mrs Tyburn'.[32] Some wore white cockades in their hats to signify defiance or, occasionally, innocence. A foreign observer commented on the festive air that marked these occasions both for the condemned and for the spectators, writing that:

> The English are a people that laugh at the delicacy of other nations who make it such a mighty matter to be hanged. He that is to be [hanged] takes great care to get himself shaved and handsomely dressed either in mourning or in the dress of a bridegroom. Sometimes the girls dress in white with great silk scarves and carry baskets full of flowers and oranges, scattering these favours all the way they go.[33]

Every opportunity was offered, and many taken, for the prisoners to make speeches and exchange witticisms with the crowd, some prisoners offering to pay for their drinks on their return journey. Highwaymen were the aristocrats of the criminal class and some onlookers would beg for a lock of their hair or a fragment of clothing in a manner reminiscent of the later treatment of popular musicians or sportsmen. Not everyone was so jovial. At a time when 14-year-olds could be executed one young boy was to be seen weeping into the lap of the father who accompanied him on his sad journey. In the vicinity of Tyburn itself the press of the excited crowd was such that fatalities occasionally occurred among the onlookers. On one occasion the scaffold collapsed and killed a spectator, and the throng was often so dense that the condemned prisoners had to descend from their carts and finish their journeys on foot. Lord Ferrers, a man with a history of violence to family and servants, took three hours to go from Newgate to Tyburn in 1760. He had murdered his steward and been convicted of the crime following a trial before his peers in the House of Lords. He had been condemned to hang at Tyburn and to have his body given up for dissection. His reputation, rank and behaviour had attracted an unusually large crowd. Such events also attracted tradesmen and pickpockets. As many as fifty could be arrested in the course of an execution morning, thus adding to the supply of criminals for trial and execution in a self-sustaining flow. Hogarth's engraving, *The Idle 'Prentice executed at Tyburn*, shows the gingerbread salesman, Tiddy Doll, plying his trade while having his pocket picked by a street urchin.

As their end approached the condemned were allowed to address the crowd, which could number more than 10,000, some of whom had paid as much as £10 for a seat in one of the wooden stands close to the scaffold itself: Mother Proctor's Pews, or those of Mammy Douglas the Tyburn Pew-opener. The anonymous author of an eighteenth-century pamphlet, which could charitably be described as a rant against the evils of modern society, was particularly censorious about a certain category of victim on these occasions. After a typically xenophobic complaint about people who employ French cooks to apply sauces to good, plain English food he decries the 'Sodomites who go to public Executions unpitied and unlamented that can neither hope or expect any Mercy in this and may justly dread the Punishments in the World to come'.[34] Some onlookers became connoisseurs of these grim spectacles. George Selwyn (1719–91) a wit, raconteur and somewhat inattentive Member of Parliament, was one such. Described as 'not merely silent but nearly always asleep' during Parliamentary sittings, he was nevertheless appreciative of a good execution and reputedly corresponded with judges about the best vantage points from which to watch them.[35]

Since they were about to die anyway the prisoners were free to make speeches in the knowledge that no further harm could come to them and a good, defiant speech was looked upon with favour by the crowd as part of the entertainment. By a strange coincidence these early examples of free speech took place close to the present site of Speaker's Corner. As previously observed, some of the supporters of the Old Pretender in the 1715 rising took advantage of the opportunity to declare their allegiance to the exiled Stuarts.[36] Some speeches were inordinately long in the hope that a reprieve would arrive in the nick of time. One such was given by a robber, Colonel James Turner, who was taken for execution on 21 January 1663, an event recorded by Samuel Pepys in his diary for that day, among a crowd of over 12,000 people. Pepys's words help to convey the extent to which these events were public entertainment. After a morning's work at the Navy Office:

> I enquired and found that Turner was not yet hanged. And so I went among them to Leadenhall Street and to St Mary Axe, where he lived, and there I got for a shilling to stand upon the wheel of a cart, in great pain, above an hour before the execution was done; he delaying the time by long discourses and prayers one after another, in hopes of a reprieve, but none came and at last was flung off the ladder in his cloak.

So long was his address and the prayers that followed that the Sheriffs became visibly impatient, but Turner's behaviour was understandable since it was not unknown for a reprieve to arrive after the execution had been carried out, too late for the victim to benefit from it. A more typical final speech, as recorded in the Account by the Ordinary of Newgate, was that of 18-year-old William Dabell, hanged at Tyburn in December 1706 for a burglary. Dabell, according to the Ordinary's pious version, 'was very devout and showed great Sorrow for his Offences against God and his Neighbour. He begged pardon of both'. A less repentant culprit, according to a contemporary, was the notorious escaper Jack Sheppard who, when finally brought to his execution, 'declared (it seems) at the Gallows, that he had laid a Foundation for raising the Reputation of the British Thievery to a greater Height'.[37] Mercy was not a feature of the behaviour of the crowd during these final moments. One female victim, Barbara Spencer, was felled by a stone while kneeling on the scaffold to offer up her final prayers.[38]

Tyburn executions took place on the 'Triple Tree'. This was constructed of three uprights which, when joined by beams, formed a triangular structure when viewed from above. Each beam could accommodate eight nooses so that twenty-four people could be hanged at once. In 1759 this gruesome memento of the penal code was demolished and replaced by a movable gallows which was taken away after each execution. Friends and relatives were allowed to mount the carts to bid a last farewell and it was at this stage that the guards would have to show special vigilance against rescue attempts made with the support of the crowd.

As the moment of execution approached the prisoners would be blindfolded or hooded and their arms would be tied. In an atmosphere akin to that of a carnival the crowd would cheer prisoners who fought the executioner unless they were unpopular, in which case they would boo. A large and fierce Irish woman, Hannah Dagoe, put up such a fight at her execution in May 1763, that she almost felled the executioner. She then ripped off much of her clothing and threw it into the crowd so that the hangman should not profit from its sale. The nooses would be placed round their necks by the hangman as the Ordinary continued to pray for their souls and then the carts would be drawn away, leaving the condemned swinging from the scaffold. Some attempts were made by more humane influences to ensure that death followed swiftly. The placing of the knot behind the right ear was believed by some to bring a quicker death from apoplexy or unconsciousness from pressure on the main blood vessels. The sudden 'drop' which broke the neck and which enabled later hangmen such as Albert Pierrepont to bring death within a fraction of a second, was not a feature of executions at Tyburn until 1760, Lord Ferrers possibly being one of the first to be executed in this way. Most prisoners died slowly from strangulation, their cries and contortions being applauded by the crowd: 'Every contortion of the limbs was hailed with a cheer or a groan according to whether the sufferer was popular or not.'[39] Some had their sufferings ended by relatives or other sympathisers who, by pulling on their legs, broke their necks. Occasionally, a merciful hangman would jump on to the shoulders of the victim to bring a swifter end. Others could swing gasping for air for over half an hour, the latter stages of their sufferings being marked by emissions of urine, a phenomenon referred to by connoisseurs of these events as 'pissing when you can't whistle'.

Some of the more sensitive spectators were deeply affected by the executions. James Boswell, having witnessed the execution of Paul Lewis, whom he had visited in Newgate,[40] wrote that he was 'most terribly shocked and thrown into a very deep melancholy'. When he went to bed two nights later he was 'still so haunted with frightful imaginations that I durst not lie by myself', but climbed into bed with a sympathetic male friend – an uncharacteristic act by the heterosexual Boswell. Some of the more celebrated prisoners were allowed to signify when they were ready for the 'drop'. One of these was James Hackman, a young soldier who had been ordained a clergyman and who in 1779 shot the mistress of the Earl of Sandwich and then failed to shoot himself. His execution at Tyburn was a matter of such public interest that James Boswell tried to persuade the *Daily Advertiser* to commission him to write an account of it, but another writer had already gained the job. When Hackman dropped his handkerchief to signify that he was ready to die the hangman immediately picked it up, recognising that it was a saleable relic. The following day a huge crowd gathered at Surgeons' Hall to view the body.

A few survived the attempts to hang them, the most celebrated being John 'Half-hanged' Smith. A former sailor, he was convicted of burglary in 1705 and sentenced to death. On Christmas Eve he was hanged at Tyburn, but took so long to die that the crowd demanded he be cut down. According to an account he gave to a witness:[41]

> After he was cut down and began to come to himself, the blood and spirits forcing themselves into his former channels put him, by a sort of pricking or shooting, to such intolerable pain that he could have wished those hanged who had cut him down.

Smith received a pardon and had a further escape when the prosecutor died as a trial for later offences was due to start. Others who suffered similar experiences were not so fortunate. Patrick O'Bryan survived a hanging at Gloucester and proceeded to murder his victim and accuser. For this offence he was hanged at Tyburn in April 1689 and then gibbeted, ensuring that he would not survive his second execution.[42]

Gruesome though it was, hanging was not the worst way of inflicting death at this time. Women who were convicted of murdering their husbands could be sentenced to burn until well into the eighteenth century, since this was regarded as petty treason – disloyalty to her lawful master. This was the fate of Catherine Hayes in 1726. It was customary in such cases for the hangman to strangle the victim beforehand to ensure that the flames consumed the corpse rather than the living body, but on this occasion the fire, already kindled, reached the hangman before his work was done. He leapt from the blaze and the wretched Catherine fought in vain to protect herself from its advance: 'The spectators beheld her pushing away the faggots while she rent the air with her cries and lamentations.'[43] In 1753 Anne Williams was the last woman to be burned for this crime. Coining (debasing the currency) was classed as high treason and for this offence Christian Murphy was condemned to be burned in March 1789, but he was spared the worst suffering by being hanged first and then committed to the fire.

THE EXECUTIONERS

It is not clear how hangmen came to their grim trade, though in a few cases the choice of men who traded as butchers suggests that some value was placed on their knowledge of how cadavers were put together and, therefore, might be taken apart. In the sixteenth century executioners were referred to as 'William Boilman' because of the hideous practice of boiling poisoners in the later years of the reign of Henry VIII. A tradition arose of victims offering payment to the executioner in the hope of a swift end. The executioners were not themselves men of irreproachable character. A butcher named Pascha Rose, and a successor named Price, were themselves executed for housebreaking, and attempted rape and murder, respectively. Another successor, William Marvell, was arrested for debt on his way to Tyburn, earning a reprieve for three condemned men. One executioner has bequeathed his name to the language. Goodman Derrick devised a structure by which several men could be hoisted aloft simultaneously, thereby executing several at once. It was later adapted for loading and unloading ships and is still used as a Derrick crane long after its original grim purpose was abandoned.

The most notorious of the Tyburn executioners was variously known as Richard Jacquet, John Catch or Jack Ketch, the last of these names being later used as a generic one for the practitioners of his craft.[44] He was the executioner from about 1663 until his death in 1686 with a brief interval during 1686 when he was in prison for insulting a Sheriff. He is remembered for his incompetence as an axeman. In 1683 he took four blows of the axe to despatch William Russell for his involvement in the Rye House Plot. He excused his clumsiness with the claim that Russell 'did not dispose himself for receiving the fatal stroke in such a position as was most suitable' and that he 'received some interruption just as he was taking aim'. When the Duke of Monmouth came to the scaffold for his rebellion two years later he paid Ketch the handsome sum of six guineas to despatch him quickly, no doubt mindful of Russell's earlier ordeal. Ketch failed to slay the Duke with the first three blows and exclaimed, 'I can't do it.' He had to be prevailed upon by the Sheriffs to administer two further blows from the axe before finally severing the head with a knife. His conduct so angered the crowd that he had to be protected from them by an armed escort. In the same year he was involved in the public chastisement of Titus Oates, whose Popish Plot had finally been unmasked as a fraud and some of whose innocent victims Ketch had helped to hang, draw and quarter six years earlier.

Titus Oates (1649–1705): one of the greatest rogues in English history, Titus Oates was the son of a dissenting preacher who had ministered to Cromwell's New Model Army during the Civil War. He became an Anglican minister, but was suspended from his livings after accusations of blasphemy and buggery. He briefly joined the Jesuits in St Omer, an action he later claimed to have taken in order to gain insights into Catholic plotting. In 1678, during the reign of Charles II, who lacked a legitimate heir, he took advantage of anxieties about the possible succession of the King's Catholic brother (later James II) to accuse a number of public figures of plotting to assassinate Charles and replace him with James. They included the Queen's physician and the secretary to James's wife, Sir Edward Coleman, who was hanged, drawn and quartered at Tyburn upon Oates's evidence while Oates watched. Charles II had never believed Oates's accusations and, by interrogating him, revealed a number of falsehoods in his accusations. This simply encouraged Oates to level ever more extravagant charges, which led to scores of arrests and a search of the Houses of Parliament for another gunpowder plot. Such was the anti-Catholic hysteria of the time that Oates was awarded an annual pension of £1,200 and an apartment in Whitehall. Oates overreached himself when he accused the Queen of plotting to poison the King and in 1681 he was imprisoned. In 1685, following the accession of James II, he was convicted of perjury, which had led to the deaths of many innocent men, imprisoned and sentenced to be whipped from Newgate to Tyburn and pilloried, the punishment to be repeated every year. According to a contemporary, Oates 'made hideous bellowings and swooned several times with the greatness of the anguish'. He was released upon the accession of the Protestant monarchs William and Mary in 1688 and died in 1705, still admired by some staunch Protestants.

THE EXECUTED: JACK SHEPPARD AND JACK RANN

On 16 November 1724, the public hangman finally managed to execute Jack Sheppard at Tyburn. It had not been easy. Sheppard (also spelled Shepherd) was born in Spitalfields in 1702, the son of a carpenter who earned an honest living but died when Jack and his brother Thomas were very young. Jack was himself apprenticed to a carpenter, a trade that he followed for about four years before becoming involved in thieving, sometimes from houses where he was working. He became involved with a number of underworld characters, including one Elizabeth Lyon, known as Edgeworth Bess, a distributor of stolen property, and the notorious gang-leader and informant Jonathan Wild. In August 1723, Jack's brother Thomas was indicted at the Old Bailey and sentenced to be branded on the hand after which the two brothers became partners in crime and carried out a series of housebreakings and thefts of goods from retailers.

Following his arrest on a tip-off from a fellow criminal, Sheppard and Edgworth Bess, passing themselves off as man and wife, were committed by a magistrate to Newgate from which he organised the first of his remarkable escapes. He acquired a file from a visitor and used it to remove his and Bess's fetters before removing an iron bar from their cell window. They descended to the yard below using a rope made of knotted sheets, scaled the external wall by using the locks and bolts of the great gate as footholds and disappeared into the underworld of St Giles, the most notorious part of London's criminal community south of the present site of Tottenham Court Road Underground station. As a result of this exploit Sheppard was now something of a celebrity and was invited to join other more experienced criminals in the execution of their illicit enterprises. These soon bore such fruit that Sheppard and a particularly active associate known as Blueskin rented a stable near the present site of Horseferry Road to use as a warehouse for the proceeds of their crimes until such time as they were able to dispose of them safely. Eventually detected, Sheppard was again sent to Newgate in August 1724 and this time he was sentenced to death. On this occasion he removed a spike from a hatch in the prison, squeezed through the gap and fled to a public house in Spitalfields where he proceeded to dispense advice to admiring fellow criminals on means of escaping from the rather ineffectual custody to which he had recently been consigned. One can only marvel both at the insouciance of Jack Sheppard and the laxity of the authorities, who not only allowed him to escape from Newgate, but also enabled him to remain in its vicinity with little fear of detection or arrest, though his spell of freedom was aided by the fact that it coincided with Bartholomew Fair, a time of more than usual mayhem in the vicinity of Newgate.

Bartholomew Fair: a fair held in West Smithfield in the last week of August each year from 1133 until 1855 when, after many failed attempts, the City authorities finally succeeded in ending this source of disorder in the life of the capital. The nearby St Bartholomew's Hospital, London's oldest, also dates from the twelfth century. In the Middle Ages, Bartholomew Fair became the principal cloth fair in the kingdom, the name being preserved in a road nearby, but by the eighteenth century it had became characterised by entertainments, including tightrope walkers, prizefighters, musicians and freak shows. By this time it had acquired a reputation for petty crime and disorder and for the rich pickings it offered for pickpockets, in which last respect it invites comparison with the Notting Hill Carnival, its nearest equivalent in the twenty-first century. In the middle of the nineteenth century the Smithfield live cattle market was relocated to an area north of Kings Cross. Once this had been done, the City authorities seized the opportunity to suppress the troublesome Bartholomew Fair and use the site for the construction of the famous Smithfield Wholesale Meat Market, designed by Sir Horace Jones and opened in 1868. The disorder associated with the event in the eighteenth century would have assisted Jack Sheppard's rudimentary attempts to hide from his pursuers.

Jack Sheppard was not one to learn from his mistakes. His enterprise was not matched by his intelligence, because a few days later he stole three watches from a watchmaker in Fleet Street. Sheppard took the uncharacteristic precaution of retreating the short distance to Finchley to avoid detection, but this was not enough to fool the authorities to whom he was now something of a challenge. He was arrested and taken to Newgate where he was confined in a cell on his own, handcuffed and chained via leg irons to a staple in the cell floor. The spectacle of the infamous Jack Sheppard thus confined offered unrivalled opportunities for profit to his gaolers, who were able to charge handsomely for the privilege of viewing him.

Sheppard had managed to equip himself with a nail, either found in the cell itself or possibly smuggled to him by a visitor. With this he unfastened the handcuffs and the padlock that attached his leg irons to the staple. Still in irons, he began to climb the chimney in his cell when he found his progress halted by an iron bar fixed across the cavity. He picked out the mortar which held the chain in place and proceeded to use the chimney to gain access to another room above his original cell. This was itself equipped with a locked door but, using the iron bar from the chimney, he wrenched off the lock and entered a passage leading to the chapel. Four further doors, all locked, along a corridor were passed with a mixture of force and enterprise, the last being opened by removing its hinges and opening it in the opposite direction to that intended by those who installed it.

Sheppard now found himself on top of a high wall from which he could descend to a neighbouring roof and thence to freedom. However, the drop would have been fatal, so Sheppard returned to his cell via doors, corridor and chimney to retrieve his blankets which, as a rope, enabled him to make the descent, enter the house via a window and fall asleep in the garret. When darkness came he left the house and made his way to a cowshed near Tottenham Court Road. Two days later he emerged from his hiding place and, with the help of a cobbler, removed his fetters and made his way to Charing Cross where he ate a supper of roast lamb while listening to his fellow citizens discussing his by now famous exploits. The next few days were spent wandering around Soho, drinking in a Rupert Street tavern, listening to ballads about his escape in the Haymarket and parading in Drury Lane, resplendent in stolen clothes and stolen jewellery, while displaying a decorated (and of course stolen) sword. It is hard to avoid the conclusion that his desire to be caught was matched only by the incompetence of the authorities who were looking for him. However, after a drinking spree in Newgate Street he was finally betrayed by a barman and conveyed, drunk, back to Newgate prison. There he boosted the earnings of his gaolers who are estimated to have taken £200 from visitors wishing to see the celebrated escapologist.[45] While in the condemned call he was visited and painted by Sir James Thornhill, sergeant painter to the Crown.

Attempts by the Ordinary to persuade Sheppard to repent met with little success. He attended the prison chapel, but gave no impression of taking the services seriously and, as noted earlier, informed the Ordinary that 'one file's worth all the Bibles in the world'. When the day of his execution arrived, 16 November 1724, the prison authorities took the unusual precaution of searching him before he left the Press Yard. A zealous officer named Watson found a sharp knife in Sheppard's pocket with which he was evidently planning to cut the rope that bound his arms, jump from the cart and flee from his pursuers with the assistance of the crowd, who were known to be more than usually well disposed to this, by now, heroic criminal. When he arrived at Tyburn he confessed to two robberies of which he had previously been acquitted. His death by strangulation in the hangman's noose was prolonged, and excited the sympathy of a crowd of unprecedented size. His body was removed by his friends, who were initially suspected by the onlookers of being emissaries of the Company of Surgeons. The crowd was determined that Sheppard's body would not be removed for dissection, so a prolonged scuffle ensued between those who wanted to remove the body for burial and onlookers anxious to frustrate the designs of the Surgeons. Reassured, the mob allowed the body to be taken to a tavern in Long Acre whence, after Sheppard's friends had refreshed themselves with suitable libations, it was removed for burial in the churchyard of St Martin-in-the-Fields. He had died at the age of 23.

After his death Jack Sheppard's reputation acquired fresh lustre. In 1725, shortly after his hanging, the *British Journal* published an account of an imaginary conversation between Jack Sheppard and Julius Caesar in which the thief's exploits bore favourable comparison with those of the general and in the following century Karl Marx's collaborator Friedrich Engels, in his *Condition of the Working Class in England* (1845), wrote that 'some children have never heard the name of Her Majesty, nor such names as Wellington, Nelson . . . there was a general knowledge of the character and course of life of Jack Sheppard, the robber and prison-breaker'. In the 1870s the exploits of the outlaw Ned Kelly were compared with those of Sheppard in the Australian press and at the same time Jesse James, in the intervals between bank robberies in the Midwest of the United States, mocked his pursuers by writing letters to the *Kansas City Star* using the pseudonym Jack Sheppard. Such is fame.

SIXTEEN STRING JACK

In the second half of the century Jack Rann, who was executed aged 24, achieved an equal degree of notoriety, though for different reasons. He was born near Bath in 1750 and acquired a taste for luxurious living while working as a servant in a wealthy household. It was at this time also that he took to lacing his knee-breeches with sixteen silk laces, thus gaining his nickname 'Sixteen String Jack', which lives on in the name of a pub in Theydon Bois, Essex, close to the scene of some of his crimes. He began his criminal career as a pickpocket, for which he escaped conviction, but then took to more profitable work as a highwayman around London, using his mistress Ellen Roche to fence the goods that he stole. He was charged with highway robbery on many occasions and scarcely attempted to conceal from his contemporaries the means by which he earned his living. In 1774 he robbed a doctor of a small sum of money and a watch. Careful investigation by a Bow Street Runner, John Clarke, under the direction of John Fielding[46] identified Rann as the thief. Ellen Roche was sentenced to transportation as an accomplice, but

Rann, upon conviction, was confined in Newgate under sentence of death. On 27 November 1774, Rann threw a dinner party in Newgate at which he entertained seven prostitutes to a fine meal in the highest of spirits. On 30 November he was hanged at Tyburn, wearing a new green suit that he had ordered for the event.

THE AFTERMATH

Further indignities could be inflicted on the corpse after death, some of them encouraged by the law itself. It had long been the practice to impale the heads of traitors on prominent sites such as London Bridge and Temple Bar, as a warning to others. A German visitor counted twenty on London Bridge in 1661, presumably a result of the vengeance wrought on the regicides following the restoration of Charles II the previous year. The visitor may have taken advantage of one of the telescopes set up by enterprising Londoners through which passers-by were invited to inspect these gruesome relics for a payment of a halfpenny. An Act of 1752, known as the Murder Act 'for the better prevention of the crime of murder' formally sanctioned the Medieval practice of gibbeting which had long been in unoffical use. To this end, the corpses were returned to Newgate where, in Jack Ketch's Kitchen[47] they were dipped in boiling pitch as a means of preserving them for the gibbet. This device was a metal cage, sometimes in the shape of a body, in which the blackened body was placed, the gibbet then being suspended from a pole. This was usually situated near the scene of the crime or close to the culprit's home and left to rot as a warning to others. To prevent relatives or other sympathisers from rescuing the cadaver from these indignities the post was often cased in lead, to prevent its being burned down, and studded with nails to deter people from climbing it to remove the gibbet.

Some cadavers were claimed for purposes of dissection, also permitted by the 1752 Murder Act. The Company of Surgeons were entitled to ten each year and the hospitals of St Bartholomew's and St Thomas's made similar claims. Further specimens could be provided by arrangement with the hangman, upon payment. The

Surgeons' accounts for the period include records of payments made, including 2*s* 6*d* as a Christmas present to the Newgate hangman and payments to the Company's beadles for injuries sustained in collecting the cadavers from Tyburn. These payments reflect the fisticuffs that could be involved in claiming the corpses. Dissection was regarded as a great indignity, so friends or relatives of the deceased would sometimes put up a stout fight to prevent its infliction, as happened in the case of Jack Sheppard. Onlookers would also struggle to touch the dead body since many believed that this would cure, or guard against, certain diseases such as scrofula.[48] Sometimes relatives would cut down the 'deceased' before death had actually occurred and smuggle the body away to be revived. William Duell, a robber, was delivered to the Surgeons in November 1740 and 'came round' on the dissecting table to the great alarm of the Surgeons. He was subsequently sentenced to transportation.

The tactic was not always successful even with the most ingenious methods of respiration. On 27 June 1777 the execution occurred at Tyburn of Dr William Dodd, known as The Macaroni Parson on account of his dandified dress habits and unconventional way of life. Dodd had been born in 1729, educated at Cambridge, ordained in 1751 and enjoyed some early success as a playwright, a profession that was still barely respectable and certainly not recommended for a clergyman. Nevertheless, his lifestyle and flamboyant personality brought him the friendship of Dr Samuel Johnson, Thomas Gainsborough and Lord Chesterfield, and helped to secure him the prestigious post of Chaplain to George III. He was instrumental in founding the Society for the Relief and Discharge of Small Debtors – a much-needed service when such debtors were frequently incarcerated in prisons like Newgate, thus denying them any chance of discharging their debts. He also founded the Humane Society for the Resuscitation of the Apparently Drowned, using an early form of artificial respiration recommended by the celebrated surgeon John Hunter.

In 1777, confronted by pressing debts, Dodd forged a bond in the name of Lord Chesterfield for the enormous sum of £4,200. He was quickly found out and prosecuted despite the fact that Chesterfield himself wanted to settle the matter without involving the criminal law. His case aroused great public interest and his conviction and the death sentence that followed provoked numerous petitions from citizens, from the universities of Oxford and Cambridge and even from the jurors who had convicted him. Samuel Johnson himself petitioned for his reprieve, but the King felt that it would be wrong to reprieve someone simply because he was a popular and prominent clergyman. Dodd was visited in Newgate by John Wesley, the founder of Methodism, a sect of people who were often more conscientious in ministering to the condemned than were the Ordinaries themselves. Dodd preached the condemned sermon himself in Newgate Chapel, the text being written by Johnson. Dodd's notoriety ensured that his execution attracted even larger crowds than normal and guaranteed a big sale for the Account prepared by the Ordinary of Newgate. On this occasion the Ordinary was the avaricious John Villette whose *Genuine Account of the Behaviour and Dying Words of William Dodd, LL.D.* included the pious final declaration, 'I was led astray from religious strictness by the delusion of show and the delights of voluptuousness. I never knew or attended to the calls of frugality.[49]

Distinctions of class were observed even on this final fatal journey. Dodd travelled to Tyburn in a carriage while Joseph Harris, a teenage highwayman who had previously attempted suicide, travelled in a cart along with his grieving father, 'a circumstance which excited the pity of the spectators, according to an eyewitness.[50] Dodd was not entirely resigned to his fate. After his execution he was cut down by sympathisers who attempted to revive him using the Hunter method that Dodd had himself advocated. This involved immersing his corpse in a warm bath at an undertaker's premises in Tottenham Court Road. On this occasion it failed. After Dodd's death the *Westminster Magazine* said of him that 'his parts were rather shining than solid'.[51] His life was celebrated in the following century in a play, *Law of the Land or London in the Last Century*, whose final scene was entitled 'The Condemned Cell in Newgate featuring Dodd's prison thoughts'.

By the late eighteenth century some of the more enlightened commentators were beginning to entertain doubts about the Tyburn rituals and their effect upon public attitudes towards crime, civil order and hangings. The novelist Henry Fielding, whose work at Bow Street Magistrates' Court is described in Chapter Four, was sufficiently repelled by the Tyburn spectacle to comment that, 'Instead of making the gallows an object of terror, our executions contribute to make it an object of contempt in the eye of the malefactor; and we sacrifice the lives of men, not for the reformation but the diversion of the populace.' The way was opening up for a more sensitive approach to capital punishment and imprisonment, though it was another half-century before the Bloody Code itself began to moderate.

FOUR

Catching the Criminals

The laws are turnstiles; only made to stop people who walk on foot, and not to interrupt those who drive through them in their coaches.

(Henry Fielding, *Rape upon Rape*, 1729)

A justice and his clerk is now little more than a blind man and his dog. The profound ignorance of the former, together with the canine impudence and rapacity of the latter, will but rarely be found wanting. The justice is as much dependent on his clerk for superior insight and guidance as the blind fellow is on his cur. Add to this that the offer of a crust will secure the conductors of either to drag their masters into a kennel.

(William Shenstone, poet and essayist, 1794, on the conduct of magistrates' courts at the time)

MEDIEVAL ENGLAND

In 1188, when Newgate prison first appears in the records, the system for identifying and detaining criminals owed much to the practices of Anglo-Saxon England. All males aged 12 or over, except noblemen, their servants and clergyman, were members of a tithing or group of ten families headed by a tithingman or chief pledge, whose office, after the Norman conquest, developed into that of parish constable. Each member of the group was responsible for identifying and apprehending any other member who had committed a crime. The tithings were themselves collected into hundreds. Twice a year, at each hundred, the king's officer, the Sheriff of the county, would hold a 'view of frankpledge' at which he would check that each man was correctly allocated to a tithing and would then preside while each tithingman gave an account of the misdeeds of members of his tithing. Following the Assize of Clarendon (1166) presentations involving serious crimes were made to a grand jury whose task was to decide whether there was enough evidence for the case to proceed to a trial, which might take place before a local baronial court or, from the time of Henry II, before the king's justices.[1] This arrangement continued until 1933 when grand juries were abolished by the Lord Chancellor, Lord Birkenhead and the prima facie case was made instead to magistrates. (Grand juries are still used for their original purpose in the United States of America.) Presentation of less serious matters, such as failure to serve in parish offices or to maintain the highways, were made to Justices of the Peace in petty sessions. In this way groups of citizens policed their own communities, though it was supplemented by the process of 'hue and cry'. This could be invoked by the Sheriff under his 'posse comitatus' (literally power of the county, the origin of the term 'Sheriff's posse') whereby the Sheriff was authorised to call upon his fellow citizens to pursue and detain a fleeing felon. The Sheriff was also responsible for ensuring that gaols were built to hold prisoners awaiting trial and that proper provision was made for holding the king's courts. From the late twelfth century the work of the Sheriff was supplemented by Keepers of the Peace, later known as Justices of the Peace from the Act of that name passed in 1361. Their task was to identify, arrest, try and sentence people whom they knew to be ne'er-do-wells, particularly vagabonds. Their role thus combined the offices of policeman, judge and jury for minor offences not tried by the royal courts.

Separate arrangements were made for certain localities, among them London, where the fragmented and mobile nature of the population, including many foreign merchants, made tithings and hundreds hard to manage. In 1285 statutes created six watchmen for each of the City's twenty-four wards and required each Alderman to 'make diligent Enquiry' into crimes committed in his ward. The Mayor, Sheriffs and Aldermen were responsible for presenting offenders to the royal courts or, in the case of minor offences, for trying and sentencing them under their own authority. The gates of the City were to be closed between sunset and sunrise each day. Offenders included suspicious people (generally speaking, strangers) who were found walking in the City after the curfew had been sounded at St Martin's Le Grand. During the Tudor period London saw the creation of the post of Provost Marshal, later known as City Marshal. This officer was responsible for policing the City of London and was, in effect, the predecessor of the Commissioner of the City of London Police Force which, to this day, remains independent of the Metropolitan Police.

In 1663 a further Act created the City watchmen known as 'Charleys' after the monarch, Charles II, who was on the throne at the time. Each ward would have a constable responsible for his ward with authority over the Charleys. The constables were technically volunteers, though many of them accepted the post with the greatest reluctance and some of them paid substitutes to do the work for them. In 1598 the men of the Hundred of Cranbrook, in Kent, were indicted at the assizes for electing as constable William Sheafe whom they knew to be 'an infirm man incapable of discharging the office'.[2] Most constables received no payment beyond some share of fines – a practice which itself encouraged corruption. The Charleys themselves, whose job was mostly concerned with patrolling the streets during the hours of darkness, were much derided. They were ill-paid and often the products of the workhouse, taking the post of watchman to escape those grim institutions. Each was equipped with a cloak, a lantern, a staff and a wooden rattle to summon help in the unlikely event of his attempting to apprehend a criminal. A post resembling a sentry box was also provided. In Westminster and other parishes outside the Square Mile the service they offered improved after 1735. From that date a series of Night Watch Acts enabled local vestries to levy rates for the purpose of increasing the numbers and quality of the watchmen. The parishes of St James and Marylebone were particularly noted for the efficiency of their watchmen whom they recruited from the ranks of the old soldiers at the Chelsea Hospital. These grizzled veterans ensured that casual thieves plied their trade elsewhere in the capital.

In addition to these measures, attempts were made to persuade criminals to betray their accomplices through announcements which were placed in the press to the effect that 'those among the suspected who will deliver themselves up to justice, constitute themselves prisoners, denounce their accomplices and give evidence against them will be pardoned'.[3] A further incentive to informants was the offer of a Tyburn Ticket, which exempted the holder from parish offices (including that of constable). Tyburn Tickets could themselves be sold to those unfortunate enough to be elected to such offices. These informants offered the beginnings of a remedy against gangs and others who violated the King's peace, but there was no effective process by which prosecutions could be raised against criminals who had robbed or otherwise injured private citizens. In such cases the injured party had to incur the risks and costs of bringing a prosecution himself so the late seventeenth century witnessed the growth of associations for the prosecution of felons. Those who subscribed to these organisations could call upon them to institute proceedings against offenders: in effect they were insurance policies. In 1767 the London Society for Prosecuting Felons, Forgers etc. was formed with the advice of Sir John Fielding who, with his half-brother Henry, was responsible for the next major development in the process of policing London, a development associated with their work at Bow Street Magistrates' Court in Covent Garden. In the earlier years of the eighteenth century less orthodox methods of catching criminals were employed.

THE CAREER OF JONATHAN WILD

The absence of an effective system for identifying and catching criminals left a gap in the judicial system which was more acute after the end of the War of Spanish Succession in 1714. Following the Peace of Utrecht of that year, the demobilisation of Marlborough's armies released tens of thousands of former soldiers with no means of support except as footpads (muggers) or highwaymen. Charles Hitchin, City Under-Marshal, told the Court of Aldermen at this time that he knew of 2,000 citizens who lived by thieving[4] and the Prime Minister, Robert Walpole, complained that 'one is forced to travel, even at noon, as if one is going into battle'. One of the consequences of this outbreak of lawlessness was the creation of the Bloody Code (see Chapter Three), but another was the emergence of the 'thief-taker' of whom the most notorious was Jonathan Wild. He made such a deep and unfavourable impression upon Henry Fielding that the author wrote an account of his career, *History of the Life of Jonathan Wild the Great*, published in 1775. 'Great' in this context was ironically defined by Fielding as 'greatness consists in bringing all manner of mischief on mankind and goodness in removing it from them' – a reference to Wild's technique of organising robberies and then profiting from reward money when the stolen goods were returned.

Jonathan Wild was born in Wolverhampton in about 1689 and apprenticed to a buckle-maker. He left his employment and appears also to have abandoned his wife and child, in order to go to London where he soon ran into debt and was imprisoned. This experience introduced him to the criminal underworld and, in particular, to one Mary Milliner, who was described as 'a common street-walker'. After his release Wild took a house near St Giles', Cripplegate, on the present site of the Barbican, and set himself up as an intermediary between the victims and culprits of crime. He had realised that thieves could obtain only a fraction of the value of the property they sold from pawnbrokers and others who acted as fences, whereas the original owners were often prepared to pay more for their return. Upon learning, from one of his underworld contacts, that an item of value had been stolen, Wild would approach the victim, inform him that an 'honest broker' of his acquaintance had come into possession of such an item, and offer to put them in touch with each other 'provided that nobody is brought into trouble and the broker has something in consideration of his care'.[5] The property having been returned to its grateful owner, Wild then collected a share of the spoils from the 'honest broker'. In this way he ensured that at no stage in the transaction did he either own the stolen merchandise or collect money directly from the victim. His hands were thereby kept clean.

As his reputation grew Jonathan Wild became bolder. He began to advertise his services and invited victims of crime to visit him in his 'Office for the Recovery of Lost and Stolen Property' and on occasion placed advertisements in newspapers such as the following in the *Daily Courant* on 20 May 1714:

> Lost on 19 March last, out of a Compting House in Durham Court, a Day Book, of no use to anyone but the owner . . . Whoever will bring them to Mr Jonathan Wild over against Cripplegate Church shall have a Guinea Reward and no Questions asked.[6]

CHARLES HITCHIN AND THE SODOMITISH ACADEMY

Wild's success soon attracted the attention of another who was engaged in the same dubious trade. Charles Hitchin, referred to above, was the City Under-Marshal, an office which Hitchin had purchased in 1712 for £700 with his wife's dowry. This investment he recovered by restoring stolen property to its owners, as Wild was doing, and also by claiming reward money for providing evidence under the Highwaymen Act of 1699, which offered £40 for information which led to a conviction. Hitchin complained to Wild that the latter was charging too little commission for his services, thereby undercutting the market, so the two briefly went into partnership in 1713. There was, however, no honour among these thieves who soon fell out over the spoils. Hitchin published a pamphlet describing Wild as 'king of the gypsies, king among the thieves and lying-master-general of England', to which Wild replied with an even more offensive publication entitled 'An Answer to a Late Insolent Libel with a Diverting Scene of a Sodomitish Academy', drawing attention to the Under-Marshal's deviant sexual tastes. The 'academy' concerned was located in Holborn and was kept by a madam whose name appears genuinely to have been Mother Clap.

After this dispute the two men went their separate ways, but the brief collaboration may have given Wild the idea of profiting from his underworld contacts in two ways: by returning stolen property and by claiming reward money for betraying the thieves who were working for him. Thus, in 1714 Wild secured the arrest of a group of thieves who had broken into the Banqueting House in Whitehall. The first member of the gang, Elizabeth Chance, was hanged and Wild then employed a technique from which he was to profit on many occasions: persuading other gang members to inform on one another in the hope of escaping the noose themselves while helping Wild to collect rewards. When necessary, Wild could himself direct his associates to carry out thefts from which reward money could later be earned. He acquired a semi-official status at this time, calling himself Thief-taker General and executing writs, as in 1719 when the Lord Chief Justice issued him with a warrant for the arrest of two highwaymen – an enterprise which required him to travel as far as Oxfordshire to make the arrests. A further source of profit at this time was a smuggling operation between the east coast and the Low Countries through which he disposed of unclaimed 'lost property' in exchange for contraband goods. Jonathan Wild could by this time be described as a prosperous businessman. One authority has estimated that Wild's earnings amounted to £25,000 – an unimaginably large sum for the period.[7]

HOSTILITY AND CONVICTION

By 1715 Wild was sufficiently well-to-do to be able to move to premises belonging to a Mrs Seagoe opposite the Old Bailey. His thief-taking business now began to overshadow his property recovery enterprise, but he also offered advice to criminals awaiting trial, advising them how to plead and helping them to establish alibis in return for payment or future service – an unorthodox version of a duty solicitor.[8] However, when it was more profitable to turn in the criminals he did not hesitate to become a guardian of the law. In the early 1720s he claimed to have broken up four London gangs and such was his reputation among the criminal community that he began to surround himself with bodyguards as well as recruiting his own people to assist him in making arrests and establishing a network of offices in cities and ports beyond London – something approaching a national enterprise. As his employees, he particularly favoured criminals who had returned, illegally, from transportation. These people, if found by the authorities, were liable to be hanged, which ensured their loyalty to Wild and further guaranteed that they would not give evidence against him in the event of his being prosecuted. He helped to secure the arrest of Jack Sheppard whose associate, Joseph 'Blueskin' Blake, earned himself much popularity by attempting to cut off Wild's head and throw it to the crowds outside the Old Bailey. This venture failed, but it was a sign of the hostility that Wild's activities had aroused – a hostility that would eventually cost him his life.

Wild was eventually arrested in February 1725 by the High Constable of Holborn. His arrest appears to have arisen from a falling-out among thieves. He was charged with, among other crimes, heading a 'corporation of thieves' and acting as an intermediary to dispose of stolen goods. The most telling indictment was that:[9]

He has often sold human blood, by procuring false evidence to swear persons into facts they were not guilty of, sometimes to prevent them being evidence against himself and at other times for the sake of the great reward given by the Government.

One of those who gave evidence against him was William Field, a friend of the Under-Marshal Charles Hitchin whom Wild had insulted. The web of deceit and betrayal that characterised the criminal justice system is further illustrated by the fact that William Field had, the previous year, betrayed Jack Sheppard to Wild.[10] On the morning of his trial at the Old Bailey Wild distributed a list of seventy-five criminals who had been hanged or transported as a result of his activities, Jack Sheppard being one of them. When this failed to prevent his conviction Wild wrote to the Earl of Dartmouth pleading for him to intervene with George I for a reprieve in view of his work as a thief-taker and when that failed he addressed a petition directly to the King from his quarters in Newgate:

> I do firmly resolve to relinquish my wicked Ways and to detest all such who persevere therein, as a Testimony of which I have a List ready to show to whom such Your Majesty shall appoint to see it.

This craven attempt to save his own skin by betraying yet more of his associates was unsuccessful, as was his final despairing attempt to escape the gallows by swallowing a large quantity of laudanum, an opium-based painkiller which normally, in a large dose, would bring about death or insensibility. In Wild's case the size of the dose, on an empty stomach, appears to have made him sick so the laudanum did not have the desired effect. Henry Fielding, in his fictional account, observed that 'the fruit of hemp seed [the rope] and not the spirit of poppy seed [laudanum] was to overcome him'. Wild therefore had to face the fury of the Tyburn mob while fully conscious.

Even by the standards of the time, Wild's last journey, from Newgate to Tyburn, on 24 May 1725, was witnessed by a particularly merciless crowd who remembered his role in the demise of the popular hero Jack Sheppard. Sheppard himself, referring to Wild and his like, had declared that, 'They hang by proxy while we do it fairly in person'.[11] Wild's dual role as grass and bent copper was no more popular then than later and an enterprising publisher printed a mock invitation to the event:

> To all the Thieves, Whores, Pickpockets,
> Family felons etc. in Great Britain & Ireland.
> Gentlemen and Ladies you are hereby
> desired to accompany your worthy Friend
> the pious Mr J....... W... from his
> seat at Whittington's College to the Triple
> Tree where he's to make his last exit.

An account published in *Mist's Weekly Journal* four days after the event stated that, 'In all that numerous crowd there was not one pitying eye to be found, or compassionate word heard; but on the contrary all the way he went nothing but hollowing and huzzas, as if it had been a triumph, particularly when he was turned off [hanged]'. His corpse was removed and sent to the Royal College of Surgeons where the skeleton remains in the Hunterian Museum.

Jonathan Wild is not a character who attracts sympathy, but it is worth reflecting on the fact that, following the death of this rather unsatisfactory policeman, there was a significant drop in the number of thieves brought to justice. He combined the offices of policeman, informant, solicitor and pioneer in the field of organised crime. More than twenty years passed before the Fielding brothers introduced a more satisfactory method of detecting criminals.

HENRY FIELDING

In his early years, Henry Fielding (1707–54) gave no reason to suppose that he would become the most celebrated magistrate ever to occupy the famous Bow Street Magistrates' Court. Indeed it seemed more likely that any appearance in a magistrates' court was likely to be in the dock rather than on the bench. He was born at Sharpham Park, near Glastonbury in Somerset, in 1707. His mother, Sarah Gould, was descended from prosperous gentry, her father serving as a judge of the King's Bench. Henry's father Edmund (who spelt his name Feilding) was a professional soldier who served in the Duke of Marlborough's campaigns against Louis XIV and eventually rose to the rank of lieutenant-general. Edmund was descended from earls, dukes, gamblers and a bigamist.[12] His younger sister Sarah (1710–68) was born when Henry was 3 years old. She became a notable author herself and a close friend of Henry's rival and fellow novelist Samuel Richardson.

In 1718, when Henry was 11, his mother died and his father sent him to Eton where he was a contemporary of William Pitt the Elder, George Lyttleton and Thomas Arne, all of whom were to play some part in his later life. While he was at Eton Henry's father remarried, his new bride being a Catholic. The union produced Henry Fielding's half-brother John who, though blind in later life, joined Henry on the Bow Street bench and continued the work of reforming the magistracy which was begun by Henry. The remarriage also provoked a family feud when Henry's maternal grandmother, Lady Gould, accused her son-in-law of many heinous acts, including bringing Henry up as a papist and giving him small beer instead of good strong ale. The case dragged on for years in the Chancery Court and Lady Gould eventually gained custody.

In 1725, upon leaving Eton, Henry's next experience of the law occurred when he attempted to abduct an heiress named Sarah Andrew. He ran away with her to Lyme Regis, was beaten up by toughs hired for the purpose by the girl's enraged guardian and taken before the mayor of the town who, as the local magistrate, bound him over to keep the peace.[13] This early experience of the judiciary may help to account for the hostility that he showed towards it in his literary works. Henry then made his way to London and soon started to make a name for himself as a playwright. The first play, *Love in Several Masques*, based on the Lyme Regis escapade, was performed in 1728 at Drury Lane. This was followed by a period of seventeen months studying humane letters (classics) at the University of Leiden in the Netherlands, after which he returned to London and resumed his career as a dramatist.

The following year saw the production of Fielding's *Rape upon Rape: or the Justice Caught in his own Trap*, the first of more than a score of biting satires on contemporary life, politics and the legal system which attracted the attention, and the wrath, of the government headed by Sir Robert Walpole, Britain's first Prime Minister. The play contains the character of Justice Squeezum, a notably corrupt magistrate with a taste for young prostitutes to whom he offered 'protection' in return for their favours. Justice Squeezum also earned a good living by despatching constables to arrest honest citizens and then extorting from them bail release fees. This was a common practice at the time among justices who regarded their status as an opportunity to earn a dishonest living, the bail release fee amounting to 1s.[14] Act II of the play contains the notable advice that 'the laws are turnstiles; only made to stop people who walk on foot, and not to interrupt those who drive through them in their coaches'.[15] In 1730 a performance was raided by constables in a crude attempt at censorship by Walpole's government. Fielding's barbs were aimed not only at Justices of the Peace, but at all levels of the legal profession. In a later play, *Don Quixote*, one character explains that 'twelve lawyers make not one honest man'.

POLITICAL SATIRE IN THE EIGHTEENTH CENTURY

At this time political satire was a marked feature of the London Theatre thanks to the works of a group of Tory writers who called themselves the Scriblerus Club, or Scriblerians, and mounted attacks on Walpole's long period of office (1721–42) under the early Hanoverians. The group included Alexander Pope, Jonathan Swift, William Congreve and John Gay. Walpole was held to represent the Whig interests of great landowners, concerned above all with maintaining peace so that they could devote themselves to making money and keeping taxes low. In 1726, *Gulliver's Travels* had satirised the world of Hanoverian politics while John Gay's *The Beggar's Opera*, produced at the Covent Garden Playhouse in 1728, compared Walpole with the notorious Jonathan Wild himself.[16] In 1733 the government had prosecuted John Harper, proprietor of the Haymarket Theatre, under the 1714 Vagrancy Act, taking advantage of the fact that the Act enabled actors to be classed as vagrants. The defence argued that, as the freeholder of a substantial property, the theatre, Harper was clearly not a vagrant. They further argued that he was unsuitable for the normal penalty for vagrancy, hard labour, because 'he being so corpulent, it is not possible for him either to labour, or to wander a great deal'.[17] In 1737 Walpole passed the Theatrical Licensing Act, which made the Lord Chamberlain responsible for issuing licences to theatres and for licensing plays before they could be staged. The office survived until 1968, but its immediate effect was to end Fielding's career as a playwright. He evaded the regulations for a while by running a puppet theatre in Panton Street, Haymarket, to which admission was free, the profits coming from the sale of tea, coffee and chocolate.

The year 1742 was a very important one for Henry Fielding. In February the government of Walpole fell and Fielding found himself faced with an administration to which he was more sympathetic and which soon came to include his Eton friends George Lyttleton and William Pitt. Within weeks of the change of government there appeared Fielding's novel *Joseph Andrews*. Less well known than the later *Tom Jones*, *Joseph Andrews* is similar in that it tells the story of two ingenuous people undertaking a journey in which they are treated with disdain by the prosperous and offered selfless help by those worse off than themselves. It contains the notably unsympathetic character Lady Booby, who is advised to have an irritating critic committed to prison on the order of a compliant magistrate. She is reassured that in gaol the critic will be 'either starved or ate up by vermin in a month's time'. Fielding sold the copyright to the publisher for £183 and thus failed to obtain the full benefit from a novel which sold 6,500 copies in its first year and was translated into French shortly afterwards. Later the same year he resumed his role as a playwright with a one-act ballad, *Miss Lucy in Town*, written in collaboration with Fielding's friend the actor David Garrick and Thomas Arne, better known as the composer of *Rule Britannia*. Another brush with the law occurred the same year when Fielding had judgment entered against him in the Court of Common Pleas in respect of a debt of £200 incurred by a friend of Fielding for which he had acted as guarantor. The debt was paid by a man named Ralph Allen whom Fielding had befriended. Allen had made a fortune from managing and developing the postal service and for many years until Fielding's death the writer was a guest at Allen's house near Bath.

BONNIE PRINCE CHARLIE AND THE 45 REBELLION

In 1745 the country was alarmed by Bonnie Prince Charlie's attempt to overthrow the Hanoverian monarchy. Fielding's support for the government was expressed in his periodical, *The True Patriot*, which supported in the struggle the administrations which succeeded Walpole's. It included lurid accounts of the consequences of a Jacobite victory, with Protestants burned at the stake, the heroic Admiral Vernon executed at Tyburn and bishoprics given to Jesuits. Fielding also applauded the young Middle Temple lawyers for forming a militia to resist the Jacobites, Fielding himself being unable to join their ranks because of gout from which he now suffered continuously.

In 1748 Fielding's most celebrated novel, *Tom Jones*, was published with its more sympathetic, if eccentric magistrate in the form of the erratic squire Western. Western however, did not altogether escape Fielding's strictures. At one point in the novel the squire is dissuaded from sending his sister's maid to prison for cheek when his clerk reminds him that he 'already had two informations [i.e. complaints] exhibited against him in the King's Bench'. Ten thousand copies were sold in the first nine months after publication and it was soon translated into French, German and Dutch. Fielding, always short of cash, sold the copyright for £600. The publisher made at least ten times that figure. Along with *Joseph Andrews* and Fielding's later novel *Amelia* (1751), it set the pattern for plot, character and contemporary references that influenced later novels in England and, later, those of Continental writers.

COVENT GARDEN

Fielding's support for the government did not pass unrewarded. In 1747 he was appointed Justice of the Peace on the Middlesex Bench, followed by appointment to the Westminster Bench a year later. He became its chairman shortly afterwards and adopted the title 'first magistrate for Westminster'. The Middlesex and Westminster benches administered justice throughout much of the Metropolis north of the Thames outside the square mile of the City of London itself, which remained the province of the Lord Mayor. In 1748 Fielding moved into a house in Bow Street, Covent Garden, which was to become the most celebrated magistrates' court in the world. Fielding was already familiar with the area because of the large number of theatres it contained. Fielding's new home had previously belonged to Thomas De Veil (1689–1746), a soldier of fortune of French ancestry who had served in Marlborough's armies and been appointed Justice of the Peace for Middlesex and Westminster in 1729. At this time there was much corruption among Middlesex justices, partly because it was difficult to find people of suitable status and quality to do the work. It therefore attracted 'basket justices' and 'trading justices' like Fielding's creation Squeezum. The expression 'basket justices' referred to their habit of carrying baskets for the gifts they solicited. The phrase 'trading justice' indicated the attitude which inspired two Justices of the Peace of the time to open a grocer's shop in the red-light district of Covent Garden from which they supplied provisions at exorbitant prices to brothel-keepers in return for turning a blind eye to their activities. Another justice, known as Sax, recently released from a debtors' prison, was observed hanging around alehouses in Wapping, peddling affidavits for cash. In 1796 Grose's *Dictionary of Vulgar Terms* defined trading justices as 'broken mechanics, discharged footmen and other low fellows smuggled into the Commission of the Peace who subsist by fomenting disputes, granting warrants and otherwise retailing justice'. Jonathan Swift suggested that much crime was actually, by predatory magistrates. In his essay *A Project for the Advancement of Religion and the Reformation of Manners* (1709) he had written:[18]

Such men are often put into the Commission of the Peace whose interest it is that virtue should be utterly banished from among us; who maintain, or at least enrich, themselves by encouraging the grossest Immoralities; to whom all the Bawds of the Ward pay Contribution for Shelter and Protection from the Laws. Thus these worthy Magistrates, instead of lessening Enormities, are the occasion of just twice as much Debauchery as there would be without them. For Infamous Women are forced upon doubling their work and Industry to answer double charges of paying the Justice and supporting themselves.

CORRUPTION

There was no shortage of evidence to support such charges of corruption. A single magistrate at this time was authorised to levy a fine of 1s upon anyone he heard uttering an oath. The money was supposed to be paid into the funds for poor relief, but in 1719 the Westminster Bench uncovered the case of one magistrate who had levied such fines to a value of 30s and pocketed the proceeds.[19]

The poet William Shenstone commented in the late eighteenth century on the corrupt relationship between magistrates and their clerks, or legal advisers:

> A justice and his clerk is now little more than a blind man and his dog. The profound ignorance of the former, together with the canine impudence and rapacity of the latter, will but rarely be found wanting. The justice is as much dependent on his clerk for superior insight and guidance as the blind fellow is on his cur. Add to this that the offer of a crust will secure the conductors of either to drag their masters into a kennel.

One justice, faced with the prospect of a debtors' prison, had himself appointed Envoy Extraordinary to the Kingdom of Bavaria so that he could claim diplomatic immunity.[20] The expression 'as corrupt as a Middlesex Justice' was recorded as common usage by one eighteenth-century writer.[21] The *Gentleman's Magazine* published a letter describing the methods employed by one trading justice at this time:[22]

> I have known a Trading Justice boast that he grants no less than forty warrants a week, makes them all special that the fees may be double and contrives to bind the parties over to the [Quarter] Sessions for the sake of unbinding them again as an Act of Grace, taking only ten shillings for his trouble.

Other magistrates showed zeal of a different kind. The poor laws of the eighteenth century made parishes responsible for the upkeep of resident paupers, the poor rate being levied by the magistrates. Magistrates therefore tried to ensure that paupers were either excluded altogether from the parishes for which they were responsible or were returned to their places of birth or residence. In 1718, a clergyman of charitable disposition at Chislehurst, in Kent, invited some pauper children from London to his church, preached a sermon for them and invited the congregation to contribute to a collection for the children. At this point two magistrates, fearing that the children would become a permanent charge upon the parish, intervened to try to prevent the collection from being taken. Having failed they then attempted to seize the collection plate, engaged in fisticuffs and ordered the congregation 'to disperse, under pain of being guilty of a riot'. In the words of Daniel Defoe, who chronicled the unhappy incident, 'if there was a riot, it was occasioned by the two Justices'.[23]

A flattering contemporary account of De Veil's life, possibly written by De Veil himself, described such characters as:[24]

Low, needy and mercenary fools who subsist on their commissions. They are hated and dreaded by the common people who fancy they have greater powers than they really have . . . they are as much afraid of being carried before *his worship* as the people of *Paris* fear the *Bastille* or the inhabitants of *Lisbon* the *Inquisition* [his italics].

De Veil established his office in Bow Street in 1740 on the site of the present magistrates' court where a plaque records the fact that he was the first holder of the office of Chief Metropolitan Magistrate. In 1738 he had been appointed to the sinecure of Inspector General of Imports and Exports at a salary of £500 with £250 for his clerk, thus placing his office on a permanent basis as long as he lived and making him, in effect, the first stipendiary (professional, paid) magistrate. He enjoyed such success in reducing corruption and improving standards of justice that he attracted assassins. The first attempt on his life occurred in 1734 when he was stabbed by a fellow Justice of the Peace, named Webster, whom De Veil had reported to the Lord Chancellor for corruption. For this injury De Veil received 'compensation' of £250 from the Secret Service fund, a source which was to be used repeatedly over the following years. The second attempt on his life occurred the following year when a gang of robbers whom he had been attempting to bring to justice was convicted of attempting to murder him. One of them was a solicitor.

His unpopularity was not confined to the criminal classes. He was also responsible for the brutal suppression of a strike by Covent Garden footmen who were complaining about their pay and conditions of service. He was knighted for his services as a magistrate in 1744. De Veil's record was not without blemish. A contemporary account suggested that he was 'friendly' to young prostitutes whom he 'interviewed' in a private closet.[25] He died a year before Henry Fielding took over as chief magistrate at Bow Street. His body was removed from his Bow Street home early in the morning to escape the attention of his many enemies.

HENRY FIELDING IN BOW STREET

De Veil had made a start, but in 1748, when Fielding moved into De Veil's former house, close to the site of the present magistrates' court, corruption was still rife. On Clerkenwell Green 'Justice Shops' run by trading justices dispensed alehouse licences, affidavits, groceries and building materials. They employed 'barkers' to solicit business for them, with some success. The Covent Garden area itself was noted for its population of prostitutes and thieves. One of the most enterprising, the pickpocket Mary Young, had a pair of false hands and arms which she folded across her lap while sitting in pews. Her real hands were used to relieve her neighbours of their possessions.[26] The area also contained many actors with whom Fielding was familiar through his work as a playwright, these being regarded by the government as little better than the criminals. The warren-like character of the area made it easy for criminals to vanish from the scenes of their crimes. In Fielding's words 'The whole city appears as a vast wood or forest in which the thief may hide in as great security as wild beasts do in Arabia and Africa.'[27]

When he took office Fielding reviewed the resources at his disposal for law enforcement. The most numerous were the 300 Charleys paid 1*s* a night to patrol the streets. Fielding described them as 'poor old decrepit people'. Then there were the constables, referred to above: reluctant volunteers who were responsible for overseeing the Charleys. Fielding continued for a time to make use of the heirs of Jonathan Wild, thief-takers such as the notorious McDaniel gang who earned handsome rewards by setting up robberies and then claiming rewards for recovering property and incriminating culprits. In 1753, when another dispute among thieves resulted in murder the ringleader, Stephen McDaniel was given the lenient sentence of seven years' imprisonment and to be pilloried twice. He was, however, spared the worst consequences of the pillory when he was protected by the keeper of Newgate and a City sheriff, which suggests a degree of official connivance at his activities.[28]

Fielding inherited eighty constables, of whom he thought he could trust six. One of these was Saunders Welch, who had been born in the workhouse in Aylesbury in 1710 and had become a prosperous grocer in Holborn and friend of Dr Samuel Johnson. In 1746 he became High Constable of Holborn, an office which required him to accompany criminals to the gallows in Tyburn. He shared Fielding's views on the measures necessary to restore order and wrote a number of pamphlets on the causes of crime and measures to prevent or detect them. They bore portentous titles such as *A Letter upon the Subject of Robbers, Causes and Prevention of Crime* (1753), but as a former resident of the workhouse he was not unsympathetic to the problems of the poor. At a dinner with Dr Samuel Johnson and the gardener Capability Brown in October 1773 Boswell records Welch as upbraiding his fellow guests for suggesting that begging was a lucrative occupation. He told them that more than 1,000 died of hunger each year in the capital and that 'what we are told about the great sums got by begging is not true: the trade is overstocked', a comment that still resonates two centuries later.[29] Fielding described Welch as 'one of the best officers who was ever concerned in the execution of justice'. Welch himself became a magistrate in 1755.

Welch wrote a booklet entitled *Observations on the Office of Constable with Cautions for the Safe Execution of that Duty etc.*, which is an instruction manual for those entering upon this hazardous task. Much of it would make a modern constable smile. The introduction explains that his purpose is 'to collect what may be useful for a body of men who perform a very troublesome task and to save them, if possible, from those enemies to their power; I mean low solicitors who are for ever preying upon their ignorance or rashness'. Having thus declared his position vis-à-vis the legal profession, he advises his constables against becoming involved in 'ale house quarrels' and to exercise great care if asked to execute a warrant against 'a person of fashion'. Discretion suggests that such warrants should be returned to the magistrate. On the other hand swearing invoked a penalty of 5s for a gentleman, but only 1s for a labourer. Traffic control was a concern, particularly 'Carmen riding upon their carts and the brickmakers in their wagons going full tilt in the streets of this town', the penalty for each being 10s. He inveighed against 'the barbarous custom of cock-throwing' (?!) and explained that 'a different conduct is necessary' when intervening in quarrels among 'neighbours of credit and fortune' than when dealing with similar disputes among vagabonds. Above all, 'let your demeanour to the magistrates in general be respectful'.[30]

ORIGINS OF THE BOW STREET RUNNERS

The six trustworthy constables, led by Welch, formed the core of Fielding's band of thief-takers who were later to develop into the famous Bow Street Runners, predecessors of the Metropolitan Police. Welch and his band were paid from reward money obtained from recovering property and gaining convictions. Welch himself became a Justice of the Peace in 1755. In Fielding's own words, 'I had the most eager desire of demolishing gangs of villains and cut-throats, so I had a set of thief-takers enlisted in my service, all men known, approved, faithful and intrepid.'

Fielding himself was paid, like De Veil before him, from the Secret Service fund and was thus relieved of the temptation to appropriate bribes and fines as many of his predecessors had done. The payment was probably £200 a year. In his last work Fielding referred to the income derived by some magistrates from court fees and fines:[31]

A predecessor of mine used to boast that he made a thousand pounds a year in his office . . . I had reduced an income of about five hundred pounds a year of the dirtiest money upon earth to little more than three hundred pounds, a considerable proportion of which remained with my clerk.

One of Fielding's first acts was to invite victims of crime to approach him for redress. In December 1748 he committed for trial a sailor who had been accused of assault and placed an advertisement in the *St James's Evening Post* inviting any citizens who had been attacked by sailors to 'give themselves the trouble of resorting to the Prison in order to view him'. The outcome of this early, if unconventional, example of an 'identity parade' is not recorded but one can say with confidence that the unfortunate sailor's defence counsel would have had no difficulty in finding fault with the process by the standards of later centuries. In February 1749 Fielding inserted an advertisement in the *General Advertiser*, which proclaimed, 'All persons who shall for the future suffer by robbers, burglars etc. are desired immediately to bring or send the best description they can to Henry Fielding Esq.,' at his office in Covent Garden. Three years later he founded the *Covent Garden Journal*, a weekly publication specifically for this purpose.

In June 1749 two sailors were arrested after wrecking a brothel where, they claimed, they had been robbed. The following day 400 of their fellow mariners rioted in protest, wrecking a pub in the Strand, The Star, and prompting Fielding to call upon troops to assist him. The mob was dispersed from around the smouldering wreckage of The Star and one culprit was hanged. In 1751 Fielding published *An Enquiry into the Causes of the Late Increase of Robbers*,[32] which drew attention to the fact that, since the end of the

War of the Austrian Succession in 1748, 54,000 men had been discharged from the army and navy, most of them being now penniless and unemployed. However, he found other, more censorious reasons for lawlessness, including 'the vast torrent of luxury which of late years hath poured itself into this nation' citing also the vice of 'drunkenness, a second consequence of Luxury among the Vulgar'. Fielding's *Enquiry* is believed to have inspired the celebrated engraving *Gin Lane* by his friend William Hogarth, depicting the consequences of drunkenness and vice. Fielding applauded a statute of Henry VIII which prohibited 'the lower sort of people' from playing numerous games, including bowls and football. This was a widely held view at the time. A contemporary of Fielding's and fellow barrister of the Middle Temple, Theodore Barlow, described the measures prescribed by this statute to stop people enjoying themselves.[33]

> Games for Diversion among the lower people tend greatly to make them idle and as such the Laws have provided against them. Every Justice may, from Time to Time, enter into any common House or Place where any are playing at Dice, Cards, Bowls, Quoits, Shove-Groat, Tennis, Football or other unlawful game new Invented, may arrest the Keepers of such places and imprison them.

Fielding particularly disapproved of gaming and on 1 February 1751 sent eighty soldiers, bayonets fixed, to close a gaming house where forty-five people were arrested. One is left wondering how he expected energetic, unemployed ex-military personnel to spend their enforced leisure time. He did have some rather strange ideas for creating jobs. He argued that wages of skilled workers should be kept high to retain their services, while wages for others should be held down to reduce prices. On the other hand, he did not think that runaway servants should be branded on the forehead by order of two magistrates. Fielding argued against the practice of advertising a reward for the return of stolen property, suggesting that this encouraged robberies, and the following year, 1752, the practice was banned. He also believed that minor offenders should have less severe punishments and should, where possible, be kept out of prison so that they could 'be kept apart from the felons and not sent to Newgate as they are now . . . the first theft will often prove the last'.

It was at this time that Fielding described Newgate as 'a prototype of Hell', reflecting not only his judgement on the suffering inflicted upon its inmates, but also its corrupting influence. Fielding also argued that evidence of previous criminal behaviour should be introduced as evidence at a trial. Both of these views were rejected at the time, though the debate on them has been renewed in the twenty-first century. Finally, he argued against the widespread use of the death sentence, which could be imposed for offences as trivial as the theft of goods worth 5s. He advocated the more widespread use of transportation instead. He particularly opposed public executions since he argued that the spectacles were conducted in an unseemly party atmosphere in which the condemned criminals attracted sympathy and were presented in an almost heroic light.

In August 1753 Fielding was summoned to see the Duke of Newcastle, soon to be Prime Minster, who asked him 'to demolish the reigning gangs' who were terrorising the Covent Garden area. Fielding proposed the recruitment of a special force of ex-constables to pursue criminals. He secured an advance of £200 from the Privy Council. Seven of the culprits were captured after a ferocious battle which involved breaking into their den and in December 1753 the *Public Advertiser* reported that 'since the apprehending of the Great Gang of Cut-Throats, not a dangerous blow, shot or wound has been given either in roads or streets'. In Fielding's words 'this hellish society were almost utterly extirpated'.[34]

By this time Fielding was exhausted, suffering from, dropsy, gout, asthma, years of overwork and possibly tuberculosis. For two years he had walked with the aid of crutches. In June 1754 he left England for Lisbon, having been advised by his doctor that the milder climate would be good for his health. He chronicled his last days in his *Journal of a Voyage to Lisbon*,[35] which also contains reflections on his life and work. He died on 8 October and is buried in that city.

BLIND JOHN FIELDING

In 1750 his half-brother, John Fielding, had moved into Henry's house in Bow Street and had been appointed to join him on the Westminster and Middlesex benches. John had been blind since 1740 as a result of an accident sustained while serving in the Royal Navy. In February 1749 he and Henry had founded a business, the Universal Register Office, on the corner of Castle Street and the Strand. It was an employment agency, but it also sold a quack medicine, known as Glastonbury Water, which claimed to be a cure for asthma and tuberculosis, though it did nothing to relieve Henry's sufferings from those conditions. John's zeal as a magistrate, if anything, exceeded that of Henry. On 14 October 1754, following the death of his brother, he inserted in the *Public Advertiser* a notice which invited victims of crime to inform John Fielding who would 'immediately despatch a set of brave fellows in pursuit, who have long been engaged for such purposes, on a quarter of an hour's notice. This became a regular feature of John Fielding's campaign against crime and in 1755 it was followed by his treatise entitled *A Plan for Preventing Robberies Within Twenty Miles of London*,[36] an ambitious scheme involving extensive patrols on foot and on horseback, which did not become fully effective until fifty years after John's death. In the meantime, he instituted eight-man mounted patrols in Westminster, paying each man 4*s* a night. Foot patrols were paid 2*s* 6*d* a night and led by a Bow Street Runner, as the constables were now called. He paid his regular Bow Street Runners 11*s* 6*d* a week and encouraged them to supplement this income with reward money from victims of crime who had recovered their possessions – an orthodox version of Jonathan Wild's methods. Fielding and Welch continued to be paid from the Secret Service fund. The Runners at this time enjoyed no official status, though Fielding did issue them with batons which carried a gilt crown to symbolise the authority which, strictly, they did not have. It is the ancestor of the police truncheon. The Runners' finest hour came in 1820 when twelve of them scaled a ladder to enter a hayloft in Cato Street where, with much violence, they arrested the Cato Street conspirators who had planned to murder the government and seize the Bank of England.

John Fielding was particularly unsympathetic to the successors of Jonathan Wild who organised crimes and then informed on the perpetrators. In 1756 four such thief-takers were convicted of inducing others to commit robberies for the purpose of informing on them. They were placed in the pillory where two of them died. Grasses were no more popular in the eighteenth century than they are today. His measures against the unsophisticated criminals who had frequented Covent Garden were so successful that many of them left town for less well-protected communities. In 1772, therefore, he

The Cato Street Conspiracy: a plot hatched by a group of radicals and named after the Marylebone Street where they met to prepare their plan to murder much of the cabinet at dinner in Grosvenor Square in February 1820. The heads of prominent members of the cabinet would then be impaled on poles and paraded about London, thereby inciting a revolution which would overthrow the government in favour of one committed to the egalitarian ideas of Thomas Spence who, before his death in 1814, had advocated the division of land equally between the population of Great Britain. The leader was a man called Arthur Thistlewood, but the plan was betrayed to the authorities and by the time the conspirators arrived at their rendezvous a Bow Street magistrate, Richard Birnie, was waiting for them with George Ruthven, a government spy and the twelve Bow Street Runners. One of the runners was killed by Thistlewood, but all the conspirators were eventually arrested and two of them agreed to give evidence against the others. According to *The Observer*, the Cato Street building became an object of macabre interest and was visited by thousands of people. Five of the conspirators, including Thistlewood, were executed at Newgate on 1 May 1820 and five were sentenced to transportation for life.

began to publish *The Weekly or Extraordinary Pursuit*, which sent to country Justices of the Peace details of crimes and of the criminals who had fled from London. This was the first attempt to establish any kind of national intelligence service on criminal activities. Its name was changed to *The Hue and Cry* and in 1883 responsibility for its publication was assumed by the Metropolitan Police under the title *The Police Gazette*. It continues to be published.

John Fielding's work had its lighter moments. In 1764 he received a complaint from the jilted fiancée of the notorious libertine Giacomo Casanova who, the unhappy girl claimed, had promised to marry her before she let him have his wicked way. Fielding interviewed Casanova who spoke flatteringly of the magistrate's excellent command of Italian. The two parted on amicable terms. Casanova was unpunished (though the brief spell that he spent in Newgate made a deep impression on him)[37] and the disappointed girl remained single.

John Fielding was not without vanity. In 1761 he suggested to the Prime Minister, the Duke of Newcastle, that he deserved a knighthood and this was duly awarded. Nor was he wanting in charity. He recognised the problems posed by homeless orphans who had little choice but to descend into criminality. This was the era of Thomas Coram's Foundling Hospital and John Fielding made his own contribution to the welfare of these unfortunate waifs. He helped to found a charity which prepared homeless boys for service in the Royal Navy and two homes in Lambeth for girls. The orphan asylum trained girls for domestic service and the Magdalen Hospital was a home for girls who wished to escape their life of prostitution.

THE AFTERMATH

A severe test of the peacekeeping system arose in 1780. As John Fielding lay on his deathbed a renegade aristocrat, Lord George Gordon, led a rioting mob in an orgy of anti-Catholic violence which for eight days in June of that year wrecked property, killed 300 citizens and brought the business of government to a standstill.

Thomas Coram's Foundling Hospital: Thomas Coram (*c.* 1668–1751) was a sea captain from Lyme Regis in Dorset who was a pioneer in the development of trade between Britain and the colonies in North America and Canada. He retired with a modest fortune and devoted himself to raising money to provide homes for abandoned children whose small bodies he had seen rotting in the streets near his home on Rotherhithe. He spent eighteen years (1721–39) lobbying and gained the support of both men and women among the aristocracy. Finally, on 17 October 1739, George II granted a charter for 'an Hospital for the Reception, Maintenance and Proper Education of such cast off Children and Foundlings as may be brought to it'. The Foundling Hospital attracted the support of many prominent citizens, including painters who donated works to raise funds, notably William Hogarth, Joshua Reynolds, Godfrey Kneller and Thomas Gainsborough. Handel gave an annual performance of *The Messiah* for the same purpose. The hospital acquired premises in Coram Fields, Holborn (close to the later site of Great Ormond Street Hospital) where mothers could leave their unwanted children in a basket. The Foundling Hospital moved to Berkhamsted, Hertfordshire in 1935 and remained in use until 1951 when the practice of fostering replaced the need for such a home. The Berkhamsted building is now Ashlyns School and the original Holborn site is the home of the Foundling Museum and Coram Fields, the only park in London which an adult may not enter unless accompanied by a child. The Thomas Coram Foundation remains active in child welfare work.

One of the most prominent casualties was the partially rebuilt Newgate prison which was burned to the ground and looted.[38] Order was eventually restored by a full-scale military operation and the rioters were taken before courts martial rather than the civil courts. Much of the blame for the disorder fell unjustly on Fielding's successor, Sir John Hawkins, who had tried to contain the disturbance with inadequate resources. He was succeeded by William Mainwaring, MP, a banker who returned to the old, corrupt ways, placing his friends and family in positions of influence and profit. The problems of corruption were thus not entirely banished. In 1780, the year of John Fielding's death, the great Parliamentarian Edmund Burke declared that, 'The Justices of Middlesex were generally the scum of the earth – carpenters, brickmakers and shoemakers; some of whom were notoriously men of such infamous character that they were unworthy of any employ whatsoever.' The quotations that open this chapter, written in 1729 and 1794, reflect the continuing corruption in provincial courts.

Henry Fielding is remembered chiefly as an early exponent of the English novel whose depiction of life in eighteenth-century England was as sharp and unflinching as that of his friend and contemporary Hogarth. But Henry and John Fielding had brought about an irrevocable change in public expectations of the office of Justice of the Peace as exercised in London. Never again would corruption be regarded as an inevitable accompaniment of the office. In the words of a recent historian of the period, 'Between them they made the name Fielding synonymous with peacekeeping for a generation of Londoners'.[39] They thereby set a pattern for the administration of justice in London and eventually elsewhere, which survives and flourishes in the twenty-first century.

THE METROPOLITAN POLICE

The work of the Fieldings was both appreciated and perpetuated, but many obstacles remained before a reasonably effective system of policing could be established. In 1785 the government introduced a Bill to extend throughout the metropolis a system of paid commissioners who would supervise a professional police force throughout the capital. The Bill failed because the Lord Mayor objected to any infringement of his jurisdiction within the square mile of the City of London itself and the Justices of the Peace, who had traditionally

The Old Whipping Post, Newgate: a device in use from Medieval times until the nineteenth century; abolished for women in 1817 thanks to Elizabeth Fry. *(Guildhall Library, London)*

Daniel Defoe stands in the pillory before Temple Bar, condemned for lampooning the established Church but protected and garlanded with flowers by an admiring mob. *(Guildhall Library, London)*

London Bridge, 1616, the entrance decorated with severed heads, some no doubt prepared in Newgate's Jack Ketch's Kitchen. *(Guildhall Library, London)*

Right: Dr Hales's ventilating machine, installed at Newgate following the death of forty-three people, including two judges, from typhus fever in 1750. Unfortunately eleven workmen died of typhus fever while installing the device. *(Guildhall Library, London)*

Far right: Surgeon's Hall: entitled to ten cadavers a year for dissection from Tyburn, though only after an exchange of blows with friends and relatives of the executed. *(Guildhall Library, London)*

The execution of Colonel James Turner in 1663, witnessed by Pepys; Turner's long final address tested the crowd's patience and failed to gain him a last-minute reprieve. *(Guildhall Library, London)*

Tyburn, 1696: a crowd gathers to watch a hanging before the introduction of the Triple Tree; in the background the Medieval process of hanging, drawing and quartering has attracted some less squeamish onlookers. *(Guildhall Library, London)*

Tyburn, 1760: the execution of Lord Ferrers by the 'sudden drop' requires grandstands to accommodate all the spectators. *(Guildhall Library, London)*

Jack Sheppard (1702–24) the notorious escaper, sketched in his Newgate prison cell by the well-known artist Sir James Thornhill, father-in-law of William Hogarth. (*NPG*)

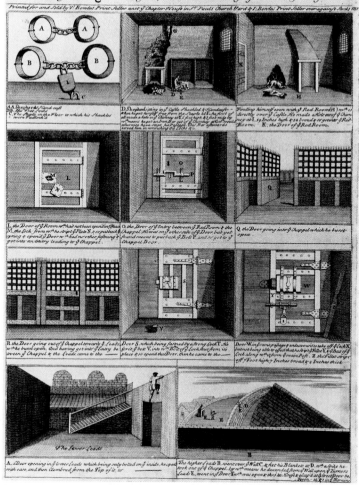

Jack Sheppard's escape: a contemporary print describing and celebrating Sheppard's last escape from Newgate. (*Guildhall Library, London*)

The London rarey Shows or who'll step into Ketch's Theatre.

Walk in Gentlemen.

Amongst the Works which Nature doth produce
As well for Admiration as for Use
A most surprizing Ostrich here we find
By Nature large & largest of its kind
His Height Prodigious but above the rest
He hardest Steel or Iron can digest.

Newgate appears & how John Sheppard lay
In heavy Irons till the fatal Day
The crowding Populace flock in to see
This Man who did the Law and Law defy
Who twice being taken twice did make escape
But now He's taught & Labour is his fate

But here's one thing to beadmir'd the most
V which the earliest Ages cannot boast
Nor England ever had the same before
two Lions young brought forth in London Towr
The like of this in such a Northern Clime
Has not been known since the first date of time

An eighteenth-century print and verse celebrating the exploits of Jack Sheppard (who peers out through the bars of his cell in the gatehouse); and those of Jonathan Wild, who sits at the door of the gatehouse negotiating with 'clients' who seek the return of their stolen property. (*Guildhall Library, London*)

St Sepulchre's, opposite Newgate, whose bells tolled the condemned to their execution:

All you that in the condemned hold do lie
Prepare yourselves, for to-morrow you shall die.

(*Guildhall Library, London*)

'Proper Charleys': Sir Robert Peel, founder of the Metropolitan Police, puts to flight a band of elderly nightwatchmen. (*Guildhall Library, London*)

Sir John Fielding (1721–80); his reforms at Bow Street, carried out with his novelist brother Henry Fielding (1707–54), put to flight the jibe that 'a justice and his clerk is now little more than a blind man and his dog'. (NPG)

The Cato Street conspirators, arrested in 1820 by Bow Street Runners, one of whom was killed. Condemned to be hanged, drawn and quartered they were allowed to die in the noose before being beheaded. (Guildhall Library, London)

The Gordon Rioters attack Newgate, 1780, a central feature of Charles Dickens's *Barnaby Rudge* and described as 'a new species of gaol delivery' by the poet George Crabbe who had paid for a vantage point from which to watch the mayhem. *(Guildhall Library, London)*

Lord George Gordon (1751–93): anti-Catholic leader of the Gordon Riots who was sent to Newgate not for inciting the riots but for libelling Marie Antoinette. He died in Newgate after converting to Judaism. *(NPG)*

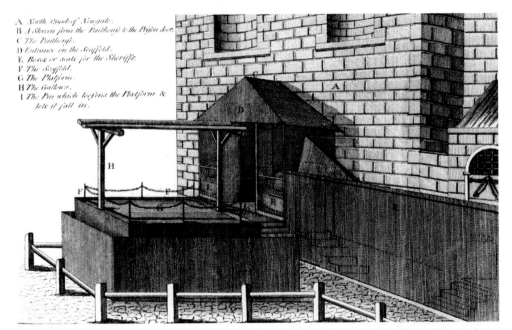

A. North Guard of Newgate.
B. A Screen from the Penthouse to the Prison door.
C. The Penthouse.
D. Entrance on the Scaffold.
E. Boxes or seats for the Sheriffs.
F. The Scaffold.
G. The Platform.
H. The Gallows.
I. The Pin which locks the Platform & lets it fall in.

'Executions are intended to draw spectators' (Dr Samuel Johnson). The execution platform outside Newgate where executions occurred from 1783 to 1868, witnessed by many including Dickens and Thackeray. *(Guildhall Library, London)*

James Boswell (1740–95), who was 'most terribly shocked' by a hanging and commended the Roman system: knock him on the head with an iron cosh and then cut his throat! *(NPG)*

'Prisoner number 31, Renwick Williams, vulgarly called the monster'; or was he just a maker of artificial flowers? *(Guildhall Library, London)*

RENWICK WILLIAMS
commonly called
THE MONSTER.

Execution Room, Newgate: executions within the walls began in 1868 and continued until Newgate was demolished in 1902. *(Guildhall Library, London)*

John Howard (*c.* 1726–90) whose death from typhus ('gaol fever') in Russia was a poor return for his work as a prison reformer. (*NPG*)

Jeremy Bentham (1748–1832) whose 'Panopticon' and 'rules of lenity, severity and economy' influenced nineteenth-century prison design and administration. (*NPG*)

Millbank prison: designed on Bentham's 'Panoptic' principles to accommodate the Silent and Solitary systems; also known as 'the fattening house', because of the quality of its food, but unfortunately vulnerable to dysentery. *(Guildhall Library, London)*

Elizabeth Fry (1780–1845): 'I have seen Elizabeth Fry in Newgate and I have witnessed there miraculous effects of true Christianity upon the most depraved of human beings.' (John Randolph, American ambassador, 1819). *(NPG)*

George Dance's design, built after the Gordon Riots of 1780, its massive, forbidding exterior surviving until the gaol was demolished in 1902 to make way for the expansion of its neighbour the Old Bailey. *(Guildhall Library, London)*

Edward Bulwer-Lytton (1803–73): better known for *The Last Days of Pompeii,* his early reputation and fortune were built on 'Newgate Novels'. *(NPG)*

Charles Dickens (1812–70) who, as a young journalist, witnessed the horrors of a Newgate execution and featured the gaol in many of his novels. (*NPG*)

supervised policing, saw the commissioners as a threat to their authority.[40] In 1792 the government managed to secure the passage of a private member's bill proposing a more restricted measure. The Middlesex Justices Act established throughout the metropolis seven other 'public offices' modelled on Bow Street. One of them was south of the river, in Southwark, though the City itself was excluded. Each office had three stipendiary magistrates, paid £400 a year, and six constables, paid 12*s* a week. One of them survives as Great Marlborough Street Magistrates' Court. The buildings and personnel were funded by the Home Secretary, but Bow Street continued to be paid for from the Secret Service fund and the Bow Street office remained the personal property of the chief magistrate until this anomaly was removed in 1842. By 1835 there were thirty stipendiary magistrates in London, all barristers, and in the meantime the system had been extended to other communities, Manchester being the first in 1813. The title stipendiary magistrate was retained until the twenty-first century when it was replaced by the designation district judge.

In 1795 a merchant and stipendiary magistrate, Patrick Colquhoun (1745–1820) who was a follower of the Utilitarian philosopher Jeremy Bentham (1748–1832) estimated that over 100,000 people in London (more than 15 per cent of the population) lived largely on the proceeds of crime. He wrote a *Treatise on the Police of the Metropolis*, which advocated a national police service. This and all subsequent attempts to establish a national service were successfully opposed despite the advocacy of such influential figures as Bentham himself and the great social reformer Edwin Chadwick (1800–90). However, Colquhoun's campaigning did bear fruit in 1798 in the creation, by a group of dockland merchants, of the private Thames River Police to protect their tempting and vulnerable premises from theft. The Thames River Police is thus the world's oldest surviving police service.

Further improvements slowly followed. In 1805 Bow Street horse patrols were instituted, following the model advocated by John Fielding exactly fifty years earlier in his 1755 *Plan for Preventing Robberies Within Twenty Miles of London*. Bow Street mounted patrols operated as far out as Kent, Essex and Surrey, and the mounted officers, who were mostly concerned with apprehending highwaymen, were issued with firearms, a pattern that was not followed elsewhere in Britain until more than a century and a half had passed. Ten years later the Home Secretary, Viscount Sidmouth, who was concerned about corruption among Bow Street Runners appointed an officer to supervise their activities. The officer himself continued to report to the magistrates.

In 1829 the Home Secretary, Sir Robert Peel, finally secured the Act which created the Metropolitan Police. The new force owed much to Peel's former post as Chief Secretary for Ireland when he had set up the Royal Irish Constabulary to prevent civil disorder. The passage of the 1829 Act was only achieved by agreeing to accommodate a number of powerful interests. The City itself remained independent of the Metropolitan Police and acquired its own separate force ten years later which it retains. The Bow Street Runners, together with the forces associated with the other seven 'public offices' remained independent, under the control of their local magistrates, until 1839, when they were absorbed into the new force. The Thames River Police remained independent until the same date when it, too, became part of the Metropolitan Police and in 1836 the Bow Street horse patrols became the Mounted Police Division of the Metropolitan Police, losing their firearms in the process. Five years earlier the first special constables were introduced – laymen with the uniform and authority of a regular constable, but working as volunteers.

The creation of the Metropolitan Police represented a decisive break with the past. On Saturday 26 September 1829 the recruits to the new force paraded in the grounds of the Foundling Hospital, Holborn, and were issued with their uniforms. The following Tuesday, at 6 p.m., they set out on their new beats. The old system of Charleys and reluctant ward constables was replaced by 3,000 'guinea a week' constables in their blue coats, blue trousers and top hats. They were supervised by two commissioners who reported to the Home Secretary. One was Charles Rowan, a former soldier who had fought at Waterloo, and the other was Richard Mayne, a barrister, both of whom were sworn in as magistrates.

The new force was not universally popular and on Guy Fawkes night, 1830, the two commissioners were burned in effigy.[41]

Many of the new constables were ex-soldiers, but their uniform had been chosen to emphasise the unmilitary character of the new force in a nation with a long-standing suspicion of standing armies – a distinction further emphasised by the decision to equip the constables with truncheons rather than firearms. Inspectors were allowed to carry pocket pistols. Three weeks training was given before launching the constables on an arduous routine of fourteen-hour days. This may account for the rapid turnover in the members of the new force. Of more than 3,000 recruits in 1829–30 three-quarters had left or been dismissed after four years. The constables' truncheons were an emblem of their authority. They were encircled by a band of copper at one end engraved with the letters WR representing the authority of the monarch (William IV) who came to the throne in 1830. These features of their equipment account for the nicknames 'coppers' and 'Old Bill', while the alternative 'Bobbies' owes its origin to the Home Secretary himself, Robert Peel. The headquarters of the new force was in Whitehall Place whose rear entrance, Scotland Yard, gave its name to the building. A few Charleys survived the advent of the new force, one being photographed in his box in Brixton Road in about 1870.

In 1835 and 1856 Acts of Parliament required boroughs to establish their own policing arrangements and the Metropolitan Police provided a model for the city, borough and county forces that swiftly followed, under the control of local authorities. Some were very small. The borough of Southwold, in Suffolk, had its own police force consisting of one constable. Detectives were introduced in the 1840s, an effective inspection regime in 1856 and in 1861 the blue lamp was installed outside police stations to give them a distinct identity. An exception was made for the police station in Bow Street to accommodate the sensibilities of Queen Victoria whose visits to the Opera House were not to be spoilt by recollections of the Blue Room at Windsor in which Prince Albert had died. Bow Street had a white lamp. In 1883 the Special Branch was formed (originally called the Special Irish Branch) to deal with terrorism and in the 1890s the Metropolitan Police began to experiment with fingerprinting, though it did not fully adopt the technique until 1901, as Newgate was about to be demolished. Formal training schemes for officers began at about the same time.

None of these developments would have been foreseen by Henry or John Fielding, let alone by Jonathan Wild. Yet it remains true that the work of the playwright and his blind half-brother in establishing a reasonably honest system of detecting and punishing crime in the eighteenth century created a pattern which was later followed in London, Britain and throughout much of the world.

POSTSCRIPT

Patterns of criminal behaviour in the nineteenth century reflected changes in society and bear some strange resemblances to those of the later centuries. Burglary and murder peaked in the 1860s, but then declined, while major frauds became a more prominent feature of criminal behaviour as large business enterprises such as railways offered richer prizes to the devious. George Hudson (1800–71), the 'railway king', lost his fortune as a result of dishonesty, but was able to retire discreetly to the Continent in 1854 on a modest annuity. Three years later Leopold Redpath, an officer of the Great Northern Railway, was sentenced to transportation to Australia for embezzling £170,000, which had been set aside by his employers to invest in the new Metropolitan underground railway from Paddington to the City – a project that was consequently delayed for six years. In 1904 Whitaker Wright (1845–1904) was convicted of defrauding investors to the tune of £5 million in connection with the construction of the Bakerloo Line and sentenced to seven years' penal servitude. A few minutes later he collapsed in the Law Courts, dead from a cyanide capsule he had been carrying. Such echoes of the twentieth century were heard again in the 1890s when the first instances of football hooliganism were recorded along with a spectacular brawl in the Old Kent Road which occurred on the August bank holiday, 1898. Many of the participants were drunk. *Plus ça change*!

FIVE

After the Riots: The Decline of the Bloody Code

Executions are intended to draw spectators. If they do not draw spectators they don't answer their purpose. The old method was most satisfactory to all parties; the public was gratified by a procession; the criminal was supported by it. Why is all this to be swept away?

(Dr Samuel Johnson)

About fifty persons of both sexes who, whether awake or asleep, are beastly drunk from drinking deeply of rum, gin and beer, while every description of the most disgusting ribaldry is going on around.

(A description of the crowd outside Newgate awaiting an execution)

There is as much moral cowardice in shrinking from the execution of a murderer as in hesitating to blow out the brains of a foreign invader . . . the plain truth is that Christianity has to have two sides. A gentle side up to a certain point, a terrific one beyond that point.

(Sir James Stephen, jurist)

115

CIVIL DISORDER

Despite the success of the Fielding brothers, the latter half of the eighteenth century continued to witness the well-established traditions of rioting and other forms of civil disorder, especially in London. They proceeded naturally from a tradition of vulgar and abusive behaviour combined with a freedom of expression which was admired by visitors such as Voltaire, but could rarely be expressed through the ballot box. They served as a substitute for democratic consultation at a time when the franchise was restricted to a privileged few and votes were bought rather than canvassed. In 1762 the Scot Boswell, commenting on the liberties enjoyed by Englishmen, noted in his diary that 'the rudeness of the English vulgar is terrible. This indeed is the liberty which they have: the liberty of bullying and being abusive with their blackguard tongues'.[1] In some cases organised bands of hooligans were directed by their leaders to attack and destroy specific targets associated with unpopular employers, institutions or public figures.

The most spectacular of these events occupied the first week of June 1780 and resulted from a piece of legislation whose intention was wholly benign. This was the Catholic Relief Act of 1778, introduced by Sir George Savile, which removed certain restrictions on the small Catholic population of England, many of these impositions dating from the time of Elizabeth I when there had been a real threat of invasion by Catholic Spain. In 1778 the American War of Independence was in progress and the Relief Act enabled Catholics to join the hard-pressed British forces as well as permitting them to own property and inherit land. This reasonable measure aroused some Tory opposition in Parliament, but it was on the streets that the real battle was fought, with fatal consequences for a new prison which was in course of construction at Newgate.

THE PROTESTANT ASSOCIATION

The first signs of trouble occurred in Scotland where a Protestant Association was formed under the presidency of Lord George

Gordon, third son of the Duke of Gordon, with the declared intention of opposing the introduction of any similar measure to Scotland. Riots in Perth and Edinburgh, accompanied by attacks on Catholic chapels and homes, prompted the Lord Provost to promise that no such legislation would be introduced in Scotland. This concession encouraged the Protestant Association and its strange leader to extend its activities to England (and to Canada where a similar Act had removed disabilities from the large population of Catholics in the French-speaking province of Quebec). The Protestant Association attracted the support of John Wesley, the founder of Methodism, though he was in no way implicated in the disorder which followed.

Lord George Gordon, born in 1751, had been elected to the House of Commons as MP for Ludgershall in 1774 after a short career in the Royal Navy. His frequent lectures to Parliament on religious questions were not appreciated and led many fellow members to doubt his sanity. One of them commented that 'the noble lord has got a twist in his head, a certain whirligig which runs away with him if anything relative to religion is mentioned'. He organised a petition for the repeal of the Catholic Relief Act which allegedly bore over 30,000 names and assembled a crowd of his supporters in St George's Fields, Lambeth on Friday 2 June 1780. The declared intention of this mob, whose size was variously estimated as anything from 20,000 to 60,000, was to present the petition to Parliament, but they were soon distracted by more tempting prospects. They proceeded to Westminster wearing blue cockades and carrying blue banners bearing the legend 'No Popery'.

In the House of Commons Gordon demanded an immediate vote on the issue as his followers ran through the Palace of Westminster threatening and maltreating any members they conceived to be hostile to their demands. The House refused to concede Gordon's demands and summoned assistance, which appeared in the form of a small number of Horse Guards. This prompted the petitioners to retreat from the building, but not before some of their number had been arrested and taken to Newgate. Enraged by these arrests the petitioners were transformed into a rioting mob who now set about the real business of the day.

117

THE RIOTS

First the mob attacked the Catholic chapels of foreign embassies, beginning with the chapel of Sardinia in Lincoln's Inn Fields and moving on to the Bavarian chapel in Warwick Street. Windows were smashed, doors forced, the contents destroyed and the furnishings burned, thereby setting fire to the buildings themselves. In the days that followed the rioters turned their attention to any buildings that were associated with Catholics, with supporters of the Relief Act, with authority or with the prospect of profitable looting. The Prime Minister, Lord North, was attacked and was lucky to escape with his life, but without his hat which was torn from his head, ripped up and distributed as trophies among the mob. The houses of Lord Chief Justice Mansfield and Sir George Savile, promoter of the Catholic Relief Act, were sacked, as was a distillery in Holborn belonging to a Catholic named Langdale. Its contents further inflamed some of the rioters while rendering others insensible and, for the moment, harmless.

The attack on Sir George Savile's house was described by Susan Burney in a letter to her sister, the writer Fanny Burney. Susan had witnessed the mayhem from the family home in St Martin's Lane, near Leicester Square. She had remained at home rather than risk venturing on to the unruly streets to attend a party at the home of Sir Joshua Reynolds nearby and she now realised the wisdom of this decision as 'the populace had broken into Sir George Savile's house and were then emptying it of furniture which, having piled it up in the midst of the square, they forced Sir George's servant to bring a candle to set fire to it'.

By now the numbers involved in the disturbances were considerably greater as opportunists joined the quest for loot. On 6 June, the fifth day of the riot, the Negro writer Ignatius Sancho (1729–80) gave an account of the rioters. Born at sea, he had worked as butler to the Duke of Manchester before opening a grocer's shop in Charles Street, Westminster, and it was from there that he witnessed the mayhem:

There is at this moment at least 100,000 poor, miserable, ragged rabble, from twelve to sixty years of age, with blue cockades in their hats, ready for any and every mischief . . . There is about a thousand mad men armed with clubs, bludgeons and crows, just now set off for Newgate, to liberate, they say, their honest comrades.

NEWGATE: 'A NEW SPECIES OF GAOL DELIVERY'

Newgate was, indeed, the next objective of the mob as it was the prison where some of their fellows had been incarcerated four days earlier. On 6 June, the last full day of the riot, they first approached the house of the keeper, Richard Akerman, who refused to admit them. His house was duly sacked and his furniture piled up against the great gate and set alight. This caused great alarm among Newgate's inmates who feared that they were to be burned to death, though Akerman bravely joined the prisoners inside the gaol rather than seeking to save his own skin. The gate soon gave way, the rioters rushed in and what followed was described by the poet George Crabbe who, on his first visit to London, had paid a householder 6*d* to watch the attack on Newgate from the roof of a nearby house: 'Here I saw a new species of gaol delivery. The captives marched out with all the honours of war, accompanied by a musical band of rattling fetters'.

Crabbe was not the only literary figure to record his impressions. The reclusive William Cowper (1731–1800), who compared London with Babylon, observed the riots which destroyed the prison and his fellow poet, William Blake (1757–1827), watched them from his new printing shop in Broad Street.[2] A total of 117 prisoners were posted as having been released from Newgate in this way. Besides the English they included Italian, German, Jewish, Irish and Afro-American offenders. Most of them were thieves. Some had robbed their employers while others were convicted of 'crack lay' (housebreaking by force) or 'dub lay' (entering with a key). There were also murderers, rapists, arsonists, counterfeiters, highway

George Crabbe (1754–1832): English poet, naturalist, clergyman and apothecary (pharmacist), Crabbe was born in Aldeburgh, Suffolk, the son of a tax collector. He studied to be an apothecary and in 1780 went to London where he witnessed and described the Gordon Riots. In 1782 he was ordained priest and became chaplain to the Duke of Rutland at Belvoir Castle, Leicestershire, eventually becoming rector of Trowbridge, Wiltshire, where he is buried. He was an early naturalist, assembling and classifying collections of plants and insects, but he is best remembered for his poetry which earned him the friendship of such contemporaries as William Wordsworth, Robert Southey and Sir Walter Scott. His poem 'The Borough', published in 1810, based upon his knowledge of Aldeburgh, became the inspiration for Benjamin Britten's opera *Peter Grimes*.

robbers and a bigamist. Most would have faced the death penalty or transportation but for their fortuitous release.[3] The effrontery of the mob was recorded by James Boswell in his *Life of Samuel Johnson*. He visited Newgate to view its ruins while they were still glowing from the destructive fires and recorded the fact that the looters were still at work on the ruins of its equally notorious neighbour:

As I went by the Protestants were plundering the Sessions House at the Old Bailey. There were not, I believe, a hundred but they did their work at leisure, in full security, without sentinels, without trepidation, as men lawfully employed, in full day.

The riots were now approaching their climax. The King's Bench, Marshalsea and Fleet prisons were attacked as was the Bank of England, but this prize was denied to the mob by the determined action of John Wilkes who, acting as City Chamberlain in an unaccustomed role as defender of the established order, commanded troops to fire upon the mob who retreated in disorder. By this time the government had recovered its nerve and deployed 12,000 troops on the streets with orders to shoot rioters and looters. Fatalities now began to mount rapidly. Almost 300 were killed and many more were wounded, about 200 seriously. Over £30,000 was paid in compensation to Catholics whose property had been destroyed, but Mr Langdale, the Holborn distiller, declined compensation, accepting instead an offer to distil spirits free of duty for a year – the foundation of a new fortune. Among the other casualties was the Bow Street office of the Fieldings, together with their records.

John Wilkes (1725–97): publisher, agitator and, despite the government, Member of Parliament, Wilkes was born in Clerkenwell, the son of a prosperous businessman. Briefly married to an heiress whose fortune enabled Wilkes to live without financial anxiety, he became MP for Aylesbury in 1757 and founded a paper, called *The North Briton*, in 1762, which mounted a series of fierce attacks on the government of George III, led by Lord Bute. This led to his prosecution for seditious libel, but the charge was dismissed by the Lord Chief Justice on the grounds that Wilkes was an MP. When Parliament amended the law to remove this impediment Wilkes fled to Paris, returning in 1768 to stand as MP for Middlesex. This led to a farcical series of elections by his constituents, expulsions from Parliament by the government faction, arrests, imprisonment, fines and riots in Wilkes's support. He campaigned for freedom of the press, Parliamentary reform and against the government's policies towards the rebellious American States. In 1774 he became Lord Mayor of London, responsible for Newgate prison and later served as City Chamberlain. Upon being informed by his former ally the Earl of Sandwich that he would die of the pox or on the gallows, he replied, 'That, my lord, will depend upon whether I embrace your principles or your mistress.'

RETRIBUTION

Considering the scale of the riots, the worst ever seen in London, the retribution exacted by the authorities was relatively mild. Twenty-one were hanged for offences arising from the riots, including three of those who had mounted the attack on Newgate. The executed did not include Lord George Gordon who was very ably defended against a charge of 'levying war on the king' (high treason) by Thomas Erskine (1750–1823), a future Lord Chancellor who successfully argued that his client had only peaceful intentions and could neither foresee nor control the actions of his unruly supporters.

Gordon's connections with Newgate were not yet at an end. In 1788 he was convicted of libelling the British government and Marie Antoinette, who at that date was still Queen of France, and was sent to Newgate where he spent the remaining five years of his life. Eccentric as ever in his religious views, he converted to Judaism and corresponded from Newgate with Baron Alvensleben, the ambassador from Hanover, to whom he complained that the Hanoverian George III had 'incorporated the system of tolerating Popery into the statute book' and that 'the Prince of Wales (if married to a Roman Catholic) might even succeed to the throne.'[4] By the time that this letter was written the Prince of Wales, later George IV, had for some years been married to the Catholic Maria Fitzherbert, albeit without the knowledge of his father King George III. Despite his imprisonment, and his conversion to the Jewish faith, Lord George continued to draw supporters to his lost cause. Upon his death a printer named Robert Hawes wrote a lament which he entitled, confusingly,[5] 'An Acrostical Tribute to the Memory of Lord George Gordon who Died in Newgate', in which he declared, in capitals throughout:

THAT THE TIME IS AT HAND FOR THE COMING OF GOD'S ANCIENT PEOPLE THE JEWS, TO THE BELIEF AND ACKNOWLEDGE-MENT OF THE TRUE MESSIAH, I AM CLEARLY SATISFIED.

Hawes ended with a long, lugubrious poem concluding:

To Lord George Gordon's memory this verse
Hawes writes who almost envieth his hearse

A greater writer than Robert Hawes drew attention to the fact that
the so-called religious motivation of the rioters was soon lost in the
looting and mayhem that the Gordon Riots soon became. In his
preface to *Barnaby Rudge, A Tale of the Riots of Eighty* Charles
Dickens wrote that 'what we falsely call a religious cry is easily raised
by men who have no religion'. The Gordon Riots were the worst anti-
Catholic riots that England ever saw, though they were not the last.
When Cardinal Wiseman re-established the Roman Catholic hierarchy
as Archbishop of Westminster in 1850 there were disturbances on the
streets of London and rumours that the cellars that John Henry
Newman was building for his oratory in Birmingham were for
murders.[6] In the meantime, despite Lord George Gordon, the Catholic
Relief Act remained on the statute book, but Newgate lay in ruins.

THE NEW NEWGATE

The prison wrecked by the rioters was in the process of being rebuilt.
For many years the condition of the gaol had been a matter of
concern to the City authorities, especially to those who had to sit at
the Old Bailey next door. As observed in Chapter Two,[7] an outbreak
of gaol fever (typhus) at Newgate in 1750 had killed forty-three
officials at the Old Bailey. In 1767 a former Lord Mayor, Sir Stephen
Janssen, wrote a pamphlet campaigning for the immediate rebuilding
of the prison.[8] He reminded his readers that in 1750, the year of the
disaster, he had been a Sheriff and therefore required to attend the
court in that capacity 'when the Newgate contagion made such
dreadful Havock in the Old Bailey Sessions House', killing the Lord
Mayor and two judges as well as others 'of less note'.

Janssen had himself later become Lord Mayor (in 1755) and was
responsible for the installation of the windmill designed by Stephen
Hales that was supposed to alleviate the problem of foul air. Hales[9]
had claimed that his device would be capable of 'drawing like large

heavy Lungs, at the rate of seven thousand Tuns of foul Air per Hour, out of several Wards at the same time', but clearly Janssen was not fully reassured.[10] He obtained a copy of the architectural drawings of the prison at York Castle, whose design he approved, and he recommended that in the new prison at Newgate each felon should have his own cell and a clean shirt once a week. In addition, each cell was to be washed once a week with vinegar and each prisoner should be swabbed down with vinegar before attending court, thus protecting the court officials from contagion. All this information was passed to the City Surveyor, George Dance, with the recommendation that he incorporate the suggestions into the design for a new prison. The design was an improvement on the old one, but the conditions within, as reported by Elizabeth Fry in the following century, were scarcely improved.[11]

GEORGE DANCE THE YOUNGER

George Dance the Younger (1741–1825) is often confused with his father, also George Dance (1700–68) who was Clerk of Works to the City of London and designed the Mansion House and the Church of St Leonard's, Shoreditch. Despite being the youngest of five brothers, George Dance the Younger was chosen to succeed his father in the architectural profession. He attended St Paul's School and then studied in Italy for six years after working in his father's practice. His experience in Italy, from which many of his sketches survive, strongly influenced him in his own designs, where classical themes are usually evident though often in combination with other motifs. His first major commission involved rebuilding the Medieval church of All Hallows, London Wall, in 1765 whose design he based on a Roman basilica. In 1768, upon the death of his father, he became architect to the City of London and produced a number of innovative designs to improve the Port of London, including a new double bridge to replace the decaying London Bridge. The two carriageways would have been 100 yards apart and fitted with drawbridges to allow shipping to pass – a precursor of Tower

Bridge. Like many of his plans, the latter was not adopted by the Corporation, the design of John Rennie being chosen instead shortly before George Dance died. He also designed the front of the Guildhall, Martin's Bank on Lombard Street and the Royal College of Surgeons in Lincoln's Inn Fields. The houses that he designed for aristocrats in Mayfair and St James's have all been destroyed, but John Wesley's house opposite Bunhill Fields survives as the only Dance-designed dwelling in London.

Dance advised his pupil, John Soane (1753–1837) on Soane's design for the Bank of England and designed the Giltspur Street Compter, almost opposite Newgate, which opened as a debtors' prison in 1819 and was demolished in 1855. In the last thirty years of his life he became rather reclusive and devoted himself more to drawing than architecture. He was a founder member of the Royal Academy, outliving all the other founders, but failed to give any lectures in the seven years (1798–1805) that he was professor of architecture there. Upon his death he left more than 200 portraits in pencil of his contemporaries, many of which were acquired by the Royal Academy, the National Portrait Gallery and the British Museum.

As architect to the City Corporation, Dance was the clear choice to design the new gaol. His proposal incorporated three courtyards with separate accommodation for debtors, male felons and female felons. It also contained a chapel and an infirmary. The external design was stark, with massive blank walls whose entrances were decorated with shackles. A later commentator, writing shortly after the building was demolished, wrote that Dance was 'determined to appeal to the emotions by the sheer bulk and proportion of his wall'[12].

First, however, the money had to be found to carry out the work. In 1766, in the face of campaigners such as Janssen, an Act of Parliament authorised a loan of £50,000 to be raised to rebuild Newgate and the Old Bailey. This was to be repaid from the coal dues, a tax originally levied on coal brought to London to repay for the rebuilding of the City after the Great Fire of 1666. In May 1770 the Lord Mayor laid the foundation stone and the reconstruction of the prison and courthouse began, though in 1778 the Corporation had to gain authorisation for a further loan of £40,000. Work on the two buildings proceeded together, though the massive, fortress-like structure of the prison contrasted with the more elegant design of the sessions house, both in its external appearance and in its internal facilities. Within the sessions house there was a single courtroom, but there was also a room for witnesses who had previously had to wait in a nearby pub. The Lord Mayor's dining room was luxuriously appointed with a mosaic, an expensive Turkish carpet, mahogany furniture and a fine wine vault.

Work on the prison was almost complete when the rioters descended upon it in 1780, but the reconstruction was completed by 1785 and Newgate remained London's principal prison until the middle of the nineteenth century when it ceased to be an ordinary prison and became a place of temporary detention for those awaiting trial at the Old Bailey and for those awaiting execution. It remained London's principal place of execution until it was demolished in 1902.

In 1797, at about the time that Newgate was being constructed, New York was building its first state prison. The newly independent citizens of the United States named their prison in New York Newgate in recognition of the fame of the original and it remained New York's principal prison until it was replaced by Sing Sing in 1828.

Dance's design for the new prison was characterised by massive, forbidding, external walls relieved only by four niches containing statues and a few narrow windows in the keeper's house, which was at the centre of the long wall which ran from Newgate Street south along the Old Bailey. The statues in the four niches represented Liberty, Justice, Peace and Plenty. The irony of these figures was not lost on the acerbic architect and garden designer Sir Reginald Blomfield (1856–1942), who wrote of the statues that 'there was a bitter irrelevance in their presence on this building for they were gracious and kindly and dearly loved by the pigeons of St Paul's'. Writing of the destruction of the building by the Gordon Rioters Blomfield added, 'The instincts of the mob of 1780 were sound, for the place with its narrow windows and gloomy yards seems to me to have been about as hopelessly human as it is possible to imagine.'[13]

The massive windowless walls were certainly forbidding and were presumably intended to emphasise the seriousness of the business that was transacted within them as well as impeding escape attempts. The building was demolished in 1902, but some comparisons have been made with the windowless lower walls of the Bank of England where security was also a concern and which was designed by Dance's pupil Sir John Soane. Much of the interior of the gaol was redesigned by the City architect Sir Horace Jones (1819–87) better remembered as the architect of Tower Bridge and Smithfield's meat market.

THE NEWGATE DROP

The reconstruction of the gaol from its charred remains coincided with the end of the notorious Tyburn processions, since in 1783 public executions were removed from Tyburn to Newgate itself, where they were carried out on a scaffold erected outside the prison the night before. On 7 November 1783 John Austin was the last man to be hanged at Tyburn (for highway robbery) and a month later, on 9 December, nine men and women were hanged on the 'New Drop' outside Newgate's Debtors Door in the Old Bailey. Not everyone welcomed the change. Dr Samuel Johnson was prominent among those who objected to the loss of the Tyburn processions, writing:

> Executions are intended to draw spectators. If they do not draw spectators they don't answer their purpose. The old method was most satisfactory to all parties; the public was gratified by a procession; the criminal was supported by it. Why is all this to be swept away?[14]

The doctor would no doubt have been consoled by the fact that the removal of the place of execution would do little to diminish either the size of the crowds that attended the executions or the unseemliness of their behaviour. Indeed, the coming of the railways in the following century ensured larger crowds than ever for executions outside Newgate, some railway companies advertising excursions for the purpose of viewing this gruesome entertainment.[15] The executions were carried out in public until May 1868, after which they took place within the prison walls. Altogether 1,167 people were executed at Newgate either outside or within the prison walls. The public executions at Newgate were compared by some writers with the gladiatorial spectacles of ancient Rome. Hepworth Dixon, who published a study of the London prisons in 1850 described the ritual whereby the scaffold would be erected at Newgate on a Sunday evening ready for the executions on Monday. He observed that 'an execution is as good as a Lord Mayor's show for the race of pickpockets' thirty or more of whom could be arrested in a single morning, and he proceeded to make such a comparison which was echoed in the works of writers such as Dickens, Thackeray and Hardy:

> This is in truth our circus, our gladiatorial arena. We Christians, who talk of Rome with measureless pity and contempt here prepare our feasts of blood. The scenes enacted in front of Newgate disgrace us in the eyes of Christendom.[16]

The seemliness of the executions gained nothing from a widespread belief that the 'death sweat' of the hanged would remove warts and other disfigurements if applied to the human body, leading to a stampede to touch the dead or expiring body.[17]

In 1840 two young writers attended the hanging at Newgate of a Swiss valet called François Courvoisier, who had been sentenced to death for killing his master, Lord William Russell. The assembled crowd was larger than usual because of the novelty of the spectacle of a servant who had murdered an aristocrat. Among them was Charles Dickens, who had rented a nearby balcony to be sure of a good view of the hanging, and the other writer, whom Dickens observed in the crowd from his vantage point, was William Thackeray. Dickens was there as a journalist while Thackeray had been persuaded to attend by his friend Richard Monkton Milnes, who hoped thereby to recruit the famous writer to the abolitionist cause. The event made a strong impression on both writers. Thackeray arrived at 4 a.m., four hours before the time appointed for the execution itself, to find a large crowd already gathered and discussing knowledgeably the finer points of this and similar occasions: 'Which executions have you attended lately? Do you think he has the rope on yet? Will he be hanged facing the crowd or facing the wall?' By 6 a.m. the space in front of the prison was full and the 'ticket-holders' like Charles Dickens, about 600 in number, were occupying their seats at windows and balconies. Ten pounds could be charged for a really good spot on the occasion of an especially notorious execution.

There were many young people in the crowd along with family parties who had arrived well victualled as for a day out at the seaside in later years. Many were drunk, some were engaged in debauchery and others were busily spotting celebrities among the crowd, such as actresses, politicians or the nobility. Six years after the event, in February and March 1846, Dickens wrote to the *Daily News*, 'I did not see one token in all the immense crowd of any one emotion suitable to the occasion; nothing but ribaldry, levity, drunkenness and flaunting vice in fifty other shapes'.[18] The only sign of decorum lay in the cry of 'Hats off!' which went round the crowd immediately before the trap was opened by the executioner.

Thackeray described the appearance of Courvoisier as he stepped on to the scaffold and his own reaction to the spectacle: 'He turned his head here and there and looked about him for a while with a wild, imploring look. His mouth was contracted into a sort of pitiful smile' and then added, 'I have been abetting an act of frightful wickedness and violence . . . I pray that it may soon be out of the power of any man in England to witness such a hideous and degrading sight.'[19]

The hideous and degrading spectacle of Courvoisier's execution was in fact quite decorous when compared with some of the events that occurred outside the Debtors Door. In 1789 the execution of William Skitch, a burglar, did not go according to plan when the rope became detached from the scaffold and Skitch simply fell through the trapdoor to the ground. The crowd was sympathetic, but Skitch called out, 'Good people, be not hurried. I can wait a little,' while the executioner prepared another rope.[20] In December, 1827, a house burglar named John Williams was sentenced to death and made a desperate attempt to escape from Newgate by scaling a drainpipe. He fell and injured or broke both legs. These were dressed by a surgeon and he was carried to the scaffold where, during his death throes, blood was seen to be pouring from the wounds in his legs.

In 1807 occurred the hangings of John Holloway and Owen Haggerty who had been convicted of a murder in Hounslow five years earlier, the only real evidence coming from their supposed accomplice, Benjamin Hanfield who, by turning King's Evidence, was pardoned. Despite a warning from the judge that such evidence should be treated with caution the jury took only fifteen minutes to return a verdict of guilty. Both men went to the scaffold protesting their innocence to the last but the notoriety of the case was such that a crowd of over 40,000 had assembled. A pieman who was plying his trade dropped his basket. Some of the crowd stumbled over it and in the ensuing mayhem more than thirty people were killed by being trampled underfoot, while many others were injured and taken, with twenty-seven of the dead, to St Bartholomew's Hospital nearby.

Last-minute confessions to a crime were usually well received. In July, 1864, Thomas Briggs was robbed and beaten to death in a train. A suspect, Franz Muller, was identified by a cabman named Matthews, who was acquainted with Muller and believed that Muller had pawned some of Briggs's property with a pawnbroker in Cheapside, appropriately called Death. By this time Muller had sailed for New York, but Matthews accompanied two policemen to New York on a faster vessel where Muller was arrested. Muller confessed to the crime only when Calcraft, the executioner, placed the hood over his head outside Newgate. Shortly afterwards the cabman, Matthews, was himself briefly jailed at the request of creditors with whom he had run up large debts on the strength of the £300 reward money that Matthews expected for identifying Muller.

More barbarous methods of execution were still in use for certain crimes after the transfer of executions to Newgate. Phoebe Harris, Margaret Sullivan and Catherine (also known as Christian or Christine) Murphy were burned at the stake for coining, which was regarded as high treason, though it was the practice to strangle the victims before confining their bodies to the flames, a merciful end compared with that of the martyrs of earlier reigns at nearby Smithfield. The last of these, Catherine Murphy, was despatched in 1789. On 1 May 1820 occurred the execution of five of the Cato Street conspirators[21] who had been sentenced to be hanged, drawn and quartered for high treason. Hanoverian justice was more merciful than its Tudor counterpart, so the conspirators were killed by hanging before being handed over to an unnamed executioner who cut off their heads. As each head was severed and raised aloft by the knifeman the crowd shouted 'Ah!' until one of the bloodied objects slipped from his grasp on to the platform itself – an action which was greeted by a cry of 'butterfingers!' The last public execution occurred on 26 May 1868 of Michael Barrett, the Fenian (Irish nationalist) whose bomb at Clerkenwell had killed seven people.

THE BLOODY CODE FADES

Although the Bloody Code[22], with its multitude of capital penalties, remained a substantial legal force until the second half of the nineteenth century, its effects were much diminished in practice. Thus in six years between 1822 and 1839 of 5,061 convicts sentenced to death in England only 302 were actually executed, the remainder being commuted by the sovereign in council.[23] Legislative changes to the code came more slowly. Sir Samuel Romilly had begun the assault on the code in 1806 when he was appointed Solicitor-General and this was the start of a process of reform which lasted for over half a century. One of his early supporters was Lord Byron (1788–1824) whose maiden speech in the House of Lords was devoted to an eloquent but unsuccessful attack on a proposal to make the destruction of machinery a capital offence.

Sir Samuel Romilly (1757–1818): grandson of a French Huguenot refugee from the persecutions of Louis XIV and son of a prosperous watchmaker, Romilly was born in Frith Street, Soho, and became a barrister of Gray's Inn. He visited France and Switzerland and became acquainted with the French leader Mirabeau (1749–91) whom Romilly advised on Mirabeau's unsuccessful attempts to establish a constitutional monarchy in France following the Revolution of 1789. He was a friend of William Wilberforce and strong supporter of the anti-slavery movement. He was offered the post of Solicitor-General by the short-lived Whig government, which took office in 1806 and subsequently sat for four constituencies. He devoted the rest of his career to mitigating the savagery of the penal codes in the face of determined Tory opposition. His limited successes included the repeal of an Elizabethan statute that made it a capital offence for a soldier or sailor to beg without a certificate from a magistrate or a commanding officer. He committed suicide in 1818, overcome by grief at the death of his wife four days earlier.

A Select Committee on the Criminal Law sat in 1819 and recommended a number of reforms which led to the abolition of the death penalty for many thefts and, in 1823, to the repeal of the anachronistic Waltham Black Act. In the 1830s a Royal Commission led to further reforms. Robert Peel's government in the 1830s repealed 278 Acts and replaced them with eight.[24] Peel himself claimed in the House of Commons, while Home Secretary 'there is not a single law connected with my name which has not had for its object some mitigation of the severity of the criminal law'.[25] By an Act of 1823, in cases not involving murder, Peel allowed a judge to 'record' the death penalty while making it clear that it would not be carried out, thereby relieving the convict of the anxiety associated with an appeal to the sovereign. By 1861 only four crimes carried the death penalty: murder, treason, piracy and arson in the royal dockyards.

In the meantime, executive action greatly diminished the effects of the code. By the 1830s only about 7 per cent of those capitally convicted were actually executed, the great majority of sentences being commuted by the sovereign, on the advice of the Privy Council, either to transportation or to service in the army or Royal Navy. About 160,000 convicts were sent to Australia between 1787 and 1864. Those thus sentenced at the Old Bailey were kept at Newgate until they were removed first to hulks (disused ships) in the Thames or Medway and thence to the transportation vessels themselves for the long voyage halfway round the world. There is some evidence that transportation was feared more than death. In June 1789 the *Morning Chronicle* reported that Mrs Fitzherbert (illegally married to the Prince of Wales) had attended the Old Bailey to listen to 16-year-old Sarah Cowan resisting attempts to persuade her that transportation was preferable to death. At the last moment she was persuaded to accept the commutation of her sentence.[26] Long prison sentences remained unusual until the latter half of the nineteenth century when more prisons were built with a view to detaining and rehabilitating prisoners rather than disposing of them to the cemetery or the colonies. Those thus imprisoned either awaiting trial or after sentence were known as prisoners while those sentenced to penal servitude or transportation were convicts.

TO KILL IN PUBLIC OR IN PRIVATE?

Since the end of the eighteenth century some campaigners had been arguing for the abolition of capital punishment altogether, though this movement was sometimes confused with more limited, if more hopeful attempts to ensure that executions were carried out in private rather than in public or that more humane methods of execution could be found. Each side of the debate attracted supporters who were eminent and others who were well informed, the two groups rarely overlapping. Thus William Cobbett, writing in 1823, was in no doubt that murderers should be executed: 'The Law of God is clear: the murderer is always positively excluded from any and from all mitigation of punishment. He shall surely be put to death.'[27] Earlier,

Dr Samuel Johnson, having presumably reconciled himself to the loss of the Tyburn procession, contented himself with arguing that the death sentence should be reserved for murder and removed from robbery since, to use his own portentous words, 'To equal robbery with murder is to reduce murder to robbery, to confound in common minds the gradations of iniquity and incite the commission of a greater crime to prevent the detection of a less.'[28] Others argued that, while capital punishment should remain on the statute book, it should never actually be carried out, acting simply as a deterrent.[29] Johnson's biographer, James Boswell, who had been moved by the spectacle of the condemned he had seen in Newgate[30] recommended a method of execution that he had seen while visiting Rome which, though crude, appeared to combine humanity and deterrence:[31]

> The criminal is placed upon a scaffold and the executioner knocks him on the head with a great iron hammer, then cuts his throat with a large knife and lastly hews him into pieces. The spectators are struck with prodigious terror; yet the poor wretch who is stunned into insensibility by the blow does not actually suffer much.

Those who were closer to the condemned were quicker to join the abolitionists and were certainly not persuaded of the deterrent effect of executions. The Reverend Brownlow Forde, Ordinary of Newgate from 1799–1814, told Jeremy Bentham in 1803 that the death penalty should be abolished altogether, reasoning from Christian principles to which the stern Utilitarian would presumably have been notably unsympathetic:

> Strange it is that our religion is so mild and our laws so sanguinary. Instead of sparing the life of a criminal in order that he may turn from his wickedness and live, our criminal code nips him in the first bud of his sin, cutting off all hope of reformation and destroying the possibility of atonement to the injured party.[32]

Cope, a nineteenth-century keeper of Newgate, declared that 'in his fifteen years' experience he had never known but one criminal hanged for murder who had not witnessed an execution',[33] a view supported by a man with his own criminal past. Edward Gibbon Wakefield had acquired his own notoriety in 1827 when he was convicted at Lancaster Assizes of abducting an heiress, Ellen Turner, taking her to Gretna Green and obliging her to marry him. A spell in Newgate as a result of this enterprise aroused his interest in prison reform and convinced him that public executions were counter-productive since the sympathy of the public lay with the victim, though his own criminal record made his arguments less persuasive in the cause of reform than they might otherwise have been.[34] The Reverend John Davis, Ordinary of Newgate for more than twenty years, could have been a more effective advocate had he known what he believed in. He told the 1864 Royal Commission on Capital Punishment that murderers 'rush into the crime . . . murders are committed in mad passion', but he also argued that the death penalty was necessary. His evidence was so confused that the Commissioners were not clear what his views were.

THE MOVEMENT FOR ABOLITION

It was as a result of the Royal Commission's report that public executions were abolished in 1868, but the case for total abolition had many more hurdles to cross. Indeed the abolition of public executions, with the unseemly behaviour they encouraged, was advocated by such eminent Victorians as Samuel Wilberforce, Bishop of Oxford, in order to ensure the continuation of the death penalty itself. Wilberforce, better known as an opponent of Charles Darwin's theories of evolution, told the House of Lords that it was important to retain capital punishment but that this worthy aim was threatened by the disorder occasioned by public executions.[35] In this respect Wilberforce was representative of many of the most pious clergymen who favoured the death penalty, because of its tendency to encourage the guilty to repent and seek forgiveness.[36] Poetry also joined the side of those who wished to maintain the death penalty when Wordsworth, in his declining years, wrote fourteen indifferent sonnets which, while sympathising with the fates of those on 'Weeping Hill' defended the retention of capital punishment as a deterrent.

The anonymous author of a pamphlet about the Newgate hangman William Calcraft argued that capital punishment was an unseemly public spectacle and an ineffective deterrent. He described a room opposite Newgate on the day of an execution as:

> Containing about fifty persons of both sexes who, whether awake or asleep, are beastly drunk from drinking deeply of rum, gin and beer, while every description of the most disgusting ribaldry is going on around.

He suggested that an Indian Brahmin, attending the spectacle, would be amazed and disgusted and went on to argue (in capital letters throughout) that SOLITARY CONFINEMENT WITH HARD LABOUR FOR LIFE WOULD BE A GREATER TERROR TO MURDERERS THAN THE MOMENTARY ONE OF HANGING AND SOCIETY WOULD THEREBY BY BETTER PROTECTED.[37]

But this was a lonely voice. More persuasive was that of the eminent jurist Sir James Stephen (1829–94), a prominent member of the Victorian intellectual aristocracy and influential commentator on legal matters. Writing in *Fraser's Magazine* in 1864, at the height of the debate on public executions, he declared:

> There is as much moral cowardice in shrinking from the execution of a murderer as in hesitating to blow out the brains of a foreign invader . . . the plain truth is that Christianity has to have two sides. A gentle side up to a certain point, a terrific one beyond that point.[38]

The case for the complete abolition of capital punishment was kept alive by a small number of determined campaigners who had found the Society for the Abolition of Capital Punishment in 1846 and whose cause in Parliament was advocated by John Bright whose Quaker upbringing underpinned his many campaigns.

John Bright (1811–89): born in Rochdale to a family whose wealth derived from the cotton trade, Bright was educated at a Quaker school and from an early age took up the causes of those whom he knew to be underprivileged. He entered Parliament in 1843 and was a prominent campaigner against the corn laws which, by taxing cheap imported corn, raised the price of bread for the poor and the price of corn for the wealthy landowners who produced it. The corn laws were repealed in 1846. He campaigned against the Crimean War, losing his seat in Parliament as a result, and blamed British misrule for the Indian Mutiny. He returned to Parliament for a new constituency and campaigned for an extension of the franchise which was eventually achieved in 1868. He kept alive within Parliament the case for the abolition of capital punishment by drawing to the attention of the House a number of injustices inflicted in its name, but in his lifetime he succeeded only in his opposition to *public* executions. He petitioned unsuccessfully for clemency for the Fenian Michael Barrett, the last to be executed publicly outside Newgate.

In the following century reforms proceeded slowly. The 1908 Children Act forbade capital punishment for those under 16 and in 1938 Parliament debated a clause in the Criminal Justice Bill which would have suspended capital punishment for an experimental period of five years. The intervention of the Second World War caused the matter to be dropped and thirteen German agents were executed during the war, William Joyce ('Lord Haw-Haw') being the last to be executed for treason in 1946. A number of controversial cases in the years that followed kept the issue before the public. Notable amongst these were the execution of Timothy Evans in 1949 for murders later found to have been committed by John Christie (hanged in 1953); the hanging of the mentally subnormal Derek Bentley, aged 19, for a murder committed by his accomplice; and the last hanging of a woman, Ruth Ellis, in 1955. These and others persuaded many politicians (though never a majority of the public) that further consideration of the matter was required.

The hanging of James Hanratty, the 'A6 murderer' in 1962 gave further impetus to the movement since many believed in his innocence. Paradoxically, DNA evidence, almost forty years later, suggested that Hanratty was indeed the murderer of the victim Michael Gregsten. Nevertheless, in 1965 the Labour MP Sidney Silverman, a long-standing campaigner against the death penalty, secured the passage of a Bill suspending the death penalty for murder in 1965, an arrangement that was made permanent in 1969. The remaining capital crimes (treason and arson in the royal docks) were removed from the statute book by a House of Lords amendment to the 1998 Crime and Disorder Act, an act further confirmed by the ratification of the European Convention on Human Rights in 1999.

THE HANGMEN

The cause of the abolitionists was frequently advanced by the behaviour of some of the hangmen associated with the Newgate drop. The most infamous of these was William Calcraft (*c.* 1800–79) who served in office for forty-five years from 1829 to 1874, thereby officiating at both public and private executions. He was born in Essex, the son of a farmer, orphaned at 10 years old and apprenticed to a shoemaker. His early life was recorded in an anti-hanging pamphlet published in 1846 entitled *The Groans of the Gallows: or the Past and Present Life of William Calcraft, the Living Hangman of Newgate*, now in the possession of the Guildhall Library.[39] Calcraft appears to have inherited the job from his predecessor, Old Tom Cheshire, to whom he acted as assistant and whose acquaintance he appears to have made as a result of his previous occupation which involved selling pies at executions. He was paid 25*s* (£1.25) a week as a retainer (a good wage for the time), plus a guinea for each hanging and half a crown (12½ pence) for a flogging, another task which went with the job.

Floggings were also carried out in public and, like the hangings, were a major source of public entertainment, especially when women were the victims, until Elizabeth Fry intervened to stop them in 1817. Such was his reputation that Calcraft's services were much in demand at other prisons, where he could charge fees of £10 or more. Further profits could be made from selling the effects of the deceased to Madame Tussaud's waxworks so that their models could be dressed in the authentic clothes of the perpetrator of the gruesome murder they were representing. The hangman's rope could also be sold for as much as 5s an inch if the criminal had been particularly celebrated. Evidence of this practice among hangman was presented in 1888 to a Parliamentary Committee enquiring into the death sentence.

After carrying out the last public hanging of the Fenian Michael Barrett in May 1868 (seats for which in nearby houses commanded a price of £10) he was then responsible for the first execution within the prison walls, that of 18-year-old Alexander Mackay, who had murdered his employer. This occurred in September 1868 on a gallows erected in a yard close to the chapel and was witnessed by representatives of the press. Calcraft was noted for his short drop, which usually failed to bring instant death by breaking the prisoner's neck and led to death by slow strangulation, as earlier at Tyburn. In the case of William Bousefield, Calcraft's miscalculation was so great that Bousefield climbed back on to the platform after the drop. Calcraft, alarmed, hurled himself upon his would-be victim and the two of them tumbled into the drop together.

Other hangmen miscalculated in the opposite direction, an excessively long drop sometimes leading to decapitation. A hangman named James Berry (1852–1913) achieved this in the 1880s and brought further notoriety upon his profession by holding court in public houses on the eve of hangings, giving accounts of executions he had carried out; and by accepting bribes from voyeurs who masqueraded as his assistants in order to view the executions themselves. After another near decapitation in 1891 Berry was not employed again, though he continued to appeal for work until 1902.[40]

Short-drop strangulation appears to have occurred in the case of Alexander Mackay, so the pressmen were obliged to watch the boy's death throes before the black flag was hoisted over the prison to tell the waiting crowds that the execution had been carried out. The hoisting of the black flag, sometimes witnessed by crowds of several thousand, continued until Newgate was closed in 1902, but pressmen continued to attend executions elsewhere until 1934. Calcraft retired in 1874 on a pension of 25s a week and died five years later. He had hanged more than eighty at Newgate itself and many others elsewhere, though one of his predecessors, William Brunskill, who was hangman while the Bloody Code was still prevalent, from 1786 to 1814, was credited with 537 executions at Newgate alone. He also carried out executions elsewhere, including several at Execution Dock, Wapping, and it was during Brunskill's time that the practice of letting three tides wash over the corpses of executed pirates was discontinued.

THE NEWGATE MONSTER

As previously observed, long periods of imprisonment, in Newgate or elsewhere, were unusual before the middle of the nineteenth century; whipping, transportation and execution were favoured as being much cheaper than incarceration. However, for six years Newgate contained one particularly celebrated prisoner who was listed in the Newgate prison calendar as prisoner number 31, 'Rhynwick alias Renwick Williams, vulgarly called The Monster', who was imprisoned from June 1790 to December 1796. This was Newgate's own monster who had been imprisoned following two trials and some rather doubtful evidence in response to public hysteria which first arose in May 1788. The case is an excellent illustration of the peculiarities of the laws and the processes which could lead a man to Newgate.

In that month Mrs Maria Smyth, the wife of a doctor with premises near Rathbone Place, north of Oxford Street, had been accosted in Fleet Street by a thin man who had indecently propositioned her.[41] She made her way hastily to a nearby house and rang the doorbell at which point her tormentor struck at her thigh with a sharp instrument causing a slight wound. Later that summer a similar experience was reported by a Mrs Franklin and her sister, Miss Kitty Wheeler, though on these occasions the assailant contented himself with making indecent propositions and there was no assault. The descriptions of the culprit varied between the incidents, as they continued to do over the next two years while the attacker, who swiftly became known as the Monster, continued his reign of terror. He was variously described as being 6ft tall; 5ft 6in tall; below medium height; short; thin and vulgar-looking; resembling a perfect gentleman; and of medium build. Many descriptions agreed that he had a prominent nose, that he wore a cocked hat and also that his behaviour was shameless. Having attacked or insulted a victim he would make no attempt to escape and would sometimes return to her home where he would stand in the street and taunt her.

In January 1790 the Monster became more active. Late in the evening of the 19th of that month he attacked a Miss Anne Porter outside her home in St James's Street, stabbing her in the thigh and buttock, and later slashed the clothes of three other ladies in the same area, though without inflicting any wounds. He also adopted a new tactic. In the same month a lady's maid was grabbed from behind and kneed several times in the buttocks while being subjected to a stream of insults. She then discovered that her buttocks had been penetrated by a sharp instrument which had evidently been attached to her assailant's knee. A similar assault was made two months later on another lady's maid in Brook Street and a few days later a Mrs Blaney was stabbed in the thigh in Bury Street, St James's, by a man who on this occasion was tall, dark, stout, gentlemanly-looking and about 35 years old. A further variation appeared in the form of nosegays among whose flowers were concealed sharp instruments which penetrated the skin when thrust into the faces of the unwary.

By now the Monster was a celebrity. Such was the interest in his activities and the anxiety felt by many to catch him that suspicion began to settle upon innocent people. One of the early victims, Mrs Maria Smyth, identified as her attacker a man whom she happened to see at an auction. He turned out to be William Tuffing, a respectable family man who had worked as a clothes salesman and hairdresser. There was no evidence in his case other than that provided by a number of witnesses who testified to his good character. The Monster's other victims did not recognise him as their attacker and, fortunately for Tuffing, another attack occurred while he was in custody.

A REWARD

A reward was now offered for information leading to the arrest and conviction of the Monster. The money was raised by John Julius Angerstein.

In April 1790, at Lloyd's Coffee-House, Angerstein himself donated five guineas to a reward fund and a sum of £100 was

John Julius Angerstein (1735–1822): born in St Petersburg of Russian and German parents, Angerstein settled in London in 1749 and worked as an office-boy before becoming an under-writer at Lloyds Coffee-House and one of the founders of this famous insurance market. He became so strongly associated with certain types of insurance that they became known as 'Julians' and he promoted an Act of Parliament which prevented ship-owners from changing the names of unseaworthy ships in order to make them insurable. He also instigated a prize of £2,000, sponsored by Lloyds, for a suitable design for a lifeboat. He devised an early state lottery which was adopted by Parliament. He profited from estates in Grenada (West Indies) worked by slaves and became a patron of the arts, much of his collection forming the nucleus of the National Gallery. He lived for many years in the Westcombe Park area of Greenwich and in 1972 his house, Woodlands, was opened by the London Borough of Greenwich as an art gallery. A Lloyds syndicate bears his name, as do various properties near his former home, including Angerstein Wharf, Angerstein Business Park and a public house. His son, also John Angerstein, became a Member of Parliament.

quickly raised. Posters were printed inviting citizens to pass any information to the Bow Street Office and their appearance prompted a series of citizens' arrests of perfectly innocent people. One person arrested a butcher whose carving knife had aroused suspicion and a few old scores were settled. One citizen arrested his employer (to whom he first administered a sound thrashing) and another delivered his brother-in-law to Bow Street as a suspect. Washer-women were asked to report anyone who approached them with bloodstained clothing, while cutlers were to look out for anyone seeking a particularly sharp instrument. One washerwoman was herself attacked, but seems to have been rather pleased by the attention: normally he only attacked the nobility and well-to-do.

The washerwoman's comment, taken together with the widely varying descriptions of the Monster's age, demeanour and appearance, may itself be significant. One of the more common types of thief at the time was the cutpurse (ancestor of the mugger), who would expertly release a victim's bag or purse by cutting the strap which attached it to its owner's arm or waist. In such an attack it was not unusual for the victim's clothing or person to be slashed either by accident or as a means of intimidation. This would not explain the bizarre behaviour such as the kneeing in the buttocks or the obscene conversation. It is, however, perfectly possible that the Monster was in reality several different cutpurses who would, of course, be more likely to attack the well-to-do than a washerwoman. There may have been other attackers who were deranged or were what later became known as copycat offenders. Moreover, since there was a good deal of hysteria surrounding the Monster's activities it is possible that some of the victims read into an attack by a cutpurse a more sensational encounter with the infamous Monster himself.

Angerstein himself certainly suspected that more than one person was involved in the attacks. In a second poster, issued a month after the first, he stated that 'there is great Reason to fear that more than ONE of the WRETCHES infests the streets' and described a number of different outfits that an attacker might wear.[42] A St Pancras Monster Patrol was formed to protect the ladies of that parish, and a debating society, striving to come up with a subject that would convey the full horror of the Monster's crimes, proposed in May 1790 the motion:

> Who is the Greater Disgrace to Humanity, the Monster who has lately cut so many women in London, or the Slave-Trading Wretches, who drag the unhappy Female African from her family and native country?[43]

A play entitled *The Monster* attracted large audiences to the spectacle of young actresses having their cheeks and buttocks pierced by the Monster's fiendish contraptions. One member of the audience was so outraged by the spectacle that he leapt on to the stage and attacked the actor who was playing the Monster's part. Some reports suggested that fashionable ladies were protecting their bottoms with copper cuirasses or shields made of cork. Cartoonists also profited from the Monster's activities. James Gillray's *The Monster Disappointed of his Afternoon Luncheon* shows the Monster, knife and fork in hand, suspending a young lady by her dress. The Monster is enraged to see that her bottom is covered by a protective shield.

RHYNWICK WILLIAMS THE NEWGATE MONSTER?

In June, 1790, with Monster mania at its height, Anne Porter, who had been a victim of the monster six months earlier outside her home in St James's Street, was walking in St James's Park with her admirer, a fishmonger named Henry Coleman. Suddenly she called out, 'There he is, the wretch' and identified a man in the crowd as the Monster. Coleman, who was more a fishmonger than a hero, followed the suspect carefully, at a distance, and eventually realised that he was someone he had met on a number of occasions at public houses. His name was Rhynwick Williams and he was about to become a most reluctant celebrity. Williams accompanied Coleman to the Porters' home in St James's Street where the hysterical Porter sisters identified him as the man who had attacked them the previous January. Williams was taken to Bow Street and his meagre lodgings were searched. Nothing suspicious was found among his few belongings.

Rhynwick Williams was the son of an apothecary who ensured that his son had a reasonably good education and paid for him to have dancing lessons with a view to a career on the stage. Nothing came of this and at the time of his arrest Williams had recently lost his job as a worker in an artificial-flower factory in Dover Street where his employer was a Frenchman. His appearances at Bow Street before the examining magistrate were accompanied by huge crowds, some curious, some determined to injure or kill him, though the evidence against him was sketchy. The hysterical Porter sisters not only identified him as their assailant, but claimed to have seen him several times before the first assault. Other victims were less sure while the most positive identifications were the most doubtful. One was from an Elizabeth Davis who had previously described her attacker as tall and gentlemanly-looking. Williams was short and very hard up. Mary Forster positively identified Williams as her attacker, but Williams was able to call a neighbour who testified that, on the day in question, Williams had been in Weymouth, 130 miles away. The neighbour was a Bow Street Runner and as such a particularly convincing witness. Williams also claimed that at the time of the assault on the Porter sisters he had been at work in the artificial-flower factory and that he had many fellow workers who would support his alibi.

FELONY OR MISDEMEANOUR?

Despite the weakness of the evidence Williams was committed for trial at the Old Bailey, but there now arose the question of what he was to be charged with. Assault, even with the intention to maim or kill, was a misdemeanour punishable usually by a flogging or imprisonment. Such a punishment would not have satisfied the mobs outside the court so a means had to be found whereby he could be charged with a felony – a more serious crime for which the sentence would be death or transportation. The magistrates found a statute of 1721, an early component of the Bloody Code, which had been directed against weavers protesting against the import of cheap cloth from India. Under this statute it was a felony to 'assault any person in the public streets with intent to tear, spoil, cut, burn or deface the garments or clothes of such person'. It was on this charge that Rhynwick Williams was to stand trial.

The trial began on 8 July 1790 at the Old Bailey, the presiding judge being Sir Francis Buller. He was known to the caricaturists as Judge Thumb, because in an earlier trial he had declared that a man might thrash his wife as long as the stick he used was no thicker than his thumb. The trial was a farce.[44] Williams's barrister, when questioning Anne Porter, the witness who most positively identified Williams, adopted an apologetic manner which conveyed to the witness and the court that he had no confidence in his client's innocence. A Lady Wallace, a supposed victim of the Monster, had offered to testify in defence of Williams by saying that he was not the person who had threatened her. She had thereby gained a front seat from which to view the proceedings. She then explained that she had in fact never been threatened by anyone and that her offer to give evidence for the defence was one of her little jokes. She nevertheless continued to occupy her front seat throughout the trial.

Despite this setback Williams's defence was strong. His employer at the artificial-flower factory, the Frenchman, Aimable Michelle, testified that, at the time of the attack upon Anne Porter, Rhynwick Williams had been working at his factory. Six fellow employees confirmed this with some convincing and precise evidence concerning timings. Seventeen character witnesses then spoke up for Williams. After a summing up by Judge Buller, which compared Michelle's evidence and that of his employees unfavourably with that of the Porter sisters, the jury immediately declared Williams guilty.

THE TWELVE JUDGES OF ENGLAND

The trial was immediately followed by the appearance of the traditional pamphlets giving an account of the crimes and the trial.

Angerstein was first off the press with *An Authentic Account of the Barbarities Lately Practised by the Monsters* (note the plural form 'Monsters'), which he had written before the trial started. His pamphlet was closely followed by *The Remarkable Trial of Rhynwick Williams*, which was from the pen of a law student from the Temple and was on sale the day after the trial. Others followed, together with likenesses of Williams. Angerstein was congratulated from all sides for his enterprise in promoting the Monster hunt, but he had his own doubts about the conviction and was impressed by Williams's alibi. So was Theophilus Swift, a relation of Jonathan Swift. Theophilus wrote a pamphlet titled *The Monster at Large* which argued that Williams was innocent. He drew attention to the discrepancies between the early descriptions given by the Porter sisters (30 years old, 6ft tall, fair hair) with their later testimony and with the appearance of Williams himself (aged 23, 5ft 6in tall, black hair). He suggested that their evidence was motivated by a desire to gain Angerstein's reward money. In the meantime, however, there was a more decisive intervention by the Twelve Judges of England.

The origins of this curious body are obscure, but certainly Medieval. The Court of Appeal, Criminal Division, was not established until 1907 and in the meantime the Twelve Judges of England acted as a primitive appeal tribunal. The body consisted of a number of judges (despite the name the number varied according to the whims of the monarch) drawn equally from the three Common Law courts of King's Bench, Common Pleas and Exchequer. It was called upon to adjudicate in cases where there were doubts in the minds of a judge or a jury about whether the correct law had been applied in a case. Upon hearing the jury's verdict in Williams's case Judge Buller had declined to pass sentence until the case had been reviewed by the Twelve Judges. Perhaps he had his own doubts about the verdict or perhaps he was simply not sure that the statute under which Williams had been tried as a felon should really have applied to the case. The judges found for Williams. The offences were misdemeanours, not felonies, so there had to be a second trial.

THE SECOND TRIAL

Since Rhynwick Williams was now being tried only for a misdemeanour his second trial was held at the Sessions House, Clerkenwell Green. This building, which remains in use in the twenty-first century as a Masonic centre, was then used for the Middlesex Quarter Sessions and the presiding magistrate at Williams's trial was William Mainwaring, a successor to the Fieldings who had not continued their reputation for probity.[45] On this occasion Williams was defended by Theophilus Swift whose enthusiasm sometimes got the better of his judgement. He reduced the principal witness Anne Porter to a swooning fit by suggesting that her home in St James's Street was little more than a brothel, but his behaviour may have alienated the jury even more than it distressed Anne Porter. Either way, the verdict was the same though on this occasion the jury took all of fifteen minutes to declare Williams guilty. He was sentenced to six years in Newgate.

Rhynwick Williams quickly became one of Newgate's principal attractions and a source of earnings for the turnkeys who continued to ply their customary trade of charging an admission fee to inquisitive visitors who wished to view the gaol's more noteworthy residents. He also enjoyed a brief notoriety as a waxwork figure in Mrs Salmon's exhibition in Fleet Street, which specialised in exotic and violent scenes. Williams also managed to prosper despite his altered circumstances. He resumed his trade of making artificial flowers, which he sold to his visitors. He also composed a pamphlet entitled *An Appeal to the Public* in an unsuccessful attempt to gain an early release. Some visitors were disappointed at his commonplace and unthreatening demeanour while Williams himself seems to have settled reasonably comfortably into the prison where one of his fellow prisoners (there were only five long-term prisoners) was the (by now Jewish) Lord George Gordon, until Gordon's death in 1793. Thereafter he was soon joined by his defence counsel, Theophilus Swift, who was sent to Newgate for a libellous attack on the Fellows of Trinity College, Dublin who had offended him by failing to award any prizes to Swift's son.

Rhynwick Williams was finally released from Newgate in December 1796 and the following February he married. He and his new wife, Elizabeth, already had a son called George who had been conceived in Newgate and baptised at nearby St Sepulchre's Church in May 1795. From these happy conjugal circumstances we may conclude that, during his stay in Newgate, Williams was living in one of the more salubrious parts of the prison, presumably on the proceeds of his flower making. Nothing certain is known of the later career of Rhynwick Williams, one of the more curious of Newgate's residents.[46]

CRITICAL DATES IN THE HISTORY OF CAPITAL PUNISHMENT
IN BRITAIN

1571	The Triple Tree built as a permanent gallows at Tyburn
1686	Alice Molland the last to be hanged for witchcraft
1723	Waltham Black Act began process of creating many capital crimes
1752	Dissection could be substituted for gibbetting of murderers
1760	Portable gallows with 'drop' replaced the Triple Tree at Tyburn
1789	Catherine Murphy last to be burned at the stake at Newgate (for coining)
1820	Last 'hanging, drawing and quartering' (of Cato Street conspirators)
1829	Thomas Maynard last to be hanged for forgery
1831	George Widgett last to be executed for sheep stealing
1832	John Barrett last to be executed for stealing Royal Mail; number of capital crimes steadily reduced from this time
1843	Practice of gibbetting abolished
1861	Criminal Law Consolidation Act limited capital punishment to murder, treason, piracy and arson in the royal dockyards
1866	Royal Commission recommended ending of public executions

1868   26 May, Michael Barrett, Fenian, executed at Newgate; the last public execution in Britain

1870   Practice of hanging and beheading traitors officially abolished

1902   Closure of Newgate; George Woolfe executed on 6 May, the last of 1,106 men and 49 women executed there

1908   Children Act; capital punishment prohibited for those aged under 16

1933   Minimum age for capital punishment raised to 18

1946   William Joyce (Lord Haw-Haw) last to be hanged for treason

1955   Ruth Ellis last woman to be hanged in Britain

1957   Homicide Act; distinguished between capital and non-capital murder

1960   Francis Forsyth, 18, last teenager to be hanged in Britain

1964   Peter Allen and Gwynne Evans last to be hanged in Britain

1965   Murder (Abolition of Death Penalty) Act suspended capital punishment for murder for five years; made indefinite in 1969

1998   Crime and Disorder Act abolished remaining capital crimes; European Convention on Human Rights adopted outlawing capital punishment for murder except 'in times of war or imminent threat of war'.

SIX

The Reformers

*Oh Mrs Fry! Why go to Newgate? Why Preach to poor rogues;
and wherefore not begin with Carlton, or with other houses?
Try Your hand at hardened and imperial sin*

(Byron, *Don Juan*, Canto X verse 85)

*The chaplain can then make the brawny navvy cry like a child;
he can work his feelings in any way he pleases.*

(A prison chaplain's comments on the 'separate system'
of imprisonment)

*I have seen Elizabeth Fry in Newgate and I have witnessed
there miraculous effects of true Christianity upon the most
depraved of human beings.*

(John Randolph, American ambassador, 1819)

JOHN HOWARD

As the eighteenth century approached the nineteenth two factors
began to focus attention on the state of Britain's prisons. First, it
came to be accepted that imprisonment should be used as a punishment in itself rather than as a means of temporarily housing those
awaiting trial or other forms of punishment. Furthermore, some

151

citizens were beginning to view the penal system, with its diet of transportation, execution and flogging, as inappropriate in a period associated with 'the enlightenment'. The name most associated with early developments in this sphere is that of John Howard (1726–90). The conditions that Howard began to confront were described by Heinrich Meister, a German-speaking citizen of Switzerland, in a vivid account of his visit to Newgate in 1792:[1]

> I was conducted the other day to see Newgate: what a horrid sight! As we crossed the courtyard I was attacked by a swarm of harpies and had no means of escaping but to throw a handful of halfpence among them for which they scrambled with all the fury of wild beasts. Others, who were shut up, stretched forth their hands through the iron bars, venting the most horrible cries.

John Howard was born in Hackney, London, in 1726, and orphaned at the age of 16, thereby inheriting from his father a substantial estate at Cardington, Bedfordshire, which relieved him of the necessity of earning his living and enabled him to spend much of his time travelling in Europe. His first experience of prison conditions was as a prisoner of the French. In 1756 he set out by sea with the intention of viewing the effects of the great earthquake that had destroyed Lisbon the previous year, imprudently overlooking the fact that Britain and France had just embarked on the Seven Years War. His ship was captured by the French and he was imprisoned for two months before an exchange of prisoners secured his release. His grim ordeal in a French dungeon aroused his interest in prison conditions in Britain. Upon his return he married his landlady and settled into a routine of happy domesticity during which much of his energy was devoted to improving the dwellings of his tenants while extolling to them the virtues of a vegetarian diet in general and the value of potatoes in particular. Howard's wife died in 1765 giving birth to their son, an event which left Howard distraught. His earlier experience of a French gaol did nothing to diminish his taste for foreign travel, or earthquakes, since in 1770 he visited Naples, another city noted for its vulnerability to movements in the earth's crust. While in Naples he underwent a conversion experience as a result of which he became a devout Congregationalist.

As a member of a dissenting sect Howard was precluded from holding paid civil or military offices, but this did not prevent him, in 1773, from accepting the honorary post of High Sheriff of Bedfordshire, a task which, among other duties, required him to inspect prisons within the county. He was appalled by the conditions that he witnessed, not least by the fact that some prisoners who had been found innocent of the charges against them were held in prison because they were unable to pay the release fee required by the gaoler. He suggested to the Justices of the Peace for Bedford that gaolers should be paid a salary in order to put an end to the need for such fees but they rejected the idea because of the cost that it would have entailed.

Following this setback, Howard spent three years, travelling 10,000 miles, visiting prisons in Britain and more than a dozen foreign countries, including France, Germany, Russia and Turkey. In March 1774 he presented some of the evidence he had gathered to a committee of the House of Commons which resulted in the passing of the Gaol Act of that year. This Act abolished gaolers' fees and proposed ways of improving the state of prisons. Howard, at his own expense, had copies of the Act printed and sent to prisons in England, but while he was on the Continent pursuing further research the Act was largely ignored both by Justices and gaolers. Upon his return he commended a prison known as Maison de Force in Ghent (later Belgium) as a model prison and published his famous account *The State of Prisons in England and Wales, with an Account of some Foreign Prisons*,[2] whose contents were so shocking that in some countries, including France, its publication was forbidden. The first entry in his famous book was Newgate itself where he recorded the continued use of entry, garnish and discharge fees together with the fact that the principal item of diet was one penny loaf per prisoner per day.[3]

Howard explained in his book that he travelled on horseback, because after visiting a prison the smell which hung about his clothing made the air in a post-chaise intolerable, while his notebook had to be sprinkled with vinegar and laid out before the fire to moderate the smell borne by its pages. He drew attention to the fact that prison food was so poor that criminals upon release were half starved and incapable of work. No bedding was provided to those who could not pay for it and the continued practice of 'ironing' (restrained by shackles, see Chapter One) prisoners caused injuries as well as making it difficult for prisoners to walk or even lie down to sleep. In some prisons insane inmates were confined with criminals to the detriment of both. Justices of the Peace were supposed to visit prisons to ensure that gaolers were not abusing their positions, but they were easily diverted from their responsibilities by gaolers who warned them that gaol fever (typhus) was rife. Howard advocated clean accommodation and clothing; adequate health care; segregation of prisoners according to sex and the seriousness of the offence; and a chaplaincy service. He also emphasised the need for useful, productive work to keep prisoners occupied and to prepare them for earning an honest living: an aim that is still to be adequately met in the twenty-first century.

In 1779 John Howard died while visiting prisons in the Crimea. Paradoxically his death was caused by typhus, the gaol fever against which he had so long campaigned. His legacy was the first systematic compilation of evidence on imprisonment, together with some ineffective legislation and some ideas which would influence later reformers. He also influenced the Penitentiary Houses Act of 1779 whose promoter in Parliament was William Blackstone[4]. This Act advocated a model for penitentiaries, which was later adopted and modified by reformers such as Jeremy Bentham whose ideas for the design of prisons acknowledged a debt to John Howard. The Act may also, paradoxically, have helped to promote the idea of prison labour of the most servile kind, including the use of the crank and the treadwheel, though it is not clear that this was Howard's intention.[5]

EARLY MOVEMENTS FOR REFORM

A decade or more after Howard's death some reforms began to make themselves felt at Newgate and elsewhere. There was certainly plenty of room for improvement at Britain's most notorious gaol. The

Ordinaries themselves were sometimes seduced by the lavish hospitality at the keeper's table so that one Ordinary 'was sometimes called upon to eat three consecutive dinners without rising from the table'.[6] The Reverend Brownlow Forde, who was Ordinary from 1799 to 1814, was a humane man who was an early opponent of the death penalty, but was frequently to be found holding court in a public house in nearby Hatton Garden, smoking a pipe and seated in a fine Masonic chair.[7] In 1817 a new keeper named Newman improved the diet, ensuring that meat was served more than once a week and that it was cooked rather than raw. He also discontinued the Medieval practice of ironing, though the humane effects of this measure were partly allayed by insisting that, henceforth, inmates would be separated from their visitors by a grille. Presumably he feared that unfettered prisoners would try to escape. By this time, also, some rudimentary instruction had been introduced to some prisons. These developments were not universally welcomed. The writer and wit Sydney Smith disapproved of the pampering that he feared was creeping into the penal system, writing in the *Edinburgh Review*:[8]

A poor man who is lucky enough to have his son committed for a felony educates him under such a system for nothing, while the virtuous simpleton who is on the other side of the wall is paying for these attainments.

Smith advocated a regime of 'beating hemp and pulling oakum' and suggested that prisoners, once freed, should be 'heartily wearied of their residence; and taught by sad experience to consider it the greatest misfortune of their lives to attend [i.e. return] to it'.

Others were more encouraging than Sydney Smith. As early as 1811 a Frenchman named Simon found prisoners playing a form of fives at Newgate, their movements only slightly impeded by an iron from knee to ankle on one leg only, the discomfort alleviated by a cushion.[9] A German visitor, Hermann Pückler-Muskau, visited Newgate in the 1820s. He saw six youths, under sentence of death, smoking and playing games, three others playing cards and another studying a French grammar, adding 'the treatment [of prisoners] is

Sydney Smith (1771–1845): born in Woodford, Essex, Smith was educated at Winchester College and New College, Oxford. While at Winchester his fellow pupils threatened to boycott competitions for college prizes unless Sydney and his younger brother were excluded from them. His wish to become a barrister was frustrated by his father's refusal to support him in this venture, so in 1796 he was ordained as a priest and became a curate at Nether Avon, near Amesbury in Wiltshire. There he so impressed the local squire that he was engaged as tutor to the squire's son and journeyed with him to Edinburgh. In that city he began to gain his formidable reputation as a preacher and was a founder of the *Edinburgh Review*, the Whig journal through which he supported such progressive causes as Catholic emancipation and Parliamentary reform. He compared opposition to the Reform Bill with an attempt to stop the incoming Atlantic tide with a mop and bucket. His preaching later drew large congregations to the fashionable Berkeley Chapel, Mayfair, and the Foundling Hospital, Holborn. His opposition to prison reform was thus out of character. His support for the Whig cause did little to advance his career. For many of his most productive years the Whigs were out of office and his sharp wit sometimes antagonised politicians who would have been better as allies. His highest office was as a canon of St Paul's Cathedral and late in life he became rector of Combe Florey, near Taunton in Somerset. The adjacent manor house, Combe Florey House, later became the residence of writers with even sharper pens: Evelyn Waugh (1903–66) and his son Auberon Waugh (1939–2001).

very mild and a most exemplary cleanliness reigns throughout'.[10] Nevertheless, in 1840 the Report of the Inspectors of Prisons wrote of the prison that, 'We most seriously protest against Newgate as a great school for crime . . . prisoners must quit this prison worse than when they first entered it'.

CAUSES OF CRIME

It was not until the late eighteenth century that some reformers began to give serious consideration to the causes of criminal behaviour, the effects of imprisonment and the implications of these matters for the future design and management of prisons. William Cobbett (1763–1835) believed that poor wages were the principal cause of crime. Henry Mayhew (1812–87) in his seminal study *London Labour and the London Poor* distinguished between settlers, criminals who resided in a locality and earned their living through crime such as theft, and wanderers, or opportunist criminals who moved from place to place. He commented that an assault on a policeman was 'the bravest act by which a coster-monger [barrow boy] can distinguish himself'.[11] Many other commentators argued that the chief cause of crime was strong liquor. Thus Friedrich Engels, Karl Marx's collaborator, wrote of the English working classes that 'while burdening them with numerous hardships the middle classes have left them only the pleasures of drink and sexual intercourse'.[12] A learned paper presented to the Statistical Society would no doubt have pleased Engels and comforted the growing temperance movement since it purported to trace a clear link between alehouses and criminality.[13]

Others of equal eminence tried to define the physical and mental characteristics of criminality. One of these was the distinguished eugenicist Sir Francis Galton (1822–1911), a cousin of Charles Darwin, who assembled a large collection of photographs of criminals with the assistance of the Prison Commissioners. His work was inconclusive, though a by-product of his research was the development of the fingerprint system of identification. His contemporary, the Italian Cesare Lombroso (1835–1909), claimed to be able to recognise 'the criminal man' and developed an atavistic theory of criminality which suggested that there was a strong hereditary element in criminal behaviour which could be observed in physical characteristics. However, an English physician, Charles Goring, compared the features of thousands of convicts with those of a group of law-abiding soldiers from the Royal Engineers and published the results in a book entitled *The English Convict* in 1913. It demonstrated that Lombroso's theories were fallacious, but a belief in the 'science' of phrenology persisted well into the twentieth century.

MORE PRISONS

In the meantime, crime continued to increase and the reaction of the authorities was to build more prisons. Whereas in previous centuries most prisons, notably Newgate, were regarded generally as temporary holding points for criminals on their way to trial, flogging, transportation, or execution, they were now increasingly used as a punishment in themselves and as a means of protecting citizens from criminal behaviour. The initial response was to cram ever more prisoners into increasingly restricted and insanitary conditions, a situation which alarmed the early reformers. In 1818 Thomas Fowell Buxton published the results of *An Inquiry Whether Crime and Misery are Produced or Prevented by our Present System of Prison Discipline*, which resulted from visits he made to prisons in Britain, the Low Countries and Philadelphia. He was particularly critical of the corrupting effects of Newgate upon untried prisoners, with mock trials being held before a prisoner arrayed in a towel serving as a wig as 'judge' and a 'pillory chair' for the accused. He commented that the purpose of imprisonment was that the inmate should be 'amerced of his freedom, *not that he should be subjected to any useless severities*' (his italics) and added that the prison staff themselves were 'of all the persons with whom I have conversed, the most sensible of the evils of our present system'. There was no consistency in the treatment of prisoners between different gaols. The practice of ironing prisoners had been discontinued in some establishments, but not in others, while dietary and medical regimes varied wildly from the comparatively benevolent to the barbaric.[14]

Thomas Fowell Buxton (1786–1845): born at Castle Hedingham in Essex, Buxton married Hannah Gurney of the wealthy Quaker family, sister of Elizabeth Fry. He became a partner in the Truman brewery and, in 1818, Member of Parliament for Weymouth. He was inspired by the Quaker ideals of public service and was a campaigner for social reform. In 1816, during the recession which followed the Napoleonic Wars, he campaigned for the relief of the starving silk workers of Spitalfields and his interest in prison reform was aroused when in 1817 he visited Tothill Fields prison (close to the present site of the Home Office in Westminster) and met a destitute sailor who had fought at Trafalgar. He was particularly interested in the reform of juvenile criminals. He worked with William Wilberforce for the complete abolition of slavery in all British possessions, assuming the leadership of the campaign after Wilberforce retired. He made many speeches in the House of Commons describing the horrors of slavery and saw the Abolition Act through Parliament in 1833. At the same time, he campaigned for prison reform and, unsuccessfully, for the ending of capital punishment, though he was instrumental in securing the reduction in the number of capital crimes from over 200 to 8 by the time of his death.

THE PANOPTICON

To accommodate the increasing number of long-stay prisoners the nineteenth century witnessed a huge increase in the number and capacity of prisons, over ninety being built or extended between 1842 and 1877. The prison-building programme was accompanied by fierce debates about prison design, prison regimes and the purpose of imprisonment – debates which continue into the twenty-first century. One of the most influential commentators was the utilitarian philosopher Jeremy Bentham (1748–1832). Bentham argued that, since punishment involved the infliction of suffering, 'all punishment is mischief: all punishment in itself is evil'.[15] For this reason punishment should be limited to the level required to reform and deter offenders and from this followed Bentham's belief that executions should take place in public because of their supposed deterrent effect. One of his many contributions to proposals for social reform included a plan for a model prison, *The Panopticon*, which may be translated as 'all-seeing'. Bentham was born in Houndsditch, London and educated at Queen's College, Oxford, and Lincoln's Inn, though he never practised law, preferring to write at length about legal reform. He visited Russia with his brother Samuel in 1785 and his idea for a model prison appears to have been devised with a view to its adoption by Tsarina Catherine the Great. He adopted from the Scottish philosopher David Hume (1711–76) the idea of 'utility', which he developed to mean that every action (or law) should be judged according to 'the tendency which it appears to have to augment or diminish the happiness of the party whose interest is in question'. In many fields his activities were entirely benevolent. He founded University College London to provide university education to Catholics, Jews, Dissenters and others whose beliefs excluded them from Oxford and Cambridge. He was a strong advocate of Parliamentary reform, which was finally achieved through the Reform Bill passed in the year of his death, and of the adoption of the secret ballot for voting. He was not always the most sympathetic of reformers. In 1780 John Franks was hanged for stealing two silver spoons from Bentham.

Bentham divided prisons into three categories. The House of Safe Custody was to house debtors and those awaiting trial. The Penitentiary was to house those who had been sentenced to relatively short sentences, while the Black House would hold prisoners serving long sentences. The Panopticon design was to be applied to the last two, though the Black House would have additional features designed to intimidate prisoners, including skeletons arrayed by the entrance doors.

The idea of the Panopticon was developed in a very lengthy correspondence whose prolix title gives a clear idea of its purpose:

Panopticon

Or

The Inspection House: containing the
Idea of a new Principle of Construction applicable to
Any sort of establishment, in which persons of
Any description are to be kept under inspection:
And in particular to Penitentiary-houses, prisons, houses of
industry, work-houses,
Poor-houses, Manufactories, Hospitals, Mad-houses and Schools

The design incorporated a central tower from which radiated cells around the circular walls of the building. The cells were thus lit from the outside wall by daylight and from the inside through windows which opened towards the central tower. The tower itself, which was thus removed from direct daylight, was comparatively dark within and this characteristic, combined with the use of blinds, ensured that the occupants of the tower could see clearly into the cells whereas the occupants of the cells could not see into the tower and could not be sure whether or not they were being watched from the observation ports. It was anticipated that the feeling of insecurity engendered when inmates did not know whether or not they were being observed ('each person should actually be in that predicament during every instant of time') would cause prisoners to modify their behaviour. Moreover, magistrates and others inspecting the prison can 'quickly inspect large numbers of prisoners without having to come near to such disgusting and repugnant objects as the prisoners themselves'.[16] Each cell was separated from the next by a thick wall which made communication between prisoners impossible, so the principle of isolation was combined with that of surveillance. Bentham believed that such a design would enable effective surveillance to be exercised over prisoners whose conduct could thus be controlled and manipulated so that they would not only behave themselves while in prison but would be reformed characters upon release. Bentham's claims for his design, in the early pages of his correspondence, were not understated and reflect his belief that it would help to reduce the burden of the Poor Laws as reflected in workhouses as well as in the penal system:

161

Morals reformed, health preserved, industry invigorated, instruction diffused, public burdens lightened, economy seated, as it were, upon a rock – the Gordian knot of the Poor laws not cut but untied, all by the simple idea in Architecture.

Bentham applauded the humanitarian sentiments which had informed the earlier work of John Howard while deploring the fact that his work contained no underlying principles to govern the penal system. His work might 'afford a rich fund of materials but a quarry is not a house: no leading principles; no order; no connection'.[17]

Bentham's 'leading principles' included three important rules. The Rule of Lenity (leniency) prescribed that imprisonment 'ought not to be accompanied by bodily suffering', which ruled out such features of the system as ironing, starvation and disease. On the other hand, the Rule of Severity stated that prison conditions should not be better than those endured by innocent victims of the same class which, at a time of great social deprivation, ensured that prisons would be unpleasant places, thereby promoting the Rule of Economy, which should merit 'first rate consideration in everything which concerns the administration of a prison' provided that it was consistent with the other rules. A Benthamite prison would be a grim place with more than a touch of Big Brother surveillance, but would not be a place of wanton cruelty. His leading principles were eventually to be adopted by the prison authorities, while his last secretary, Edwin Chadwick, applied them ruthlessly to workhouses through the Poor Law.

THE SILENT SYSTEM

The Panopticon was well suited to the application of the Silent System of imprisonment, though the system was also used in other prisons which did not follow all the principles of Bentham's design. The system became widespread in the 1830s, after Bentham's death, inspired by the earlier advocacy of Jonas Hanway (1712–86). Hanway, a victualler to the navy, adopted a number of eccentric

Sir Edwin Chadwick (1800–90): Chadwick's zeal as a campaigner for praiseworthy philanthropic causes was matched only by his capacity for antagonising others who shared his aims and could have been allies. He campaigned for the reform of the Poor Law and became Secretary to the Poor Law Commission, a position he used with ruthless ingenuity to whip into line local Poor Law Guardians who did not approach their tasks with sufficient zeal. He insisted that food, accommodation and employment, while supporting existence, should be no more 'eligible' (attractive) than conditions outside the workhouses in order to discourage the idle from seeking admission: a principle applied by Bentham to prisons. The Commission was dissolved as a result of the antagonism his activities aroused. He then turned his attention to the cause of sanitary reform and in 1848 he became a member of the General Board of Health and the Metropolitan Sewers Commission. The following year he (and his principal antagonist) were removed by the Home Secretary from the Metropolitan Sewers Commission in order to bring peace to that body. This left more time for Chadwick to use his position on the General Board of Health to interfere with the work of local boards and this was one of the factors that led first to Chadwick's removal from the Board and then to its abolition. Chadwick never held public office again. He was knighted in 1889, the year before his death.

causes. He advocated the use of umbrellas, opposed the practice of tipping and the granting of citizenship to Jews, launched fierce onslaughts on the practice of drinking tea and argued that prisoners should be isolated from one another. The object of the system was to prevent prisoners from communicating with and, in the process, 'contaminating' one another with evil ideas and thoughts. At this time the 'miasmatic' theory of disease propagation was held by many eminent citizens (notably Edwin Chadwick himself). It proposed that diseases such as cholera and typhoid were propagated by airborne organisms rather than polluted water (the true cause) and some authorities maintained that criminal behaviour was contagious through a similar mechanism. Under the Silent System prisoners would be protected from such contagion and would, instead, be obliged to commune with themselves, reflect upon the error of their ways and, in the process, become law-abiding citizens. A separate process, sometimes associated with the Silent System, required that prisoners be kept occupied with hard, unremitting and sometimes pointless toil. This was designed to make the prison experience so unpleasant that no one would want to repeat it once he was released.

The words of Sir Edmund du Cane, chairman of the Prison Commission in the latter half of the century, sum up this philosophy: 'Hard labour, hard fare and hard board'. Under this regime the new prisoner would often be required to sleep on a hard, plank bed and work alone in his cell picking oakum (separating strands of old, tarred rope). Oscar Wilde was subjected to this punishment in the final years of the century. In May 1895, following his disastrous decision to prosecute the Marquess of Queensberry for libel, Wilde was found guilty of committing indecent (i.e. homosexual) acts and was sentenced to two years' imprisonment with hard labour. After a brief sojourn in Newgate, Wilde was taken to Pentonville where he was subjected to the full rigours of the Silent System as adopted by that prison: six hours daily on the treadmill; sleeping on a plank board; oakum picking; and one day's exercise in Indian file with other prisoners with whom he was not allowed to converse. He suffered from cold, insomnia and disease, his attacks of diarrhoea being so frequent and severe that on three occasions warders were sick when they entered his cell. He lost a stone and a half in weight during the weeks he spent in Pentonville before his transfer to Reading.[18]

A detailed account of the pointless and degrading process of oakum picking as executed in Newgate was given by a writer called James Greenwood in 1874:[19]

My day's work was brought to me, consisting of a pound and a quarter of oakum. Along with the oakum was an iron hook, with a strap attached to it and this was to fasten to the knee to help tear the tarred rope, which is as tough almost as catgut. A pound and a quarter does not sound much, and it doesn't look much, but a pound and a quarter to a man whose fingers are as soft as a woman's and who hasn't the least idea how to go about it, is a tremendous day's work. I know that for the first four or five days I was at work on it from morning till night, with my nails broken and my fingers bleeding.

At other times the prisoner might be required to walk on a 6ft-diameter treadwheel, holding a bar as he did so, for 8 hours, with 5 minute rests every 10 minutes, climbing the equivalent of 8,000ft. Talking was strictly forbidden during this process and failure to observe this rule was punished by such measures as withdrawal of meat from the diet. An alternative labour was the crank, which required the prisoner to turn a handle a prescribed number of times, the mechanism lifting a heavy weight. Hard labour was not finally abolished until 1948. James Greenwood left an account of the techniques developed by prisoners to frustrate the Silent System. While in Pentonville, which adopted the Silent System, he described the methods used by prisoners to converse during chapel services, despite the attentions of warders:

The prisoners sit in gangs all in a row of a dozen or so, every prisoner having a space of about six feet between himself and his neighbour, a warder being attached to each gang to see that order is kept. Some of the old hands, however, are too knowing for him. Long practice has taught them how to talk without moving their lips, and it is not uncommon to see the warder in command staring his hardest along the row and scrutinising the face of every man with a most perplexed face of his own. He is certain that talking in an undertone is going on. He can hear the mysterious sounds but every face is to the right and every eye fixed devoutly on the parson.

Oscar Wilde failed to master this system and his overwhelming need to converse with his fellow inmates, many of whom were sympathetic to him, earned him the customary punishments of a bread and water diet and solitary confinement. The hardest labour that Greenwood encountered during his journey through the prison system was at Portland gaol where prisoners were to required to work in the quarry blasting, breaking and moving huge lumps of Portland stone by hand or by barrow, the materials being borne to London by rail for use in the city's great construction projects.

THE SEPARATE SYSTEM

A harsher variation of the Silent System was the Separate System in which prisoners had no contact at all with their fellow inmates. In 1834 William Crawford, on behalf of the Quaker-inspired Society for the Improvement of Prison Discipline, visited Philadelphia and reported favourably on the adoption of the Silent and Separate Systems in the city's gaol, echoing Bentham by commenting that it used 'the passive weight of architecture to secure its ends'. As a result of such encouraging words a House of Lords Committee in 1835 recommended the more widespread adoption of the system, but others were not so sure. The sanity of some prisoners was tested to breaking point by the process. At Pentonville, whose first governor, Sir Joshua Jebb (1793–1863) was an enthusiastic advocate of the Separate System, the regime was particularly severe. The prison was designed on Panopticon principles and opened in 1842. All 520 identical cells were observable from a central point. The rule of silence would have made a Trappist monastery seem disorderly. The warders wore padded shoes and when prisoners left their cells they wore hoods to prevent them communicating with or clearly seeing other inmates. Even the prison chapel was designed so that panels prevented prisoners from seeing the person sitting in the adjacent seat. The routine included hard labour, which involved such arduous tasks as breaking stones for road-making. A report of 1845 on Pentonville prison referred to several cases of insanity resulting from the Separate System while a comment by the chaplain of Preston gaol carried a sinister note. The Revd John Clay claimed that 'a few months in the separate cell render a prisoner strangely impressible. The chaplain can then make the brawny navvy cry like a child; he can work his feelings in any way he pleases'.[20]

MILLBANK

Bentham, a skilled and persistent lobbyist, succeeded in persuading the Prime Minister, William Pitt, of the merits of his Panopticon, but the Younger Pitt had more important matters on his mind during the Napoleonic Wars than Bentham's ingenious schemes. It was not until 1816 that Bentham's ideas took concrete shape in the form of the first prison to be built under the authority of the Home Office. This was the huge penitentiary at Millbank. It opened in 1821 with a capacity of over 1,000 prisoners, many of whom would previously have been sentenced to transportation or death. It was built on a site now occupied by the Tate Gallery (Tate Britain). Its architect was Sir Robert Smirke (1781–1867) in his capacity as architect to the Office of Works (in effect the government's chief architect), though Smirke is better remembered as a leader of the neo-classical revival in the nineteenth century and architect of the British Museum. Millbank penitentiary was built on such swampy ground that it partially collapsed while being built. The unhealthy site was soon to take its toll. The prison's design consisted of a hexagonal core with a pentagon radiating from each of the six sides like petals. Each pentagon was designed on panoptic principles to enable constant surveillance of prisoners along the lines recommended by Bentham. A system of reflecting mirrors enabled the officer at the central point of each pentagon to see into the cells while a speaking tube enabled him to admonish the prisoners. It was used as a holding depot for prisoners awaiting transportation or dispersal to local prisons and also for some long-stay prisoners. Millbank was easily adapted to the Silent and Separate Systems when these were widely adopted from the 1830s, after which a similar routine was followed for all prisoners.

Upon admission prisoners were bathed, had their hair cut and were issued with a uniform. Those sentenced to penal servitude had their heads shaved and they were issued with the notorious uniform decorated with arrows as additional marks of humiliation. For the first six months the Separate System applied in what was designated the first class. Prisoners were kept isolated from one another in separate cells and exercised for one hour each day, during which time they were not allowed to converse with other prisoners. Thereafter they were transferred to the second class or Silent System, working in concert with other prisoners, but not allowed to converse with them on pain of penalties. Misbehaviour could lead to the culprit being back-squadded to the first-class regime. The great scientist Michael Faraday was consulted as to the best materials to ensure 'acoustic silence' in the building.

In some ways the Millbank regime was an enlightened one. Male and female prisoners were separated and females were supervised by officers of their own sex. Some attempt was made to find useful employment for the inmates, tailoring and shoemaking being the principal occupations. The prisoners made uniforms for the prison officers and boots for the Royal Naval dockyard at Chatham. The governor strongly supported these activities, informing inspectors that 'the grand secret was employment: when work ended his troubles began'. The prison, however, quickly became mired in controversy.

The damp, marshy site was always unhealthy and in 1823 an outbreak of dysentery among the prisoners led to several deaths. After that date female prisoners were accommodated elsewhere and the diet was improved. Breakfast consisted of cocoa, molasses, milk and bread; dinner included meat, potatoes and bread; supper was a pint of gruel made with oatmeal or wheat flour, molasses and bread. The punishment diet allowed only 1lb of bread per day with water to drink. The prison then became known among the local populace as 'the fattening house' because the food (notably the meat) was better than that which could be afforded by many honest but impoverished citizens. It was closed temporarily in 1832 following an outbreak of severe diarrhoea and it was also plagued by riots among the long-term prisoners. In the 1850s each prisoner passing through Millbank was ill, on average, more than four times each year. At Brixton, by comparison, one in four prisoners was ill each year. In 1843 it ceased to be a model prison for long-term inmates and became a convict assembly depot from which convicts were transferred to prison hulks before being transported to Australia or South Africa, a function which became redundant when transportation ended in the 1850s. Millbank penitentiary was closed in 1890 and the building was demolished to make way for the Tate Gallery, which incorporated many of the prison's bricks in its own structure.

The hulks consisted of old warships, no longer required by the exigencies of the Napoleonic Wars, which were moored in the Thames and the Medway for the accommodation of prisoners for whom there was no space in conventional prisons. Many of Nelson's Trafalgar fleet ended their days in this ignoble way, including the *Bellerophon* on which Napoleon had been taken prisoner and which had taken the defeated emperor to his final exile in St Helena. The use of the hulks had been enacted in 1776 as a temporary measure when the American War of Independence prevented the transportation of prisoners to the American colonies, but the practice survived for eighty years, ending only when transportation itself ceased. A degrading consequence of the use of the hulks was the spectacle of prisoners being taken to them from Newgate in readiness for transportation. Jeering crowds would gather as the prisoners were conveyed, chained, in carts from the prison to the riverbank where they began their long and often fatal journey to the penal colonies.

An even larger prison than Millbank was the one at Cold Bath Fields, close to the present site of the Royal Mail's Mount Pleasant sorting office. It had existed since the sixteenth century, but was rebuilt in 1794 and enlarged in the following century to the point that it could accommodate more than 1,000 prisoners, male and female, most of them serving short sentences imposed by magistrates. It had more than 300 cells and more spacious quarters could be provided on payment of half a guinea (52½p) per week. In mid-century almost 10,000 prisoners passed through Cold Bath Fields, with as many as 1,200 men and women being held there at any one time.

LEGISLATIVE CHANGES

From the 1820s onwards, under the enlightened rule of Sir Robert Peel as Home Secretary, a series of Acts introduced improvements to the prison system. Uniform codes of discipline, punishment and dietary regimes were introduced and applied both to prisons like Millbank, which were the responsibility of the Home Office, and to local prisons which were governed by county magistrates until the Home Office assumed responsibility for all prisons in 1877. In this way the Separate and Silent Systems were gradually extended to local prisons. Tobacco was to be prohibited, but, on the other hand, the prison authorities were made responsible for providing adequate food for inmates.

Nevertheless, the first report of the prison inspectors (who had been appointed in 1835)[21] on Newgate itself indicated that extra food was still being brought into the gaol for some prisoners to supplement their meagre diets and that other features of the eighteenth-century regime had survived unscathed. The prison was less under the control of the keeper than the wardsmen, the prisoners who supervised each ward and charged their fellows for legal advice. Wrestling, boxing, shove-halfpenny and associated gaming were among the more popular occupations of prisoners, though it was noted that *The Times* and the *Morning Chronicle* were regularly available in the wards to keep prisoners informed of events outside the prison walls. Some prisoners in Newgate occupied themselves in making lead tokens with sentimental inscriptions such as 'True for Ever' or 'Love for Life', which were either pressed on female companions or worn by the prisoners themselves upon discharge. A more sinister note added that a 'young, rosy-cheeked girl' had been spared transportation so that she could act as the keeper's servant girl. Since by this time Newgate was only being used for prisoners awaiting trial and others expecting 'the final penalty' it was possible to close much of the prison and convert the wards to cells, thus enabling some aspects of the Separate System to be introduced to Newgate. This conversion did not take place until the 1850s.

ELIZABETH FRY AND NEWGATE

The appearance of the portrait of Elizabeth Fry (1780–1845) on the £5 note in 2002 was a recognition of the critical role she had assumed in reforming Britain's gaols in the nineteenth century. She is most often associated with her work in Newgate itself, but her influence extended to every part of the prison system as a result of her persuasive testimony before Parliamentary Committees. Elizabeth Fry was born in Norwich in 1780 and lived as a child at Earlham Hall, two miles from the centre of the city. Her father was John Gurney, a successful Quaker businessman and her mother, Catherine, was descended from the Barclays who founded the bank of that name. When Elizabeth was 12 years old her mother Catherine died soon after giving birth to her twelfth child and much of the responsibility for bringing up the young family fell upon Elizabeth. They included her brother Joseph, who was to be associated with her in her prison work, and her sister Hannah, the future wife of the prison reformer and anti-slavery campaigner Thomas Fowell Buxton.[22]

The Quakers, or Society of Friends, had themselves suffered greatly at the hands of the prison system during the time of their persecution in the late seventeenth and eighteenth centuries. George Foxe (1624–91), the founder of the movement, recorded his own sufferings at the hands of brutal gaolers and many Quaker preachers fell foul of the Five Mile Act of 1665, which forbade dissenting preachers from coming to preach within five miles of towns. Many were arrested at the City Meeting House in Gracechurch Street and, like William Penn, were sent to Newgate, where some of them died.[23] The Quaker connection was a great influence in Elizabeth Fry's life. Apart from the strong moral influence exercised by the Society, it also gave her valuable contacts since the family was connected with other leading figures in business and politics such as the Lloyds, founders of Lloyds Bank, and the Wilberforces. The extraordinary success of Quakers in founding businesses such as Barclays and Lloyds Bank and Cadbury's, Rowntree's and Fry's confectioners, owed much to the fact that their faith debarred them from many professions.

At the age of 18 Elizabeth heard the American Quaker William Savery preach in Norwich and was so moved by him that she asked her father to invite him to dinner. Following her meeting with Savery she became very active in ministering to the poor of Norwich. In January 1799 she recorded in her diary, 'Most of this morning I spent in Norwich seeing after the poor; I do little for them and I do not like it should appear I do much.'[24] In August 1800 she married the son of another distinguished Quaker family, Joseph Fry. The couple lived in the premises of the family business at Saint Mildred's Court, close to the site of the Bank of England and, after his father's death, at Joseph's family home at Plashet, near East Ham.[25] There she settled to a domestic routine of childbearing (the Frys eventually had eleven children), though she also found time to start a school and soup kitchen for the poor close to her home.

A VISIT TO NEWGATE

Elizabeth Fry's interest in Newgate was aroused by a family friend named Stephen Grellet (1773–1855). Born a French nobleman, Etienne de Grellet, he had fled the French Revolution, settled in America and joined the Society of Friends through which he met the Gurneys and the Frys. He visited Newgate prison in 1813 and was deeply shocked by the conditions he witnessed, especially in the women's section which he had entered against advice of the keeper who feared that in that unruly place harm would befall the distinguished American visitor. His account of his experiences at the gaol prompted a visit from Elizabeth, which she briefly recorded in her journal of 16 February 1813: 'Yesterday we were some hours at Newgate.'[26] The previous year Elizabeth had noted in her journal, 'I fear that my life is slipping away to little purpose,' a surprising statement from the mother of a large family. Grellet's account of Newgate gave her the sense of purpose that she had previously lacked.

As with Grellet, the gaolers were reluctant to admit Elizabeth to the women's section of the prison through concerns for her own safety, but, once admitted, she was deeply shocked at what she saw.

The prison at that time contained fourteen children as prisoners, aged 9 to 13, as well as the children and babies of convicted adults.[27] She was dismayed by the filth, depravity and squalor that she found in the gaol, and noted disapprovingly that many of the women wore men's clothing, presumably because they had no other. She was appalled to witness two women stripping clothes from a dead baby to give them to another child. She expressed her feelings in a letter written to her children at about the same time:

I have lately been twice to Newgate to see after the poor prisoners who had poor little infants without clothing, or with very little and I think if you saw how small a piece of bread they are allowed each day you would be very sorry.

She gave a more censorious account to her brother-in-law, Thomas Buxton, at the same time:

All I tell thee is a faint picture of reality; the filth, the closeness of the rooms, the furious manner and expressions of the women towards each other and the abandoned wickedness, which everything bespoke, are quite indescribable.[28]

Family concerns, including the bearing of more children, fully occupied her for the next four years, but she returned to the gaol shortly before Christmas in 1816 where she was confronted by the spectacle of women fighting. She later gave an account to a Parliamentary committee of one of these visits when 'we were witnesses to the dreadful proceedings that went forward on the female side of the prison; the begging, swearing, gaming, fighting, singing, dancing, dressing up in men's clothes' and observed that some of the women had spoons on long sticks which they thrust through the gratings of their cells in order to beg from visitors, who naturally kept their distance from the noisome multitude.[29] Any money received through this demeaning process was likely to be spent on drink from the prison 'tap'. Elizabeth, despite the further entreaties of the governor, entered the women's section, picked up a small child and proposed to establish a school in the prison. An inmate named Mary Connor, a thief, was proposed by other prisoners as the teacher and by February 1817 Elizabeth was writing in her diary, 'I have lately been much occupied in forming a school in Newgate for the children of the poor prisoners as well as the young criminals but my mind has also been deeply affected in attending a poor woman who was executed this morning . . . the poor creature murdered her baby; and how inexpressibly awful now to have her life taken away.' Elizabeth Fry's opposition to capital punishment and campaigns for more humane practices in prisons led the Home Secretary, Lord Sidmouth, to criticise her for trying to remove 'the dread of punishment in the criminal classes'.

Elizabeth was unable to save the condemned mother, but the school, for children and young women, flourished with the assistance of the Association for the Improvement of the Female Prisoners in Newgate, which was run by a committee of Quaker women. The objects of the association were expressed in terms which showed their Quaker origins:

> To provide for the clothing, instruction and employment of the women; to introduce them to knowledge of the Holy Scriptures; and to form in them, as much as possible, those habits of order, sobriety and industry, which may render them docile and peaceable while in prison, and respectable when they leave it.

With the at first hesitant support of the keeper, who had previously regarded his female charges as beyond hope, they appointed a matron to supervise the female prisoners and the matron was herself assisted by monitors, elected by the prisoners themselves, who were responsible for maintaining cleanliness and order in the women's quarters. The female inmates reacted very positively to this unaccustomed rule of kindness, and needlework classes for the women were soon added to the work of the school itself. Elizabeth then conceived the idea of selling the garments the women made to the convict settlement in Botany Bay and, to this end, she approached Richard Dixon and Co., in Fenchurch Street, who held the contract for the penal colony. In the words of her brother-in-law, Sir Thomas Buxton, she 'candidly told them that she was desirous of depriving them of this branch of their trade'.[30] Richard Dixon was only too happy to cooperate with Elizabeth and, in effect, appointed her Newgate venture as a sub-contractor, thus ensuring a steady if modest stream of income to her enterprise, which was used for 'small extra indulgences' for the prisoners.

At the end of February 1817 Elizabeth recorded, 'Newgate prison and myself are becoming quite a show, which is a very serious thing. I believe that it certainly does much good to the cause in spreading amongst all ranks of society a considerable interest in the subject.' Among those whose interest was thus aroused was the Lord Mayor, who visited the gaol and was confronted by an unexpected spectacle, 'instead of being peopled with beings scarcely human, blaspheming, fighting, tearing each other's hair . . . a scene where stillness and propriety reigned'.[31] So impressed was he by what he saw that he agreed, on behalf of the City Corporation, to pay some of the expenses of the matron and the school. Other equally eminent visitors followed, including John Randolph, American ambassador to England, who wrote in February 1819, 'I have seen Elizabeth Fry in Newgate and I have witnessed there miraculous effects of true Christianity upon the most depraved of human beings.' The attention of the industrial philanthropist Robert Owen was also drawn to Elizabeth's work and he wrote to newspapers commending her methods as 'proof of the effects of kindness and regular habits' and suggesting that they should be followed elsewhere.[32] Not all her contemporaries showed unqualified enthusiasm. In his poem 'Don Juan', Lord Byron (1788–1824), who died while Elizabeth's work was gathering pace, encouraged her to turn from the reprobates of Newgate towards the real sinners who were to be found at a much more elevated point in society. At the time he wrote, Carlton House was the home of the dissolute George IV:

> Oh Mrs Fry! Why go to Newgate? Why
> Preach to poor rogues; and wherefore not begin with
> Carlton, or with other houses? Try
> Your hand at hardened and imperial sin

Robert Owen (1771–1858): born in Wales, Owen was sent at the age of 10 to work as a draper, a trade he quickly mastered. At the age of 19 he set up in partnership as a manufacturer of spinning machinery and in 1799 he raised enough money to be able to buy textile factories in New Lanark, near Glasgow, from his father-in-law. Here he discontinued the practice of employing children under 10 years of age and built a school for them to attend. He appeared before Parliamentary committees to argue the case for a more humane management of industry, but antagonised other advocates of change, such as William Wilberforce and William Cobbett, by criticising the attitudes of the Church of England. When his ideas were not as well received as he had hoped in England he moved to the USA and bought some land in Indiana where he created the community of New Harmony based upon his socialist principles, which were extended to agriculture. The inhabitants proved to be more disputatious than he had hoped so he returned to England and made a further unsuccessful attempt to found such a community in Hampshire. He continued to campaign for these and other causes in what he called his 'new moral order', including prison reform, until his death and formed the Grand National Consolidated Trade Union (1834) and the Association of all Classes and all Nations (1835).

OTHER GAOLS

By this time Elizabeth Fry was a celebrity and, as Owen had suggested, she began to turn her attention to wider issues of reform. In 1821 she formed The British Ladies' Society for Promoting the Reformation of Female Prisoners, which campaigned for the supervision of female prisoners by female officers. She was wise enough to add, for the benefit of those who wished to support her, that, 'Those who engage in the interesting task of visiting criminals must not be impatient if they find the work of reformation a very slow one'.[33] She argued that a more humane regime should be extended also to inmates of workhouses and lunatic asylums. She also campaigned for better training for nurses and founded the first nurse training school at Guy's Hospital. Florence Nightingale acknowledged the influence of Elizabeth Fry's example and took some of her trained nurses with her to the Crimea after Elizabeth's death.

In 1818 Elizabeth Fry began to visit prisons elsewhere in the company of her brother Joseph Gurney who recorded the experience in his book *Notes of a Visit Made to Some of the Prisons in Scotland and the North of England in Company with Elizabeth Fry*, published in London in 1819.[34] They visited thirty-three gaols and some, such as the one at York Castle, received a relatively favourable verdict, though most were criticised. In 1825 Elizabeth published *Observations on the Siting, Superintendence and Government of Female Prisoners*, in which she advocated a regime of 'hard labour, which properly pertains to a reforming discipline and forms an important part of the system of punishment', along with education and religious instruction based, of course, upon Bible readings.[35] She also proposed regular inspections of visiting committees of magistrates and others and supported the regime of surveillance earlier advocated by Bentham and others. However, she opposed the Separate System as being cruel and as rendering its victims ill-equipped to return to civil society upon their release. In the words of her daughters: 'No delusion did she consider greater than that man can be treated as a machine and remodelled through having his conduct bent to obedience through strong coercion and dread of punishment.' She was also opposed to capital punishment because it was 'evil and produced evil results'. Her work was only briefly interrupted by the failure of her husband's bank in 1828 and his own bankruptcy, which prompted a move from Plashet to more modest premises in nearby Upton Lane. The family's financial problems were mitigated by the generosity of her wealthy brother Joseph, who arranged for her to receive an annual allowance of over £1,000.

By this time Elizabeth's celebrity had caught the attention of the highest circles of aristocratic as well as intellectual society. She met Louis Philippe, then King of France, when visiting that country to

Debtors' prisons: Joseph was fortunate. He could have been sent to prison as a debtor, a fate which befell many of his contemporaries. By the time of his bankruptcy there were five debtors' prisons in London: King's Bench, Marshalsea, Fleet; White Cross Street and Horsemonger Lane. In the 1730s James Oglethorpe (1696–1785) had founded the colony of Georgia in the present United States as a settlement for debtors after one of his friends had died of smallpox in the Fleet prison. Nevertheless, it remained possible for creditors to pursue their debtors and have them sent to prison until their debts were discharged, though their incarceration prevented them from earning anything with which to discharge such debts. In 1821 Marc Brunel (father of Isambard) was sent to the King's Bench prison as a debtor, a misfortune he attributed to the Admiralty which had failed to pay him for an invention which facilitated the production of pulley blocks for the Royal Navy. The Admiralty paid up when Marc threatened to sell his invention to the Tsar of Russia and Marc was released. Three years later Charles Dickens's father suffered the same fate in Marshalsea, an episode that haunted the author for the rest of his life. The remnants of Marshalsea may still be seen north of St George's Church off Borough High Street, Southwark, where a wall plaque commemorates the brief residence of John Dickens. The practice of gaoling debtors largely ended in 1869 with the passing of the Debtors' Act.

inspect the prison at Saint Lazare and the King of Prussia visited Newgate to hear Elizabeth reading to the prisoners from the Bible, later dining with her at her home. Elizabeth herself visited Prussia in 1839 with her husband, where they heard about the work of the Rhenish Westphalian Prison Association, founded by a pastor who had been influenced by Elizabeth's example. In 1831 she had met the Duchess of Kent with her young daughter, the future Queen Victoria, and Queen Adelaide, wife of William IV. In 1839 she held a fund-raising sale at Crosby Hall, in Bishopsgate (formerly the City home of Sir Thomas More),[36] which raised over £1,000. Victoria herself, by now Queen, contributed £50 to Elizabeth's fund-raising, which led to a meeting between those two formidable ladies in 1840. Two years later she was a guest at the Lord Mayor's banquet at the Mansion House (a most unusual honour for a woman at that time), where she met Prince Albert. She also drew the approbation of Hannah More (1745–1833) and particularly valued a copy of the writer's *Practical Piety: The Influence of the Religion of the Heart on the Conduct of Life*, a pietistic work of great significance to the devout Quaker which Hannah More dedicated in glowing terms:

> To Mrs Fry,
> Presented by Hannah More
> As a token of veneration
> Of her heroic zeal,
> Christian charity,
> And persevering kindness
> To the most forlorn
> Of humans beings

Elizabeth was also called upon to give evidence to Parliamentary Committees. Her evidence influenced Sir Robert Peel's Gaols Act of 1823, which prescribed that female prisoners should be governed by female officers and that gaolers should be paid so that they did not need to exact charges from their inmates. The Act also provided for the inspection of gaols by Justices of the Peace. In 1835 she gave evidence to the House of Lords Committee on The State of Gaols and Houses of Correction in England and Wales, before whom she advocated the complete separation of male and female prisoners and further argued that even preaching to females would be better undertaken by women, though she acknowledged that the lack of suitably qualified females might necessitate the occasional employment of men in this important role. She opposed the use of the treadwheel by women (while approving it for men), but allowed the use of the crank for women prisoners. She also proposed to divide

Hannah More (1745–1833): was the most active female member of the movement dedicated to the abolition of slavery. She was born near Bristol, the daughter of a headmaster, and educated in that city which owed much of its prosperity to the slave trade. She worked in a school for young ladies, which had been started by her older sisters, and started to write plays while in her 20s, an activity which brought her the acquaintance of figures such as Samuel Johnson, David Garrick and Sir Joshua Reynolds. Through an early friendship with William Wilberforce she was drawn into the Clapham Sect, a group of evangelical Christians and reformers based in that village, then on the outskirts of London, who campaigned for such causes as the establishment of Sunday schools and the abolition of slavery. The Clapham Sect included such figures as the abolitionists Thomas Clarkson and John Newton. She was a philanthropist rather than a revolutionary who, though sympathetic to the poor, believed that the practice of religion would teach them that deprivation in this life was a price paid for joy in heaven and that they could be taught to make the best use of what little they had. She died in the year that slavery was abolished and may be regarded as one of the first of the female philanthropists of the period, of whom Elizabeth Fry is a later example.

the female prisoners into four classes according to their previous records and the nature of their crimes, ranging from those afflicted by 'no deep moral dye' to the worst offenders who should 'undergo peculiar privations and hardships'. The last group should also have their hair cut short to promote 'humiliation of spirit which, for persons so circumstanced, is an indispensable step to improvement and reformation'.[37] The four groups should be separately accommodated and in Newgate she marked their distinction with different uniforms and badges. Many of her ideas were accepted by the committee, including the provision of adequate food for inmates, but their Lordships were not persuaded by her arguments against the Separate and Silent Systems which were more widely adopted as a result of their report. They did, however, give the Home Secretary powers to appoint prison inspectors to ensure that certain minimum standards were observed within the system.

By the time of her death in 1845 Elizabeth had acquired an almost mythical status. Queen Victoria described her in her journal as 'a very superior person' and the Bishop of Norwich, where she had been born, stated that it would be unsuitable to bury her among the 'emblems of heathen mythology' in Westminster Abbey though that stern Anglican may have been influenced in this judgement by her Quaker faith. Instead, her memorial took the form of the Elizabeth Fry Refuge in Hackney, for the 'temporary reception of repentant females on their release from the Metropolitan gaols', as described in *The Times*.[38] More than 1,000 people attended her burial in the Quaker graveyard in Barking near her home.

LATER DEVELOPMENTS

At the time of her death the prison system was no longer merely a place of squalor and disease for incarcerating, at minimum cost, people who were awaiting execution or transportation or who were not deemed fit to be at large. Bentham and others had begun to think, in rather mechanical terms, about how those in the prison system could be prepared to live peaceful lives outside its walls and Elizabeth Fry and her collaborators had introduced a note of humanity to this process. She had also ended the humiliating spec-tacle of crowds jeering at prisoners and throwing missiles as they were taken from Newgate to the hulks for transportation, insisting that they be conveyed in covered carriages instead of open wagons and accompanying them herself when necessary to avoid the riots among the prisoners that had frequently accompanied this ritual. She also regularly visited the prisoners on the hulks and campaigned for improvements in their living conditions. Other reforms followed her death. In 1857 remission of up to a third of the sentence was made available to prisoners whose conduct had merited it and in 1859 Newgate's open wards were converted to cells. At about the same time the practice of transportation also ceased.

Further improvements to the system resulted from the report of the Gladstone Committee, which sat in 1895, fifty years after Elizabeth's death, and many of whose recommendations were reflected in the Prison Act of 1898. The chairman of the Prison Commission, Sir Edmund Du Cane ('hard labour, hard fare and hard board')[39] resigned and some humane reforms were introduced.[40] The committee recommended that 'unproductive labour should be abolished wherever possible' and that 'the number of skilled teachers of industries in the prison service should be increased' thereby preparing prisoners to pursue useful occupations upon release. 'Habitual criminals should be kept as a class apart from other criminals', though the committee cast doubt on the values of the Separate System, as Elizabeth Fry had done. Nevertheless, the system survived in some places until 1922 and oakum picking until well into the twentieth century – its abolition coming too late to spare Oscar Wilde this humiliation. As previously observed, hard labour survived until 1948. The 1898 Act was followed in 1902 by the introduction of Borstals for young offenders believed to be capable of reform. The institutions were named after the village of Borstal, near Rochester in Kent, where the first one was established. Shortly afterwards the 'convict crop' haircut and arrow uniform were abolished.

Today, 160 years after Elizabeth Fry's death, habitual criminals still turn prisons into universities of crime for less experienced and more naive inmates and the authorities continue to wrestle with the problem of introducing purposeful education and training into gaols whose inmates are too often on the move because of overcrowding. Many of Elizabeth Fry's ideas, based upon her experiences among the prisoners in Newgate, remain aspirations rather than achievements within the prison system of the twenty-first century.

SEVEN

Newgate in Literature; Final Days

Several thieves and street robbers confessed in Newgate that they raised their courage at the playhouse by the songs of their hero Macheath, before they sallied forth in their desperate nocturnal exploits

> (A disapproving comment on the effect on the criminal community of John Gay's *Beggar's Opera*, 1728)

For the last fourteen days, so salutary has the impression of this butchery been upon me, I have had the man's face continually before my eyes; I can see Mr Ketch at this moment, with an easy air, taking his rope from his pocket

> (William Makepeace Thackeray's account of *Going to See a Man Hanged*, 1840)

Everything told of life and animation but one dark cluster of objects in the centre of all – the black stage, the cross beam, the rope and all the hideous apparatus of death.

> (Charles Dickens describes Oliver Twist's departure from Newgate after visiting Fagin in the condemned cell)

Newgate has spawned its own literary heritage, a testimony to the hold that the notorious gaol exerted on the literary imagination. A century after the building was demolished the Newgate Novel still enjoyed the unusual distinction of its own entry in the *Oxford Companion to English Literature*.[1] Much of its influence on subsequent literature may be traced back to the collection of works loosely described as *The Newgate Calendar*. The literary merit of these works is debatable, as is their accuracy but their influence may clearly be recognised in the works of writers and artists as distinguished and diverse as Daniel Defoe, Charles Dickens, William Makepeace Thackeray, John Gay and William Hogarth, as well as less well-known writers such as Harrison Ainsworth, William Godwin and Edward Bulwer-Lytton. It was the source of crude morality tales as well as featuring in major works like *Barnaby Rudge, Oliver Twist and Great Expectations*.

THE NEWGATE CALENDAR

The original *Newgate Calendar* was a document compiled each month by the keeper of the gaol which recorded the names of those entering the gaol each month: in effect a gaol register. However the notoriety of Newgate was such that the title also became attached to accounts of the trials and misdeeds of the inmates, or indeed to others whose connections with Newgate itself were tenuous or non-existent. Some reference to such accounts has been made in previous pages, including the *Memoirs of the Right Villainous John Hall*.[2] They were privately produced by enterprising publishers with an eye to profiting from sensational literature. The first account to refer to a calendar was published in about 1705 under the title *The Tyburn Calendar or Malefactors Bloody Register*. The others that followed over the next two centuries were given similar titles, their publishers showing no wish to understate their contents. In 1719 Captain Alexander Smith published in the Newgate series an account of the *Most Notorious Highwaymen* and in the years that followed the reading public was able to buy *Villainy Displayed in all its Branches* (1720); *Plunders of the Most Noted Pirates Interspersed with Several Remarkable Trials of the most Notorious Malefactors* (1734); and in 1780 *Accounts of Executions, Dying Speeches and other Curious Particulars Relating to the Most Notorious Violators of the Laws of their Country who have Suffered Death*. Many versions of the work amounted to morality tales. A stern warning of the consequences of criminality would preface the volume and most offenders were presented as inadequate rather than heroic, though exceptions were made for celebrities such as Jack Sheppard and villains like Jonathan Wild.[3] The typical subject was idle and feckless, sometimes led astray by others and guilty of stealing items or money of little value before being caught. Murders often arose from robberies which went wrong, but the criminal was always caught and almost always executed.

In the 1820s two lawyers, Andrew Knapp and William Baldwin, published four edited volumes entitled *The Newgate Calendar Comprising Interesting Memoirs of the Most Notorious Characters* and they sold so well that, two years later, they published six volumes of *The New Newgate Calendar*. Young writers who were struggling to become established took on the work of compiling these titles, one of them being George Borrow (1803–81), the son of an army recruiting officer. He was born at East Dereham, Norfolk, and spent much of his childhood sharing his father's nomadic existence, moving from place to place as his father sought out candidates for the king's shilling. He was educated first in Norwich and later in Edinburgh and was briefly articled to a solicitor, but the settled life did not suit him and he continued his wanderings on the Continent, visiting France, Germany, Spain, Russia and Portugal, acquiring a knowledge of many foreign languages including that of gypsies for whom his wandering life gave him an affinity. He published a dictionary of the Romany language and earned his living partly from translating works such as the Bible from English into other languages. He contributed to *The New Newgate Calendar* in 1825, though in his fanciful, semi-autobiographical work *Lavengro*, published in 1851, he gave an exaggerated account of his role in the compilation of this massive work. He described a meeting with a publisher in which the latter offered him £50 for a compilation of Newgate lives and trials, to comprise six volumes of at least 1,000 pages each. Hardly a generous offer, even for the early nineteenth century, though later in the same work he claimed to have completed the task and to have enjoyed it more than any of his other literary works.

Most of the accounts of crimes, trials and confessions included in the various versions of the calendar were very short, amounting to two or three pages of the most alarming facts. Longer accounts were reserved for criminals who were particularly infamous or who had carried out especially gruesome crimes. Thus one edition of the work, *The Complete Newgate Calendar*, allowed Jack Sheppard fourteen pages while the less notorious Elizabeth Brownrigg had five pages devoted to her because of the horrible cruelty she inflicted on the servant girls that had been sent to her care by the Foundling Hospital. The compiler recorded with satisfaction that Brownrigg's corpse was sent to Surgeons' Hall for dissection.[4] Many versions of *The Newgate Calendar* did not feel obliged to confine their accounts to crimes which had any connection with the prison, the main criterion for inclusion being that the events described should be sensational. Thus the same edition includes the tale of Dick Turpin, who was executed at York, while another is that of the unfortunate Jonathan Bradford, who was 'executed at Oxford for a murder he had contemplated but did not commit'. Margaret Dixon is included, having been hanged at Edinburgh in 1728 for supposedly murdering her child (a crime she firmly denied), but when the coffin lid was seen to move she was revived by those of the mourners who had not fled in terror. A few days later she remarried her husband according to the compiler of this version of the *Calendar*. As far as is known this lady never set foot outside Scotland. Sawney Beane, another Scot who never went near Newgate, was included because he was 'an incredible monster who, with his wife, lived by murder and cannibalism in a cave' and was executed in Leith in the reign of James I.

The fact that multi-volume works of this kind could sell in sufficient quantities to reward their publishers at a time when only a small proportion of the population could read invites comparison with the popular press of the twenty-first century. However, the sales of this version of *The Newgate Calendar* were far outstripped by those of individual trials, especially when the notoriety of the crime was followed by the confession and death of the condemned. The pre-eminent practitioner of this branch of sensational literature was the printer James Catnach (1792–1841). He was born in Alnwick, Northumberland, and inherited a printing business from his father, also called James. It was based in Monmouth Court in the notorious St Giles district of London, which was the heart of London's criminal community and close to the route which criminals had taken on their way to execution at Tyburn. His publications were illustrated with crude woodcuts to attract the semi-literate and included a twopenny broadsheet, *Life in London; Or the Sprees of Tom and Jerry*, the first reference to this notable pair of names. However, his greatest sales were for accounts of sensational trials such as that of *Maria Marten and the Murder in the Old Red Barn*, which was itself recorded in *The Newgate Calendar*, though the trial and execution of the murderer, William Corder, took place close to the scene of his crime at Bury St Edmunds in Suffolk. Some accounts suggested that in 1828 Catnach sold a million copies of his broadsheet on this notorious crime, which was soon turned into one of the most popular of Victorian melodramas.

Other writers traded on the name of Newgate simply by including it the titles of works which implied improbable claims. An example of this, written as late as 1873 when the gaol was in its final years, was *How to Get Out of Newgate by One who has Done It and Can Do It Again*. The writer recommends that the escaper should bribe the governor, ply the gaolers with brandy and distract them with magic lantern slides.[5] Newgate, or lurid accounts of It, thus generated one of the earliest forms of really popular literature, a fact which helps to explain its influence on later more celebrated writers.

THE BEGGAR'S OPERA

One of the most famous literary works based on the affairs of Newgate was John Gay's *The Beggar's Opera*, which was revived in 1928 by the German Marxist writer Bertold Brecht as *The Threepenny Opera*. John Gay (1685–1732) was born in

Barnstaple, Devon, and sent to London as an apprentice to a silk merchant, but was soon drawn to the world of literature. He demonstrated his familiarity with London low life in 1712 by his essay entitled *An Argument Proving that the Present Mohocks and Hawkubites are the Gog and Magog of Revelation*. The Mohocks and Hawkubites were street ruffians of the early eighteenth century. Gay earned a modest living as secretary to members of the aristocracy and as a writer of verses, which drew him into the circle of writers such as Richard Steele, Alexander Pope and Jonathan Swift. It was Swift who suggested to him that a tale based upon 'a Newgate pastoral, among the whores and thieves there' would find a ready market, as a result of which *The Beggar's Opera* was produced in 1728. The principal character, Peachum, who is both a receiver of stolen goods and an informant, is clearly based upon Jonathan Wild who had exercised both these professions and been hanged at Tyburn three years before the musical play was produced, at enormous profit to Gay and to the producer John Rich. The production was said to have made Gay rich and Rich gay. Its memorable characters included Captain Macheath, the gallant highwayman, Lucy Lockit, the Newgate gaoler's pretty daughter, and Polly Peachum, Lucy's rival in love for the affections of Macheath and so popular that Gay wrote a sequel for her simply called *Polly*. The music was based upon popular ballads whose tunes would have been familiar to the large audiences which attended it at the New Theatre in Lincoln's Inn Fields. At the end of the play Macheath is reprieved from the condemned cell at Newgate.

The sympathetic portrayal of Macheath and his escape from execution meant that *The Beggar's Opera* was not a tale of virtue rewarded, a feature which ensured that it became an object of controversy as a possible source of moral decay. Macheath was perceived as gallant and sympathetic despite his criminal activities, whereas the normal formula for Newgate tales was that criminals should be condemned and punished. One contemporary writer recorded, with dismay, that 'several thieves and street robbers confessed in Newgate that they raised their courage at the playhouse by the songs of their hero Macheath, before they sallied forth in their desperate nocturnal exploits' thereby suggesting that crime was actually being promoted by the entertainment.[6] Further offence was caused to the Prime Minister, Sir Robert Walpole, whose politics and private life were both satirised in the drama. Walpole retaliated by depriving Gay of a comfortable apartment he occupied in Whitehall as holder of the sinecure post of Commissioner of Lotteries. When Gay's friend Henry Fielding continued the attack on Walpole the enraged Prime Minister passed the Theatrical Licensing Act, which made the Lord Chamberlain responsible for issuing licences to theatres and for licensing plays before they could be staged. The office survived until 1968 but its immediate effect was to end Fielding's career as a playwright and to precipitate a decline in English drama, an outcome that was not foreseen by these 'Newgate' writers.

THE NEWGATE NOVEL

Henceforth tales about Newgate would take the form of the novel, which remained free of the ministrations of the Lord Chamberlain, and the Newgate Novel became a recognised category within the genre of historical fiction: a precursor of the crime fiction of the centuries that followed. Two of Britain's earliest novelists based their Newgate tales upon direct experience of the gaol, though from different perspectives. Reference has already been made to the short and relatively painless period that Daniel Defoe (1660–1731) spent in Newgate as a result of his satirical pamphlet *The Shortest Way with Dissenters*.[7] The author of *Robinson Crusoe* drew on his experience as a prisoner there for a novel whose full title was *The Fortunes and Misfortunes of the Famous Moll Flanders Who was Born in Newgate and During a Life of Continued Variety for Threescore Years was Twelve Years a Whore, Five Times a Wife (whereof once to her own Brother), Twelve Years a Thief, Eight Years a Transported Felon in Virginia, at Last Grew Rich, Lived Honest and Died a Penitent*. It purported to be the autobiography of the daughter of a woman who was spared the gallows because of her pregnancy and was instead transported to Virginia shortly after Moll, the daughter's, birth. The story, which is well summarised in its prolix title, was a morality tale of an altogether superior quality to those of *The Newgate Calendar* itself and shows the unlikely heroine, Moll herself, as a woman in charge of her destiny in a way that was unfamiliar to eighteenth-century readers. Defoe's description of the gaol in *Moll Flanders* no doubt reflects his own experience of the place:

It was impossible to describe the terror of my mind when I was first brought in; and when I looked round upon all the horrors of that dismal place, the hellish noise, the roaring, swearing and clamour, the stench and nastiness and all the dreadful afflicting things that I saw there joined to make the place seem an emblem of hell itself and a kind of entrance to it.

Defoe also produced his own potboiler account of the activities of Jonathan Wild, one of many written by authors of widely varying abilities during the centuries that followed the execution of the notorious thief-taker. The full title of Defoe's version, like that of *Moll Flanders*, could not be described as pithy and emphasises the author's supposedly superior credentials as a reliable reporter: *The Life and Actions of the Late Jonathan Wild, not made up of Fiction and Fable but Taken from his Own Mouth and Collected from Papers of his Own Writing.*

The second of these early novelists, Henry Fielding (1707–54) was acquainted with Newgate and its practices in his capacity as a magistrate at Bow Street and his horrified view of the gaol reflects Defoe's. Fielding's description of Newgate as 'a prototype of hell' and 'the dearest place on earth' has already been recorded. Many of the most important episodes in his novel *Amelia* are set in Newgate, which is relentlessly portrayed as a place of filth, brutality and corruption, many of whose inmates are innocent victims of Trading Justices whom Fielding was endeavouring to exclude from the capital.[8] The principal character, Amelia, is based upon Fielding's much-loved wife Charlotte who, unlike Moll Flanders, is presented as an honest, loving and innocent woman who is a victim of the corrupt and powerful. Her charming, brave but rather helpless husband William is imprisoned in Newgate on a false charge, but it is also while in Newgate that Amelia is shown to have been defrauded of her inheritance by a dishonest lawyer who is duly taken to the prison for execution while Amelia, her fortune restored, retires to a prosperous life in the country far from the corrupt metropolis: another morality tale.

OPPRESSED INNOCENCE

William Godwin (1756–1836) is better remembered for his family life than for his writings, though the latter were very influential during his lifetime. He was born in Wisbech, Cambridgeshire, the son of a Presbyterian minister and he himself followed that profession for some years with excursions into a number of unorthodox religious views, which caused anxiety to his teachers and fellow ministers. He eventually left the ministry and turned to radical politics, inspired by a belief that humans were susceptible to rational argument; that such reasoning would promote feelings of benevolence; and that as a result such persons could live harmoniously without the need for laws. In March 1797 he married Mary Wollstonecraft, the early advocate of women's rights and author of *A Vindication of the Rights of Women* published in 1790. Godwin appears to have married Mary because she was pregnant, her daughter being born in September 1797. The mother died shortly after the birth and the daughter went on to become Mary Shelley, wife of the poet, and author of *Frankenstein*.

Godwin's Newgate Novel is *Caleb Williams: Or Things as They Are*, an early novel of crime and detection and a powerful satire on the oppression of the honest and weak by the vicious and strong. The text includes numerous references to *The Newgate Calendar* and to John Howard's *State of the Prisons in England and Wales*.[9] The principal character, Caleb Williams, is secretary to Squire

Falkland, a man of charm and goodwill who has himself been corrupted by his tyrannical neighbour Squire Tyrrel. Having killed Tyrrel in a quarrel the previously benevolent Falkland escapes justice by falsely incriminating an innocent tenant and his son. Caleb Williams learns of Falkland's guilt but loyalty to his master prevents him from making his suspicions known. Instead of showing gratitude the shameless Falkland persecutes Williams but is eventually driven to relent by Williams's honesty and innocence. This happy outcome was excluded from the original, much darker version which ended with a demented Williams in gaol. The theme of oppressed innocence is thus mitigated at the end, but William Hazlitt underlined the power of the characterisation when he wrote that 'no-one ever began *Caleb Williams* that did not read it through'.

HARRISON AINSWORTH AND EDWARD BULWER-LYTTON

William Harrison Ainsworth (1805–82) carried the Newgate Novel a step further with historical fiction explicitly based on characters and events from the prison. He was the son of a lawyer who had an interest in legal and criminal history which he imparted to his son whose first success, *Rookwood*, published in 1834, created the entirely fictional legend of Dick Turpin's ride to York. He followed this with the very successful *Jack Sheppard* (1839) in which he narrates the exploits of three real Newgate characters: Jack Sheppard, Jonathan Wild and Sheppard's collaborator 'Blueskin'. To these he adds fictional characters such as the virtuous Darrell whose path deviates from that of Sheppard as Darrell chooses a life of work while Sheppard takes to crime. The reader is encouraged to harbour some feelings of sympathy for Sheppard as he is pursued by the wicked and relentless thief-taker Wild, but Sheppard's life of crime leads to the gallows, as convention required, while justice is further served by the hanging of the more vicious and corrupt Wild.

Ainsworth's much more famous contemporary was Edward Bulwer-Lytton (1803–73) best known for his historical novel

The Last Days of Pompeii (1834) and, during his lifetime, for his relentless pursuit by his troublesome wife Rosina, also a writer. She dedicated her life after their estrangement to embarrassing him by writing libellous novels and abusing him at public meetings when he was campaigning as a Member of Parliament. His Newgate Novels included *Paul Clifford* and *Eugene Aram*, the latter based on a real case of murder, both novels being characterised by criminals who engage the sympathy of the reader. Both of them were very successful in Bulwer-Lytton's lifetime and the first, *Paul Clifford*, influenced a novelist of more enduring stature.

WILLIAM MAKEPEACE THACKERAY

William Thackeray (1811–63) was born in Calcutta, the son of an employee of the East India Company who died when he was three years old. Educated at Charterhouse and Trinity College, Cambridge, he left the latter without a degree, dabbled in the law and soon drifted into the world of journalism, scratching a modest living working for *The Times*, the *Morning Chronicle* and *Fraser's Magazine*. Misgivings about the penal code prompted in him deep misgivings about what he regarded as the glamorous depiction of crime by writers such as Harrison Ainsworth and Edward Bulwer-Lytton, both of whom he satirised in *Fraser's Magazine*. It was in reaction to such works that he wrote *Catherine*, also serialised in *Fraser's Magazine* in 1839–40 and narrated under the pseudonym 'Ikey Solomons Junior'.

Thackeray took the story of Catherine Hayes from a particularly lurid version of *The Malefactors' Bloody Register* published in the 1770s. Catherine had been burned at the stake in 1726 for the murder of her husband.[10] Thackeray's intention, in choosing such an unsympathetic subject and such a gruesome fate, was to demonstrate the grim and squalid nature of crime in contrast to the sympathetic and even heroic representations of Ainsworth and Bulwer-Lytton. This noble purpose was set out in a preface to the published book which took the form of an 'advertisement' and explained:

The story of *Catherine* which appeared in *Fraser's Magazine* in 1839–40 was written by Mr Thackeray under the name of Ikey Solomons Junior to counteract the injurious influence of some popular fictions of that day, which made heroes of highwaymen and burglars and created a false sympathy for the vicious and criminal. With this purpose the author chose for the subject of his story a woman named Catherine Hayes who was burned at Tyburn in 1726, in very revolting circumstances. Mr Thackeray's aim obviously was to describe the career of this wretched woman and her associates with such fidelity to truth as to exhibit the danger and folly of investing such persons with heroic and romantic qualities.

To strengthen his anti-Newgate arguments Thackeray drew in features of other gruesome crimes, including the activities of two grave-robbers who, unable to find suitable candidates for the dissection tables from their customary sources, created their own corpse by drugging and drowning a young Italian boy whom they had abducted from the streets of London. One of the abductors was a butcher whose special skill was gouging teeth from the gums of corpses with a bradawl and the site of the murder, Nova Scotia Gardens in Bethnal Green, was a popular place for voyeurs to visit. The crime was a cause célèbre when Thackeray wrote his novel and should have added to the feelings of revulsion among his readers.[11]

The novel was a great popular success, though not in the way that Thackeray had intended. The strong characterisation of the principal character, Catherine herself, and of Catherine's seducer (a fictional character), evoked the sympathies of the readers in a way that Thackeray had not intended. The ironies of the work were lost upon the readers, to Thackeray's annoyance, though it did succeed in stirring up the so-called 'Newgate controversy' in the weekly magazines. John Forster, friend, colleague and biographer of Dickens, led the arguments against the romanticising of crime in Newgate Novels and Thackeray followed up with indignant articles in *Punch*. The correspondence ran for weeks

The controversy surrounding Newgate Novels was sharpened when it was argued in the trial of the valet François Courvoisier that he had read Ainsworth's *Jack Sheppard* before murdering his master Lord William Russell. The implication was that the novel had prompted the crime, an allegation echoed in similar charges two centuries later in controversies over violent and pornographic forms of entertainment. It was in *Fraser's Magazine* that Thackeray recorded his reactions to the hanging of Courvoisier under the title 'On Going to See a Man Hanged'.[12] The event made a lasting impression on Thackeray who wrote about the experience a fortnight later:

> For the last fourteen days, so salutary has the impression of this butchery been upon me, I have had the man's face continually before my eyes; I can see Mr Ketch at this moment, with an easy air, taking his rope from his pocket; I feel myself shamed and degraded at the brutal curiosity that took me to that brutal sight; and I pray to Almighty God to cause this disgraceful sin to pass from among us, and to cleanse our land of blood.[13]

In the same crowd was an even more celebrated writer upon whom the events of the day made an equally strong impression.

CHARLES DICKENS AND NEWGATE NOVELS

Charles Dickens (1812–70), who named his eldest son after his friend and fellow novelist Lytton, experienced the judicial and prison systems early in life in most distressing circumstances. His father, John Dickens, an improvident clerk in the navy pay office, managed his finances in the ways later adopted by Wilkins Micawber, in *David Copperfield*. Consequently, in 1824 he was committed for debt to the Marshalsea prison in Southwark, a humiliation which hung upon the 12-year-old Charles for the rest of his life. The ordeal was made more bitter by the fact that his father's incarceration coincided with Charles's period of employment in a blacking factory owned by a friend of the family near Charing Cross. Here the boy worked twelve hours a day, lodging first in

Camden Town and then in Southwark close to the Marshalsea where the rest of the family resided until John Dickens discharged his debt by means of a legacy from his mother.

Many of Dickens's most memorable characters spend time in a debtors' prison. One of his earliest characters, Samuel Pickwick, spends an uncomfortable time in the Fleet prison for debt as a result of the ludicrous *Bardell vs Pickwick* case in which the innocent Pickwick is sued for breach of promise by his landlady. *Pickwick Papers* was published in 1837 but twenty years later Dickens returned to the theme in *Little Dorritt*. The whole Dorritt family lives in the Marshalsea, as Dickens's father had done, the patriarch of the family and the gaol's longest-serving inmate being William Dorritt (Old Dorritt), who is the victim of a contract with the Circumlocution Office, an unflattering portrait of a government department. Amy, the 'Little Dorritt' of the title, is born in the Marshalsea and when her father is released after twenty-three years he is unable to adjust to the ways of the world despite inheriting a fortune.

DICKENS AND THE PENAL SYSTEM

Following the release of the family from the Marshalsea, Charles was first articled as a clerk to a solicitor and learned shorthand, using this attribute first to become a Parliamentary reporter and later to enter the profession of journalist, making contributions to the *Morning Chronicle* under the pseudonym Boz. His family's experience of prison led Dickens to take an interest both in prison regimes and in the death penalty, an interest reflected in his journalism as well as his great works of fiction. One of his earliest forays as a journalist was recorded in *Sketches by Boz* and concerned a visit to Newgate in 1836.[14] He recorded the casts of the heads of notorious prisoners and the irons allegedly worn by Jack Sheppard together with the yard set aside for 'prisoners of the more respectable class'. He then made his way to the chapel and described:

The condemned pew; a huge black pen in which the wretched people who are singled out for death are placed on the Sunday preceding their execution, to hear prayers for their own souls, to join in the responses of their own burial service and to listen to an address urging themselves, while there is yet time to 'turn and flee from the wrath to come'.

He observed almost thirty awaiting execution, from a grizzled old man to a boy of under 14 (though it was at this stage normal for such young offenders to have their death sentences commuted). Dickens also saw fourteen infant pickpockets 'drawn up in line for our inspection – not one redeeming feature among them – not a glance of honesty, not a wink expressive of anything but the gallows or the hulks'.

In his *American Notes* written in 1842, he recorded a visit to a prison in Philadelphia.[15] He took the opportunity to judge and condemn the Solitary System which he witnessed there.[16] In a long account of his visit to the Eastern Penitentiary in that city he wrote:

The system here is rigid, strict and hopeless solitary confinement. I believe it, in its effects, to be cruel and wrong . . . I believe that very few men are capable of estimating the immense amount of torture and agony which this dreadful punishment, prolonged for years, inflicts upon the sufferers.

He described the process by which each prisoner was compelled to wear a black hood to prevent any visual contact with other prisoners. Apart from an occasional glimpse of his gaolers 'he never looks upon a human countenance or hears a human voice. He is a man buried alive, to be dug out in the slow round of years and in the meantime dead to everything but torturing anxieties and horrible despair'. One prisoner was allowed to keep rabbits but, despite this concession, he looked 'as wan and unearthly as if he had been summoned from the grave'. Another, who had endured eleven years of this solitary confinement, would say nothing, but would 'stare at his hands and pick the flesh upon his fingers'. Upon release some of the prisoners were so disorientated that they could not hold the pen steadily with which to sign the discharge book and, upon being let through the prison gate into the daylight, could only lean against the prison wall, unsure of where to go or what to do. Some of the prisoners had become deaf. He also visited prisons in Boston, Massachusetts and Maryland. It is not hard to make the connection between these disorientated prisoners and the inability of Old Dorritt to cope with life outside the Marshalsea.

Dickens's comments caused great offence to his American hosts, but his visits to English and American gaols, combined with his own family's experience of the Marshalsea, helped to form his ambivalent attitude towards the justice system, imprisonment, capital punishment and the criminal classes. His works of fiction are littered with references which reflect an attitude composed of indignation at injustice, compassion for its victims and loathing for the incorrigible. *Bleak House* (1852–3) satirises the corruption and delays of the Court of Chancery in the case of *Jarndyce and Jarndyce* in which corrupt lawyers profit from the law's delay. The long shadow of the Bastille hangs over the character of Dr Manette after his unjust incarceration in *A Tale of Two Cities*.

Dickens's attitude to criminal behaviour and penal reform was ambivalent. On one occasion he was reported as having marched a young woman to a police station for swearing in public[17] and he frequently emphasised the need for prisoners to undertake hard, futile labour as an antidote to crime. In *Great Expectations* he makes some sarcastic comments on prison conditions when Pip, the principal character of the story, visits Newgate with the good-hearted clerk Wemmick to interview clients of Wemmick's master, Jaggers. Pip noted that:

At that time gaols were much neglected and the period of exaggerated reaction consequent on all public wrongdoing was still far off. So, felons were not lodged and fed better than soldiers (to say nothing of paupers) and seldom set fire to their prisons with the excusable object of improving the flavour of their soup.[18]

The reference to the soup concerned an incident at Chatham prison in February, 1861, as Dickens was writing this instalment, when some prisoners had set fire to the gaol in protest against the quality of their food. Reference has already been made to public resentment at the 'fattening house' at Millbank gaol after the diet was improved in the 1820s and from Dickens's reference to soldiers and paupers we may judge that he had some sympathy for the critics of the reformers.[19] By the time that Dickens came to write his favourite book, the semi-autobiographical *David Copperfield*, he was still sufficiently interested in prison regimes to send David and his friend Tom Traddles to investigate the separate system where David comments on the prison diet:[20]

> I wondered whether it occurred to anybody that there was a striking contrast between these plentiful repasts of choice quality and the dinners, not to say of paupers but of soldiers, sailors, labourers, the great bulk of the honest working community, of whom not one man in five hundred ever dined half so well.

DICKENS AND CAPITAL PUNISHMENT

His attitude towards capital punishment was particularly complex. He was influenced by the arguments of a clergyman, Henry Christmas, that the Bible, and particularly the New Testament, did not support the practice, a belief that was strengthened by his attendance at the execution of Courvoisier in July 1840, the occasion also witnessed by Thackeray and described in *Fraser's Magazine* as 'Going to See a Man Hanged'.[21] Five years after the Courvoisier execution he saw a beheading in Rome, following which he wrote a series of letters to the *Daily News* in February and March 1846[22] in which he argued for 'the total abolition of the Punishment of Death, as a general principle, for the advantage of society, for the prevention of crime and without the least reference to, or tenderness for any individual malefactor whatever'. Dickens thought that public executions might actually promote crime because of their impact on the criminally inclined, arguing that:

> Present this black idea of violence to a bad mind contemplating violence; hold up before a man remotely compassing the death of another person, the spectacle of his own ghastly and untimely death by man's hands; and out of the depths of his own nature you shall assuredly raise up that which lures and tempts him on.

Three years later, in 1849, Dickens again attended a public execution, that of Frederick and Marie Manning who had murdered Marie's lover. They were the first married couple to be executed for more than a century, a feature of the spectacle which prompted almost unprecedented interest. A grandstand was erected by some entrepreneurs and Dickens paid two guineas, a substantial sum, to be sure of a good view from a nearby roof. This prompted further letters from him, on this occasion to *The Times*, but Dickens was no longer advocating outright abolition. Rather, he expressed the hope that 'the Government might be induced to give its support to a measure making the infliction of capital punishment a private solemnity within the prison walls'.[23] It is not clear whether this change of heart was caused by a belief that murderers deserved to die though without promoting an unseemly public spectacle; or whether he was simply recognising, as others did, that total abolition was a lost cause and that the ending of public executions was an acceptable half measure. He later declined to attend a meeting calling for the complete abolition of capital punishment.[24]

DICKENS'S NEWGATE FICTION

In his fiction Dickens resolved some of his feelings about the system which Newgate represented by distinguishing between the incorruptible, the incorrigible and those who fell somewhere between these two categories. Thus in *Oliver Twist* (1838) Fagin attempts to teach Oliver to be a thief by encouraging Oliver to pick

Fagin's own pockets and by telling him amusing stories about Fagin's early criminal exploits. The corruption of Oliver will deprive him of his inheritance and earn Fagin a reward, but Oliver's character is such that Fagin completely fails to draw Oliver into a life of crime.[25] Bill Sikes, on the other hand, and Fagin himself are incorrigible villains for whom no penalty is too harsh. Sikes comes to a horrible end, hanging himself by accident as he tries to escape. Fagin is tried at the Old Bailey, next to Newgate, where the spectators in the public gallery give 'looks expressive of abhorrence' towards Fagin as he stands in the dock and when the death sentence is pronounced by the judge he hears 'a peal of joy from the populace outside, greeting the news that he would die on Monday'.[26]

Fagin's ordeal in the condemned cell is one of Dickens's darkest passages. Oliver visits his former tormentor within 'those dreadful walls of Newgate' and sees his 'face retaining no human expression but rage and terror'. Fagin is angry and indignant rather than repentant and refuses Oliver's plea to say a prayer with him. As he leaves the gaol, Oliver sees the world outside the gates where 'everything told of life and animation but one dark cluster of objects in the centre of all – the black stage, the cross beam, the rope and all the hideous apparatus of death'. The bells of the neighbouring church clocks (St Sepulchre's among them) signal Fagin's approaching death. For Fagin there is no hope just as for Oliver there is no possibility of corruption, while some of the characters surrounding Fagin learn from their experiences and adopt honest means of earning a living – one of them becoming a police informer. The work was published in 1838 and in a preface to the third edition, in 1841, Dickens dissociated it from the earlier Newgate Novels and insisted that it did not glamorise crime.

Other prisoners are treated with more sympathy by Dickens. Thus in *The Old Curiosity Shop* (1841) the saintly errand boy Kit Nubbles, who is devoted to Little Nell, is framed by the evil dwarf Quilp and committed to prison for a while. However, Dickens was clearly uneasy with the idea of the honest Kit suffering the same discomforts as the evil Fagin. Kit is 'lodged, like some few others in the jail, apart from the masses of prisoners because he was not

201

supposed to be utterly depraved and irreclaimable and had never occupied apartments in that mansion before'. Whether these reassurances were designed to comfort the reader or Dickens himself is not clear: probably both. In *David Copperfield* even the profoundly unsympathetic character Uriah Heep is shown to be a model prisoner following his unmasking by Micawber, though whether this is evidence of his redemptive qualities or of his well-known capacity for dissimulation is not quite clear.

BARNABY RUDGE

Of all Dickens's novels *Barnaby Rudge: A Tale of the Riots of 'Eighty* is the novel most strongly associated with Newgate. It was published both in serial form, and as a single volume, in 1841. It includes the most vivid account of the Gordon Riots of 1780, which had destroyed much of London including the recently rebuilt Newgate prison[27], but the gaol itself and the punitive system it represents cast longer shadows over some of the principal characters in the narrative. Moreover, many passages reflect Dickens's experiences of attending public executions. Barnaby Rudge himself, the simpleton after whom the book is named, is inveigled into taking part in the riots by being allowed to carry a silken flag in the ranks of the rioters. He is sent to Newgate where he is the subject of one of the most famous of Phiz's illustrations, fettered and bewildered in a dark cell.

Barnaby is rescued from Newgate by the rioters and, recaptured, is condemned to death, but reprieved at the eleventh hour. Further references to Newgate and the penal system are made in the fate of Hugh the ostler, who is the son of one of the principal villains of the story. Hugh's mother, a gypsy, had been hanged at Tyburn and Hugh himself is hanged outside Newgate after the riots, his demeanour as he approaches the scaffold echoing the defiance of some of those executed earlier:

Upon these human shambles I, who never raised a hand in prayer till now, call down the wrath of God! On that black tree, of which

Phiz, whose real name was Hablot Knight Browne (1815–82), was descended from French Huguenots and apprenticed to an engraver of steel plates, but had his indentures cancelled because he spent too much of his employer's time preparing his own illustrations. In 1836 Dickens fell out with Robert Seymour, illustrator of the *Posthumous Papers of the Pickwick Club,* and the comparatively unknown Browne took over, adopting first the pseudonym Nemo (Latin for 'nobody') which he soon changed to Phiz. He subsequently illustrated ten of Dickens's novels. One of his most important qualities appears to have been the easy tolerance with which he accommodated the needs and whims of the imperious Dickens. The relationship was ended by Dickens in about 1860 after Browne had illustrated *A Tale of Two Cities.* *Barnaby Rudge* was the fruit of one of their earlier collaborations and contains the famous illustration of the hapless Barnaby in Newgate. Browne also illustrated works by the Newgate novelists Harrison Ainsworth and Edward Bulwer-Lytton, as well as editions of Henry Fielding, Sir Walter Scott and Lord Byron. Despite his falling-out with Dickens he continued to work as an illustrator until his death at the age of 67 in 1882.

I am the ripened fruit, I do invoke the curse of all its victims past, and present and to come.

The behaviour of the crowd reflects the earlier observations that Dickens and others had recorded when attending Newgate executions themselves. Thus the crowd swells with 'every chime of St Sepulchre's clock' which also brings nearer the moment of execution and the traditional cry of 'Hats off' greets the condemned men as they emerge from the prison. Dickens, who in the preface to the book described the riots as 'those shameful tumults [which] reflect indelible disgrace upon the time in which they occurred' shows sympathy for those whose executions followed except for the wretched former hangman Dennis who is presented as a craven coward begging for a reprieve. Thus he writes that 'those who suffered as rioters were for the most part the weakest, meanest and most miserable among them' and he adds a moving description of a grey-haired man greeting and embracing his son as the boy ascends the scaffold. Perhaps he had read the account of the father accompanying his condemned son to Tyburn.[28]

FINAL DAYS

Dickens died in 1870 as Newgate entered its final phase. The prison-building programme of the first half of the nineteenth century had ensured that, from 1850, Newgate had been used to hold only those prisoners awaiting trial at the Old Bailey and those awaiting execution. Its design did not lend itself to adaptation to 'panoptic' or other principles embraced by the reformers and the recommendations of the Gladstone Committee, already noted,[29] and the replacement of the Du Cane prison regime by a more humane one ensured that the days of Newgate as a gaol were numbered. Moreover, the Old Bailey next door needed larger premises from which to conduct its grim business and the City Corporation was actively seeking ways of extending the building. The government considered offering a site for a new sessions house on the Victoria Embankment, but this idea was abandoned and in 1898 the Newgate site was sold to the City for £40,000, the money being used to extend Brixton prison. This cleared the way for the demolition of Newgate, an event which was lamented by no one. In July 1900 *The Sphere* published an illustrated article to mark the forthcoming destruction of Newgate, commenting, 'This is not to be regretted, for its history is of the most unsavoury order.' On 6 May 1902 George Woolfe became the last of over 1,100 people to be executed at Newgate, after which the remaining male inmates were sent to Pentonville while the females went to Holloway. The scaffold also went to Pentonville, where it was soon in use.

On 15 August 1902 demolition of the old gaol began, an event recorded by the *Daily Mail* with the words 'the doom of the gaol was being carried out at last'. It was also noted by the *Illustrated London News*, though most of the emphasis in that publication was on the architectural designs for the new sessions house, the Old Bailey, and the occasion was overshadowed by the extensive coverage of the delayed coronation of Edward VII.[30] A few months later, on 4 February 1903, occurred an auction of Newgate relics which was recorded in the *City Press* under the heading 'The Passing of Newgate: Historic Sale of Relics'. The auction took place 'within the gloomy precincts of crime-stricken Newgate'.[31] The newspaper commended the jovial manner of the auctioneer, but noted that the 214 lots of the auction managed to raise only the modest sum of £980. Nine plaster casts of the heads of some of the most notorious former inmates were sold for only £5 and some of the furniture fetched less than its value as firewood. The equipment from the execution shed fetched only five guineas, while the flagstaff on which the black flag had been hoisted to mark an execution was sold for eleven and a half guineas to a citizen of Cape Province, South Africa. Twelve pounds ten shillings was paid for a key cupboard which, according to the auctioneer, was the very same one (or almost the very same one) as had been mentioned in *Barnaby Rudge*. The highest price by far was the £100 paid by Madame Tussaud's for the great bell of Newgate, which had tolled away the hours to executions. This event was Newgate's last rite. None mourned its passing. It is commemorated now only in the name of the street in which it once stood and in a macabre phrase of uncertain origin, which has become a simile for blackness and filth:

As black as Newgate's knocker.

Notes

CHAPTER ONE

1 Gordon Home, *Roman London*, London, Benn, 1926, has a good account of the Roman gates of London.
2 John Stow, *Survey of London*, 1603 edn., Oxford, 1971, p. 35.
3 The term 'Lord Mayor' was not used before the sixteenth century; Edward III's concession is recorded in *Liber Albus*, compiled by John Carpenter in 1419, 1861 edn., London, p. 357.
4 W.J. Loftie, *History of London*, London, Edward Stanford, 1884, vol. 1, p. 437.
5 John Stow, *Survey of London*, p. 36.
6 *Ibid.*, p. 50.
7 *Ibid.*, p. 36.
8 A. Marks, *Tyburn Tree*, London, Brown Langham, 1908, p. 104.
9 A. Griffith, *Chronicles of Newgate*, 1987 edn., London, Bracken Books, 1883, pp. 17–22.
10 These cases and those that follow are to be found in *Memorials of London Life in the 13th 14th and 15th Centuries*, ed. H.T. Riley, London, Longmans Green, 1868, pp. 229, 470, 562.
11 A. Babington, *The English Bastille*, London, Macdonald, 1971, pp. 26 *et seq.*

12 Sir Thomas Skyrme, *History of the Justices of the Peace*, Chichester, Barry Rose Publishers, 1991, vol. 1, p. 174.

13 See Chapter 6 for an account of Elizabeth Fry's work.

14 Sir Thomas Skyrme, *History of the Justices of the Peace*, vol. 1, p. 174.

15 A. Babington, *The English Bastille*, p. 27.

16 John Stow, *Survey of London*, p. 191.

17 *British Mercury*, London, 1790, pp. 336–7.

18 Sir Thomas Skyrme, *History of the Justices of the Peace*, vol. 1, p. 173.

19 A. Griffith, *Chronicles of Newgate*, p. 24.

20 Sir Thomas Smith, *De Republica Anglorum*, London, 1583, chapter 23 .

21 A. Babington, *The English Bastille*, p. 30.

22 John Stow, *Survey of London*, p. 37.

23 R. Sharpe, *Memorials of Newgate and the Old Bailey*, London, Blades, 1907, p. 4.

24 *Memorials of London Life in the 13th 14th and 15th Centuries*, H.T. Riley, ed., p. 673.

25 The expression 'Lord Mayor' did not come into use until Tudor times, a century after Whittington.

26 Hard to translate into twenty-first century terms, but certainly the equivalent of a multi-millionaire.

27 John Stow, *Survey of London*, p. 35.

28 A. Babington, *The English Bastille*, p. 18.

29 *Ibid.*, p. 23.

30 See Chapter 2 for an account of later sponging houses.

31 A. Babington, *The English Bastille*, p. 20.

32 *Ibid.*, p. 6.

33 P. Ackroyd, *London, the Biography*, London, Vintage, 2001, p. 247.

34 John Stow, *Survey of London*, p. 351.

35 P. Ackroyd, *London, the Biography*, p. 248.

36 There are many editions of Foxe's famous book; these extracts quoted are taken from a version available on the Internet at www.bible.crosswalk.com/Historey/Ad/FoxsBookofMartyrs

37 Yale edition of the complete works of More, Yale University Press, 1963, vol. 8, p. 21.
38 A. Griffith, *Chronicles of Newgate*, p. 45.
39 Luke Hutton, *The Discovery of a London Monster Called the Black Dog of Newgate*, London, 1612.
40 A. Griffith, *Chronicles of Newgate*, p. 41.
41 *Ibid.*, p. 63.
42 *Ibid.*, p. 67.
43 *Ibid.*, p. 67.
44 *Journal of the House of Commons*, vol. 2, 1641, p. 394.
45 A. Griffith, *Chronicles of Newgate*, p. 123.
46 D. Lupton, *London Carbonadoed*, 1632, p. 70, Guildhall Library Ref. 2464ii.

CHAPTER TWO

1 For an account of the New River Company see S. Halliday, *Water: A Turbulent History*, Stroud, Sutton Publishing, 2004.
2 Henry Chamberlain, *History and Survey of the Cities of London and Westminster*, London, 1770, p. 120; a similar account is found in William Maitland, FRS, *History of London from its Foundation to the Present Time*, London, 1775, p. 950.
3 *Pennant's Tour of London*, 1805, Guildhall Library ref. SL 84.
4 A. Babington, *The English Bastille*, London, Macdonald, 1971, p. 56
5 B.L., London, *An Accurate Description of Newgate*, 1724, Guildhall Library no. A 8.7 no. 2.
6 Five new pence are worth one shilling; one new penny is worth 2.4 old pennies.
7 H. Chamberlain, *History and Survey of the Cities of London and Westminster*, London, 1770, p. 14.
8 B.L., London, *An Accurate Description of Newgate*, p. 12 *et seq.*
9 *Ibid.*, p. iv.
10 *Ibid.*, p. 21.

11 A. Babington, *The English Bastille*, p. 83.

12 C. De Saussure, *A Foreign View of England 1725–30*, London, Caliban Books, 1994, p. 189.

13 B.L., London, *An Accurate Description of Newgate*, pp. 35 and 45.

14 See pp. 189–90 below for a fuller account of Newgate as represented in *Moll Flanders*.

15 B.L. London, *An Accurate Description of Newgate*, p. 45.

16 P. Ackroyd, *London, the Biography*, London, Vintage, 2001, p. 250.

17 J. Cockburn, (ed.), *Crime in England, 1550–1800*, Princeton University Press, 1977, p. 250.

18 J. Cockburn (ed.), *Crime in England, 1550–1800*, contains an account of the Newgate routine.

19 *History of the Press Yard*, London, 1717, p. 4.

20 The Habeas Corpus Act of 1679 had formalised the subject's right (established by writ since the fourteenth century) to be brought before a court to answer for alleged crimes, but it was suspended during emergencies such as the 1715 rebellion.

21 Misspelt 'Goal' in the original text; Phoenix Court, Newgate, survived as a street name.

22 *History of the Press Yard*, London, 1717, p. 5.

23 See Chapter 1, pp. 9–10, for an account of this gruesome process.

24 *History of the Press Yard*, London, 1717, p. 9.

25 *Ibid.*, p. 53.

26 *Ibid.*, p. 85.

27 *Ibid.*, p. 122.

28 *Ibid.*, p. 62.

29 A. Griffith, *Chronicles of Newgate*, 1987 edn., London, Bracken Books, 1883, p. 132.

30 B.L., London, *An Accurate Description of Newgate*, p. 56.

31 *Ibid.*, p. 36.

32 A. Griffith, *Chronicles of Newgate*, p. 98.

33 W.E. Hooper, *History of Newgate and the Old Bailey*, London, Underwood Press, 1935, p. 48.

34 *Ibid.*, p. 44.
35 M. Waller, *1700: Scenes from London Life*, London, Hodder and Stoughton, 2000, p. 310.
36 B.L., London, *An Accurate Description of Newgate*, p. 36.
37 John Hall, *Memoirs of the Right Villainous John Hall*, London, 1708, p. 27.
38 W.E. Hooper, *History of Newgate and the Old Bailey*, p. 62.
39 Hall, *Memoirs of the Right Villainous John Hall*, p. 24.
40 *Ibid.*, p. 30.
41 See pp. 62–3 for an account of this ritual.
42 Hall, *Memoirs of the Right Villainous John Hall*, p. 38.
43 *Ibid.*, p. 5.
44 A. Griffith, *Chronicles of Newgate*, p. 96.
45 J. Cockburn (ed.), *Crime in England, 1550–1800*, p. 240.
46 A. Babington, *The English Bastille*, p. 66.
47 J. Cockburn, (ed.), *Crime in England, 1550–1800*, p. 241.
48 A. Griffith, *Chronicles of Newgate*, p. 102.
49 J. Cockburn (ed.), *Crime in England, 1550–1800*, p. 242.
50 Sir Thomas Skyrme, *History of the Justices of the Peace*, Chichester, Barry Rose Publishers, 1991, vol. 1, p. 175.
51 The Lord Mayor sat as a judge at the Old Bailey until the Supreme Court of Judicature Act, 1873.
52 A. Babington, *The English Bastille*, p. 60.

CHAPTER THREE

1 *Eirenarcha, or of the Office of the Justices of Peace*, London, 1619, p. 60.
2 *Eirenarcha, or of the Office of the Justices of Peace*, London, 1619, pp. 204–5.
3 See Chapter 5 pp. 145–6 for this curious anomaly.
4 H. Dixon, *London Prisons*, London, Jackson & Walford, 1850, pp. 216–17.
5 *The Times*, editorial, 25 July 1872.

6 H. Potter, *Hanging in Judgment: Religion and the Death Penalty in England*, London, SCM Press, 1993, p. 10.

7 H. Potter, *Hanging in Judgment: Religion and the Death Penalty in England*, p. 13, gives an account of Paley's views.

8 D. Taylor, *Crime, Policing and Punishment in England, 1750–1914*, London, Macmillan, 1998, p. 114.

9 Thomas Wontner, *Old Bailey Experience*, London, 1833, p. 59.

10 *Ibid.*, p. 162 and p. 175.

11 See pp. 72–7 for an account of Sheppard's exploits.

12 See Chapter 2 for an account of Batty Langley's time in Newgate.

13 B.L., London, *An Accurate Description of Newgate*, 1724, p. 50 *et seq.*

14 John Hall, *Memoirs of the Right Villainous John Hall*, London, 1708, p. 38.

15 P. Linebaugh (ed.), *Crime in England, 1550–1800*, Princeton University Press, 1977, p. 236 *et seq.*

16 P. Linebaugh, *The London Hanged: Crime and Civil Society in the Eighteenth Century*, London, Allen Lane at the Penguin Press, 2003, p. xxi.

17 *Dictionary of National Biography*, vol. 12, pp. 140–1 gives an account of Lorraine's career.

18 P. Linebaugh (ed.), *Crime in England, 1550–1800*, p. 250.

19 See Chapter 2 for Defoe's experience of Newgate.

20 *A Narrative of all the Robberies, Escapes etc. of John Sheppard . . . Written by Himself [or rather, written by D. Defoe]*, London, 1724, p. 14.

21 G. Howson, *The Macaroni Parson*, London, Hutchinson, 1973, p. 219.

22 T. Wontner, *Old Bailey Experience*, p. 167.

23 M. Waller, *1700: Scenes from London Life*, London, Hodder and Stoughton, 2000, p. 322 *et seq.*

24 *Crime in England, 1550–1800*, P. Linebaugh (ed.), p. 252.

25 *Ibid.*, p. 236.

26 *Punch*, June 1842, p. 240.

27 *Boswell's London Journal, a Visit to Tyburn and Newgate*, 3 May 1762.

28 The money was bequeathed either by Robert Dow *or* Elizabeth Elliott according to different sources. See *The Complete Newgate Calendar*, ed. J. Rayer and G. Crook, Navarre Society Reprint, 1926.

29 B.L., London, *An Accurate Description of Newgate*, 1724, p. 48.

30 M. Waller, *1700: Scenes from London Life*, p. 325 *et seq.* describes the procession.

31 H. Chamberlain, *History and Survey of the Cities of London and Westminster*, London, 1770, p. 14.

32 Hall, *Memoirs of the Right Villainous John Hall*, p. 38.

33 P. Ackroyd, *London, the Biography*, London, Vintage Publications, 2001, p. 293.

34 *Hell Upon Earth or the Town in an Uproar*, London, 1729, p. 42.

35 *Dictionary of National Biography*, vol. 17, p. 1169; this macabre element of his personality has been denied by some; see *DNB* entry.

36 See Chapter 2 for the example of William Paul.

37 *Hell Upon Earth or the Town in an Uproar*, p. 51.

38 A. Griffith, *Chronicles of Newgate*, 1987 edn., London, Bracken Books, 1883, p. 167.

39 J. Laurence, *History of Capital Punishment*, London, Sampson Low, 1932, p. 44.

40 See above p. 63 for this incident.

41 M. Waller, *1700: Scenes from London Life*, p. 330.

42 *The Complete Newgate Calendar*, Navarre Society Reprint, 1926, vol. 3, p. 4.

43 *Ibid.*, vol. 3, p. 40.

44 *Dictionary of National Biography*, vol. 11, p. 71, gives an account of Ketch's career.

45 A. Babington, *The English Bastille*, London, Macdonald, 1971, p. 34.

46 See Chapter 4 for an account of the work of John and Henry Fielding at Bow Street Magistrates' Court.

47 See Chapter 2 for an account of this room.

48 A form of tuberculosis also known as The King's Evil since in some quarters the royal touch was also believed to cure it.

49 J. Villette, *A Genuine Account of the Behaviour and Dying Words of William Dodd, LL.D.*, London, 1777, p. 23.

50 *Ibid.*, p. 25

51 Guildhall pamphlet A 7.7 no. 54.

CHAPTER FOUR

1 See Chapter 1 for this early development of the Common Law.

2 C. Emsley, *The English Police: A Political and Social History*, London, Longman, 1996, p. 11.

3 C. de Saussure, *A Foreign View of England, 1725–30*, London, Caliban Books, 1994, p. 73.

4 G. Howson, *Thief-taker General: The Rise and Fall of Jonathan Wild*, London, Hutchinson, 1970, p. 4.

5 *The Complete Newgate Calendar*, Navarre Society Reprint, 1926, vol. 3, p. 15 *et seq.*

6 Howson, *Thief-taker General*, p. 36.

7 *Ibid.*, p. 282.

8 D. Rumbelow, *The Triple Tree*, London, Harrap, 1982, p. 88.

9 *The Complete Newgate Calendar*, vol. 3, p. 29.

10 *Ibid.*, vol. 3, p. 6.

11 D. Defoe, *A Narrative of all the Robberies, Escapes etc. of John Sheppard*, London, 1724, p. 14.

12 D. Nokes, *Henry Fielding, Joseph Andrews*, London, Penguin, 1987, contains an account of Fielding's ancestry.

13 *The Times Literary Supplement*, 4 June 1931, p. 447, contains an account of the event.

14 William Blizard described this practice in *Desultory Reflections on Police; with an Essay on the Means of Preventing Crimes and Amending Criminals*, London, 1785, p. 16.

15 Possibly the origin of the expression 'to drive a coach and horses through'; there are alternative claims; see *Oxford English Dictionary*.

16 The character Peachum in the drama is a barely disguised portrait of Wild.

17 *London Magazine*, 1734, p. 87.

18 London, 1709, pp. 15–16, British Library reference T.756 (2).

19 Minutes of Westminster Petty Sessions, 6 August 1719.

20 C.A. Beard, *The Office of the Justice of the Peace in England*, New York, Columbia University Press, 1904, p. 330, describes this episode.

21 T. Baston, *Thoughts on Trade and Public Spirit*, London, 1716, p. 127.

22 *Gentleman's Magazine*, December 1769, p. 539.

23 D. Defoe, *Charity Still a Christian Virtue*, London, 1719.

24 Deveil, *Memoirs of the Life and Times of Sir Thomas Deveil, Knight, One of his Majesty's Justices of the Peace*, London, 1748; British Library ref. 1201.c.21.

25 A. Babington, *A House in Bow Street*, Chichester, Barry Rose Publications, 1999, pp. 46 *et seq.*, contains an account of De Veil's life.

26 *Ibid.*, p. 16, has an account of Mary Young's exploits.

27 H. Fielding, *An Enquiry into the Causes of the Late Increase of Robbers*, London, 1757, p. 116.

28 D. Hay and F. Snyder, *Policing and Prosecution in Britain, 1750–1850*, Oxford, Clarendon Press, 1989, p. 335.

29 J. Boswell, *Life of Johnson*, Chapter 30.

30 *Observations on the Office of Constable*, Saunders Welch, London, 1754, BL shelfmark 1417.i.31.

31 *The Journal of a Voyage to Lisbon*, T. Keymer (ed.), London, Penguin, 1996, p. 15.

32 The edition quoted is that of the Clarendon Press, Oxford, 1988, ed. Malvin R. Zirker.

33 T. Barlow, *The Justice of Peace: a Treatise Concerning the Power and Duty of that Magistrate*, London, 1745, British Library reference 516.m.3.

34 *The Journal of a Voyage to Lisbon*, T. Keymer, (ed.), p. 14.

35 *Ibid*.

36 London, 1755, available in British Library ref. T.1086.(3).

37 See Chapter 2.

38 See Chapter 5 for an account of the attack upon Newgate.

39 P. Langford, *A Polite and Commercial People; England, 1727–83*, Oxford University Press, 1989, p. 161.

40 T.A. Critchley, *A History of Police in England and Wales*, London, Constable, 1978, pp. 36–7.

41 D. Taylor, *Crime, Policing and Punishment in England, 1750–1914*, London, Macmillan, 1998, p. 83.

CHAPTER FIVE

1 P. Ackroyd, *London, the Biography*, London, Vintage Publications, 2001, p. 482 *et seq.*, describes the activities of the London mobs at this time.

2 Now Broadwick Street.

3 P. Linebaugh, *The London Hanged: Crime and Civil Society in the Eighteenth Century*, London, Allen Lane at the Penguin Press, 2003, pp. 336 *et seq.*

4 *A Letter from Lord George Gordon in Newgate*, London, 1792, British Library catalogue no. 8135.c.49.

5 The present author could find no acrostical word puzzle in the work.

6 B. Martin, *John Henry Newman, His Life and Work*, London, Continuum, 2000, pp. 92 and 96.

7 See p. 46 above.

8 Sir Stephen Theodore Janssen, *A Letter to the Lord Mayor*, London 1767, BL reference 1608/3254.

9 See panel on p. 47 for a brief account of the career of Stephen Hales.

10 Sir Stephen Theodore Janssen, *A Letter to the Lord Mayor*, p. 33.

11 See Chapter 6 for an account of Elizabeth Fry's work in Newgate and elsewhere.

12 R. Blomfield, *The Architect of Newgate*, in *Studies in Architecture*, London, Macmillan, 1905.

13 R. Blomfield, *Studies in Architecture*, London, Macmillan, 1905, p. 74 *et seq.*

14 J. Boswell, *Life of Johnson*, London, Everyman, 1992, vol. 4, p. 188.

15 D. Taylor, *Crime, Policing and Punishment in England, 1750–1914*, London, MacMillan, 1998, pp. 136–7.

16 W. Hepworth Dixon, *The London Prisons*, London, Jackson & Walford, 1850, p. 193 and 196.

17 M. Cheney, *Chronicles of the Damned*, Yeovil, Marston House, 1993, p. 105.

18 *Daily News*, 23 February, 9, 13 and 16 March, contains the correspondence.

19 X. Baron, *London 1066–1914, Literary Sources and Documents*, London, 1997, vol. 2, pp. 394–5.

20 J. Bondeson, *The London Monster; A Sanguinary Tale*, London, Da Capo Press, 2002, p. 5.

21 See panel on p. 107 for an account of this bizarre episode.

22 See Chapter 3 for a discussion of this phenomenon.

23 *History and Biography: Essays in Honour of Derek Beales*, T. Blanning and D. Cannadine, (eds), Cambridge, Cambridge University Press, 1996, p. 91.

24 D. Taylor, *Crime, Policing and Punishment in England, 1750–1914*, pp. 131–3.

25 Hansard, 2nd series, vol. 17, p. 411, 1 May 1827.

26 *Morning Chronicle*, 9 June 1789.

27 W. Cobbett, *Twelve Sermons*, 1823, p. 154, British Library shelfmark 08408.e.61.

28 *The Rambler*, 20 April, 1751.

29 See for example *Hansard* 29 March, 1811, col. 625–6, Mr Frankland on the Dwelling House Robbery Bill.

30 See Chapter 3 for Boswell's reactions to his Newgate visits.

31 *The Hypochondriack*, M. Bailey (ed.), California, Stanford University Press, 1928, vol. 2, p. 284; British Library no. 012272.dd.1.

32 B. Montagu, *An Enquiry into the Aspersions upon the late Ordinary of Newgate*, London, 1815, Appendix B in H. Potter, Hanging in Judgment: Religion and the Death Penalty in England, SCM Press, 1993, p. 16.

33 H. Potter, *Hanging in Judgment: Religion and the Death Penalty in England*, London, 1993, p. 69.

34 *The Shrigley Abduction*, Abby Ashby and Audrey Jones, Stroud, Sutton Publishing, 2004 gives an account of this extraordinary tale.

35 *Parliamentary Debates* (House of Lords) 3rd series, 15 May 1854, vol. 133, cols 306–11.

36 H. Potter, *Hanging in Judgment: Religion and the Death Penalty in England*, p. 111, discusses this tendency among clergymen.

37 *The Groans of the Gallows or, the Past and Present Life of William Calcraft, the Living Hangman of Newgate*, London, 1846, pp. 10 and 12; Guildhall pamphlet 1490.

38 *Fraser's Magazine*, vol. 49, June 1864; James Stephen was the brother of Leslie Stephen and uncle of Virginia Woolf.

39 Pamphlet 1490.

40 H. Potter, *Hanging in Judgment: Religion and the Death Penalty in England*, p. 103.

41 J. Bondeson, *The London Monster: A Sanguinary Tale*, is the definitive source of this strange tale and the source of many of the facts that follow.

42 J. Bondeson, *The London Monster: A Sanguinary Tale*, pp. 31 and 39, show both of Angerstein's posters.

43 *Ibid.*, p. 47.

44 *Ibid.*, p. 92 *et seq.*, tells the sorry tale.

45 See Chapter 4 for an account of Mainwaring's activities.

46 He may have changed his name to Henry Williams and continued to work as an artificial-flower maker; see J. Bondeson, *The London Monster: A Sanguinary Tale*, pp. 159–60.

CHAPTER SIX

1 F.M. Wilson, *Strange Island*, London, Longmans, 1955, p. 135.

2 British Library, ref. X.203/2091.

3 J. Howard, *The State of the Prisons*, Abingdon, Professional Books, 1977, p. 151.

4 See Chapter 1 for an account of Blackstone's career.

5 J. Howard, *The State of the Prisons*, introduction, p. ii.

6 A. Griffith, *Chronicles of Newgate*, 1987 edn., London, Bracken Books, 1883 pp. 368 and 374.

7 J. Smith, *A Book for a Rainy Day*, London, Methuen, 1905, pp. 177–80.

8 A. Griffith, *Chronicles of Newgate*, p. 396.

9 M. Letts, *As the Foreigner Saw Us*, London, Methuen, 1935, vol. 2, p. 272.

10 H. Pückler-Muskau, *Tour in England in the Years 1825–6*, London, Collins, 1987, vol. 4, p. 72.

11 D. Taylor, *Crime, Policing and Punishment in England, 1750–1914*, London, Macmillan, 1998, p. 83.

12 F. Engels, *The Condition of the Working Class in England*, London, Macmillan, 1973 edn., pp. 144–5.

13 *Journal of the Statistical Society*, 1857, pp. 22–32.

14 T.F. Buxton, *An Inquiry etc.*, London, 1818, pp. vii, 7, 48 *et seq.*

15 J. Bentham, *An Introduction to the Principles and Morals of Legislation*, London, 1823, chapter 13.

16 J. Bentham, *Panopticon*, vol. 1, p. 28.

17 J. Bentham, *Panopticon*, postscript, part 2, 1791.

18 R. Ellmann, *Oscar Wilde*, Hamish Hamilton, 1987, pp. 454–5, describes Wilde's ordeals in Newgate and Pentonville.

19 J. Greenwood, *Three Years of Penal Servitude*, London, 1874, British Library shelfmark 12356.e.35.

20 J. Clay, *The Prison Chaplain: Memoirs of the Rev. John Clay*, London, 1861.

21 A. Griffith, *Chronicles of Newgate*, pp. 402–12.

22 See p. 158 for an account of the life of Thomas Fowell Buxton

23 See Chapter 2 for an account of William Penn's sojourn in Newgate.

24 *Memoir of the Life of Elizabeth Fry*, edited by her daughters Katherine and Rachel, London, 1848.

25 Now the site of a school.

26 *Memoir of the Life of Elizabeth Fry*, edited by her daughters Katherine and Rachel, p. 201.

27 W.E. Hooper, *History of Newgate and the Old Bailey*, London, Underwood Press, 1935, p. 124.

28 R. Dobash et al., *The Imprisonment of Women*, London, Blackwell, 1986, p. 45.

29 *Memoir of the Life of Elizabeth Fry*, edited by her daughters Katherine and Rachel, p. 257.

30 Sir Thomas Buxton, *An Enquiry whether Crime and Misery are Produced or Prevented by our Present System of Prison Discipline*, London, 1818, p. 124–6.

31 J. Kingsmill, *Chapters on Prison and Prisoners*, London, 1852, pp. 383–4.

32 A. Griffith, *Chronicles of Newgate*, p. 383.

33 E. Fry, *Observations on the Visiting, Superintendance and Government of Female Prisoners*, London, 1827, p. 23.

34 British Library shelfmark 1127c9 (4).

35 E. Fry, *Observations on the Siting, Superintendence and Government of Female Prisoners*, p. 50.

36 In 1910 Crosby Hall was moved from Bishopsgate to Chelsea where it stands in what was once the orchard of Sir Thomas More's Chelsea home.

37 E. Fry, *Observations on the Siting, Superintendance and Government of Female Prisoners*, p. 61.

38 *The Times*, 18 June, 1846.

39 See p. 164 above for this reference.

40 *Parliamentary Papers*, 1895, vol. 56, contains the committee's recommendations.

CHAPTER SEVEN

1 *Oxford Companion to Literature*, ed. Margaret Drabble, Oxford University Press, 6th edn., 2000, pp. 483 and 719.

2 See Chapter 3.

3 See Chapter 4 for an account of their exploits.

4 Chapters 33 and 36 respectively.

5 The title is credited to Sir Francis Burnand; British Library shelfmark 12331.aaa.10.

6 P. Ackroyd, *London, the Biography*, London, Vintage Publications, 2001, p. 279.

7 See Chapter 2.

8 See Chapter 4 for an account of the activities of these corrupt justices.

9 See Chapter 6 above for an account of this work.

10 See Chapter 3 for an account of her gruesome death.

11 S. Wise, *The Italian Boy: Murder and Grave-Robbery in 1830s London*, London, Cape, 2004, gives a full account of the episode.

12 See Chapter 5 for a description of this event.

13 *London 1066–1914, Literary Sources and Documents*, ed. X. Baron, Robertsbridge, Helm, 1997, vol. 2, pp. 394–5.

14 C. Dickens, *Sketches by Boz*, Oxford University Press, 1989, pp. 201–14.

15 C. Dickens, *American Notes*, London, Hazell, Watson and Viney, 1842, 'Philadelphia and its Solitary Prison', chapter 7.

16 See Chapter 6.

17 P. Ackroyd, *Dickens: Public Life and Private Passion*, London, BBC Publications, 2002, p. 111.

18 C. Dickens, *Great Expectations*, Oxford University Press, 1998, p. 257.

19 See Chapter 6.

20 See C. Dickens, *David Copperfield* for a description of the visit, Chapter 61.

21 See Chapter 5.

22 *Daily News*, 28 February, 9, 13 and 16 March 1846.

23 *The Times*, 19 November 1849.

24 H. Potter, *Hanging in Judgement, Religion and the Death Penalty in England*, London, SCM Press, 1993, p. 78.

25 C. Dickens, *Oliver Twist*, London, Penguin, 1994, chapters 9, 10 and 18 describe Fagin's attempts to corrupt Oliver.

26 C. Dickens, *Oliver Twist*, London, Penguin, 1994, p. 498.

27 See Chapter 5.

28 See Chapter 3. The references to the novel are from the Dent paperback, 1996, p. xxxiii (Preface), 448 (illustration of Barnaby in Newgate) and 572 *et seq.* (concluding chapters).
29 See Chapter 6.
30 *Illustrated London News*, 4 October 1902, pp. 486 and 497.
31 *City Press*, 7 February 1903.

Bibliography

BOOKS AND PAMPHLETS

Ackroyd, P. *London, the Biography*, London, Vintage Publications, 2001
——. *Dickens: Public Life and Private Passion*, London, BBC Publications, 2002
Anon. *A Genuine Account of the Behaviour and Dying Words of William Dodd*, London, 1777
Anon. *A Letter to the Lord Mayor, Sir Stephen Theodore Janssen*, London 1767, BL shelfmark 1608/3254
Anon. *Eirenarcha, or of the Office of the Justices of Peace*, London, 1619
Anon. *Hell Upon Earth or the Town in an Uproar*, London, 1729
Anon. *History of the Press Yard*, London, 1717
Anon. *The Groans of the Gallows or, the Past and Present Life of William Calcraft, the Living Hangman of Newgate*, London, 1846, Guildhall pamphlet, 1490
Ashby, A. and Jones, A. *The Shrigley Abduction*, Stroud, Sutton Publishing, 2004
Babington, A., *The English Bastille*, London, Macdonald, 1971
——. *A House in Bow Street*, Chichester, Barry Rose Publishers, 1999
Bailey, M. (ed.). *The Hypochondriack*, California, Stanford University Press, 1928, vol. 2, BL shelfmark no. 012272.dd.1

Barlow, T. *The Justice of Peace: A Treatise concerning the Power and Duty of that Magistrate*, London, 1745, British Library shelfmark 516.m.3

Baron, X. (ed.). *London 1066–1914, Literary Sources and Documents*, Robertsbridge, Helm, 1997

Baston, Thomas. *Thoughts on Trade and Public Spirit*, London, 1716, p. 127

Beard, C.A. *The Office of the Justice of the Peace in England*, New York, Columbia University Press, 1904

Bentham, J. *Panopticon*, postscript, part 2, London, 1791

——. *An Introduction to the Principles and Morals of Legislation*, London, 1823

Blomfield, R. 'The Architect of Newgate', in *Studies in Architecture*, ed. R. Blomfield, London, Macmillan, 1905

Bondeson, J. *The London Monster: A Sanguinary Tale*, London, Da Capo Press, 2002

Boswell, J. 'A Visit to Tyburn and Newgate', *London Journal*, 3 May 1762

——. *Life of Johnson*, London, Everyman edition, 1992

B.L. *A Description of Newgate by B.L.*, London, 1724, Guildhall Library reference A 8.7 no.2

Buxton, Sir Thomas. *An Enquiry whether Crime and Misery are Produced or Prevented by our Present System of Prison Discipline*, 1818

Blanning, T. and Cannadine, D. (ed.). *History and Biography: Essays in Honour of Derek Beales*, Cambridge University Press, 1996

Chamberlain, H. *History and Survey of the Cities of London and Westminster*, London, 1770

Cheney, M. *Chronicles of the Damned*, Yeovil, Marston House, 1993

Clay, J. *The Prison Chaplain: Memoirs of the Rev. John Clay*, London, 1861

Cobbett, W. *Twelve Sermons*, 1823, British Library shelfmark 08408.e.61

Cockburn, J. (ed.). *Crime in England, 1550–1800*, Princeton University Press, 1977

Critchley, T.A. *A History of Police in England and Wales*, London, Constable, 1978

Defoe, Daniel, *Charity Still a Christian Virtue*, London, 1719

——. *A Narrative of all the Robberies, Escapes etc. of John Sheppard*, London, 1724

Deveil, T. *Memoirs of the Life and Times of Sir Thomas Deveil, Knight, one of his Majesty's Justices of the Peace*, London, 1748, British Library reference 1201.c.21

Dickens, Charles. *American Notes*, London, Penguin Books, 2000

——. *David Copperfield*, London, Penguin Books, 2004

——. *Great Expectations*, London, Penguin Books, 1994

——. *Oliver Twist*, London, Penguin Books, 1994

——. *Sketches by Boz*, London, Penguin Books, 1994

Dixon, W.H. *The London Prisons*, London, 1850

Dobash, R. *et al. The Imprisonment of Women*, London, Blackwell, 1986

Ellmann, R. *Oscar Wilde*, London, Hamish Hamilton, 1987

Emsley, C. *The English Police: a Political and Social History*, London, Longman, 1996

Engels, F. *The Condition of the Working Class in England*, London, Macmillan, 1973

Fielding, H. *An Enquiry into the Causes of the Late Increase of Robbers*, London, 1757

——. *Joseph Andrews*, London, Penguin, 1987

Fry, E. *Observations on the Siting, Superintendance and Government of Female Prisoners*, London, 1825

Fry, K. and R. *Memoir of the Life of Elizabeth Fry, Edited by her Daughters*, London, 1848

Gordon, Lord George. *A Letter from Lord George Gordon in Newgate*, London, 1792, British Library shelfmark no. 8135.c.49

Greenwood, J. *Three Years of Penal Servitude*, London, 1874, British Library shelfmark 12356.e.35

Griffith, A. *Chronicles of Newgate*, London, Bracken Books, 1883

Hall, J. *Memoirs of the Right Villainous John Hall*, London, 1708

Halliday, S. *Water: a Turbulent History*, Stroud, Sutton Publishing, 2004

Bibliography

Hay, D. and Snyder, F. *Policing and Prosecution in Britain, 1750–1850*, Oxford, Clarendon Press, 1989

Hooper, W.E. *History of Newgate and the Old Bailey*, London, Underwood Press, 1935

Howard, J. *The State of the Prisons*, Abingdon, Professional Books, 1977

Howson, G. *Thief-taker General: the Rise and Fall of Jonathan Wild*, London, Hutchinson, 1970

——. *The Macaroni Parson*, London, Hutchinson, 1973

Hutton, L. *The Discovery of a London Monster called the Black Dog of Newgate*, London, 1612

Keymer, T. (ed.). *The Journal of a Voyage to Lisbon*, London, Penguin, 1996

Kingsmill, J. *Chapters on Prison and Prisoners*, London, 1852

Langford, P. *A Polite and Commercial People; England, 1727–83*, Oxford University Press, 1994

Laurence, J. *History of Capital Punishment*, London, 1932

Letts, M. *As the Foreigner Saw us*, London, Methuen, 1935

Linebaugh, P. (ed.). *Crime in England, 1550–1800*, Princeton University Press, 1977

Linebaugh, P. *The London Hanged: Crime and Civil Society in the Eighteenth Century*, London, Allen Lane at the Penguin Press, 2003

Loftie, W.J. *History of London*, London, Stanford University Press, 1884

Lupton, D. *London Carbonadoed*, 1632, Guildhall Library Ref. 2464ii

Maitland, William, FRS. *History of London from its Foundation to the Present Time*, London, 1775

Marks, A. *Tyburn Tree*, London, Brown Langham, 1908

Martin, B. *John Henry Newman, His Life and Work*, London, Continuum, 2000

Montagu, B. *An Enquiry into the Aspersions upon the late Ordinary of Newgate*, London, 1815

More, Sir Thomas. *Yale Edition of the Complete Works of Sir Thomas More*, ed. R. Sylvester, Yale University Press, 1976

Potter, H. *Hanging in Judgment: Religion and the Death Penalty in England*, London, SCM Press, 1993

Pückler-Muskau, H. *Tour in England in the Years 1825–6*, London, Collins, 1987, vol. 4

Riley, H.T. (ed.). *Memorials of London Life in the 13th, 14th and 15th Centuries*, London, Longmans Green, 1868

Rumbelow, D. *The Triple Tree*, London, Harrap, 1982

Sharpe, R. *Memorials of Newgate and the Old Bailey*, London, Blades, 1907

Skyrme, Sir Thomas. *History of the Justices of the Peace*, Chichester, Barry Rose Publishers, 1991

Smith, J. *A Book for a Rainy Day*, London, Methuen, 1905

Smith, Sir Thomas. *De Republica Anglorum*, London, 1583

Stow, J. *Survey of London*, 1603 edition, Oxford, 1908

Taylor, D. *Crime, Policing and Punishment in England, 1750–1914*, Basingstoke, Macmillan, 1998

Waller, M. *1700: Scenes from London Life*, London, Hodder & Stoughton, 2000

Welch, Saunders. *Observations on the Office of Constable*, London, 1754, BL shelfmark 1417.i.31

Wilson, F.M. *Strange Island*, London, Longmans, 1955

Wise, S. *The Italian Boy: Murder and Grave-Robbery in 1830s London*, London, Cape, 2004

Wontner, T. *Old Bailey Experience*, London, 1833

NEWSPAPERS AND MAGAZINES

City Press, 7 February 1903

Daily News, 23, 28 February, 9, 13 and 16 March 1846

Fraser's Magazine, vol. 49, June 1864

Gentleman's Magazine, December 1769

Illustrated London News, 4 October 1902

London Magazine, 1734

Morning Chronicle, 9 June 1789

Punch, June 1842, p. 240

Bibliography

The Rambler, 20 April 1751
The Times, 18 June 1846, 19 November 1849, 25 July 1872

PARLIAMENTARY MATERIALS

Hansard, 29 March 1811, 1 May 1827
Journal of the House of Commons, vol. 2, 1641
Parliamentary Debates (House of Lords), 3rd series, 15 May 1854
Parliamentary Papers, vol. 56, 1895

MISCELLANEOUS MATERIALS

The Complete Newgate Calendar, Navarre Society Reprint, 1926
Journal of the Statistical Society, 1857
Minutes of Westminster Petty Sessions, 6 August 1719
Pennant's Tour of London, 1805, Guildhall Library reference SL 84

Index